Power and Politics in Organizations

The Social Psychology of Conflict, Coalitions, and Bargaining

Samuel B. Bacharach

Edward J. Lawler

Power and Politics in Organizations

Jossey-Bass Publishers

San Francisco • Washington • London • 1981

POWER AND POLITICS IN ORGANIZATIONS
The Social Psychology of Conflict, Coalitions, and Bargaining
by Samuel B. Bacharach and Edward J. Lawler

Library of Congress Cataloging in Publication Data

Bacharach, Samuel B
    Power and politics in organizations.

    Bibliography: p. 225
    Includes index.
    1. Organizational behavior—Political aspects.
2. Political action. 3. Power (Social sciences)
4. Coalition (Social sciences) 5. Social conflict.
I. Lawler, Edward J., joint author. II. Title.
HM131.B134   302.3'5   79-92460
ISBN 0-87589-458-5

Manufactured in the United States of America

JACKET DESIGN BY WILLI BAUM

FIRST EDITION
First printing: August 1980
Second printing: May 1981

Code 8020

The Jossey-Bass
Social and Behavioral Science Series

Preface

Power and Politics in Organizations presents a political analysis of intraorganizational relations; in it, we theoretically examine the key dimensions of such an approach. While a number of other writers have maintained that organizations are political systems (Cyert and March, 1963; Crozier, 1964; Thompson, 1967; Karpik, 1972), few of them have systematically laid out a paradigm for the political analysis of intraorganizational structure and processes. Cyert and March (1959) come closest to such a systematic analysis, but the potential of their work has not been realized in that it has not led to the development of an explicit framework applicable to a comparative organizational analysis. The assumptions that guided their work also relate to our theoretical concerns.

In developing our paradigm of intraorganizational politics, we have attempted to integrate the social psychology of politics with the structural analysis of organizations. To this end, we have broken from the three perspectives that currently dominate intraorganizational analysis. That is, we do not see organizational actors as the passive entities presented in organizational psychology; we do not view organizations as loosely coupled systems or as structurally coordinated monoliths. All of these perspectives ignore the power politics involved in interest groups and coalitional bargaining. Indeed, we believe that the main void in organizational theory is a lack of concern with politics. We have directed our energies toward filling this void. What we offer here is a middle-range theoretical orientation, which will help in generating the type of research that will move intraorganizational political analysis away from the realm of descriptive anecdotes toward the realm of comparative, quantitative analysis.

Specifically, the book examines *intra*coalition and *inter*-coalition processes. With social psychological theory as a backdrop, we address two basic issues: (a) the formation or mobilization of interest groups into coalitions and (b) the nature or pattern of conflict between different coalitions. We distinguish between two dimensions of power—authority and influence—and examine how they facilitate or constrain the mobilization of interest groups into coalitions. We compare interest group politics with coalition politics and argue that the type of political alignment has an important effect on relations within organizations. Our theory of bargaining relationships and bargaining tactics is relevant to power struggle and the conflict between coalitions within organizations.

An understanding of organizational politics requires an analysis of power, coalitions, and bargaining. The power relationship is the context for political action and encompasses the most basic issues underlying organizational politics. As the primary mechanism through which individuals and subgroups acquire, maintain, and use power, coalitions crystallize and bring to the foreground the conflicting interests of organizational subgroups. Through bargaining, distinct coalitions attempt to achieve their political objectives and protect themselves from encroachments by opposing coalitions. Power, coalitions, and bargaining, therefore, constitute the three basic themes in our theoretical treatise on organizational politics.

Chapter One is a critique of the literature on organizations and the inadequate picture of organizational politics provided by contemporary perspectives on organizations. The study of organizational politics requires a new perspective: an image of organizations grounded in social psychological research on power, coalitions, and bargaining.

The second and third chapters organize and extend prior approaches to the issue of power in organizations. Simmel's (1950) distinction between form and content provides the backdrop for our analysis. Chapter Two examines the form of power and identifies three dimensions of power: its relational aspect, its dependency aspect, and its sanctioning aspect. Chapter Three focuses on the content of power in organizational settings. Authority and influence are the two dimensions of content, with authority being stable, formal, and normatively sanctioned and influence being fluid, informal, and dynamic. This distinction between authority and influence has implications for organizational change, the flow of power, and the relation of bases and sources of power in organizations.

The fourth and fifth chapters deal with coalition processes. Chapter Four analyzes social psychological theories of coalitions and argues that these theories have implications for the way in which authority structure or formal stratification of an organization constrains or facilitates coalitions between disparate subgroups. Chapter Five considers coalitions as means of influence independent of the authority structure. We distinguish coalition politics from interest group politics and analyze the organizational conditions under which interest groups ally with other interest groups, thereby creating coalition politics.

Chapters Six, Seven, and Eight are concerned with the bargaining relationships and processes of conflicting coalitions. Chapter Six uses Schelling's (1960) contrast of tacit versus explicit bargaining and the contrast between distributive versus integrative bargaining (Pruitt and Lewis, 1977; Walton and McKersie, 1965) to construct a typology of bargaining relationships. In addition, this chapter analyzes the importance of basic tactical and constituent-representative issues for intergroup bargaining. Chapter Seven presents a general theory of bargaining tactics grounded in notions of power dependence (Emerson, 1962, 1972; Blau, 1964). The theory provides a basis for predicting tactical choice in bargaining and for analyzing the dynamics of power struggle. Chapter Eight concerns the role of coercion in bargaining and contrasts deterrence and conflict spiral theories. We also examine the methods of coercive communication and their relationship to compliance to organizational dictates.

Chapter Nine treats the emergent properties of the coalition network in organizations and identifies various dimensions of the coalitions network, such as size, density, centrality, and fit with the formal structure. These characteristics simultaneously grow out of organizational politics and identify parameters that constrain organizational politics at a given time.

This theoretical work transcends conventional disciplinary boundaries. It will interest scholars in organizational sociology, organizational behavior, and organizational psychology, as well as social psychologists concerned about extensions of work on power, coalitions, and bargaining to macro settings. This book is also of relevance to political scientists interested in formal organizations, and it is one of the few volumes that develops the interface between the fields of collective bargaining and organizations.

Acknowledgements

In writing this book we have been greatly assisted by colleagues, friends, and family. Donald E. Cullen has been of great assistance to us in the past two years in seeing the larger implications of many of our concerns. Joseph Shedd, in making numerous detailed comments, helped us see the implications of our work for collective bargaining. Stephen Mitchell commented on many of our chapters and was particularly helpful in relating our discussion to the mainstream of organizational behavior. Jonathan Reader, as always, gave us some excellent suggestions. Rose Malanowski spent months working closely with us on this volume. Her warmth, sense of humor, and intellectual insights assisted greatly in the completion of this book. Pamela Kline, who put up with all of us, was the professional who assured that the manuscript was typed to look like a book. Barbara Smalley did a professional job in typing and retyping a number of chapters. We also thank Howard Aldrich for his intellectual and personal support throughout the writing of this book. At times he gave insights to our work that both of us had overlooked. We both have our private debts outside the professional world. Samuel Bacharach is especially indebted to Nancy McGuy, who provided tenderness and support during a year and a half of difficult work. Edward Lawler would like to thank his wife, Joan, for her patience and understanding during this difficult process. He would also like to thank his son, Michael, for putting up with a year in Ithaca.

Finally, we want to emphasize that this was a joint work in every respect.

February 1980
Samuel B. Bacharach
Ithaca, New York

Edward J. Lawler
Iowa City, Iowa

Contents

The Authors

Samuel B. Bacharach is an associate professor in the Department of Organizational Behavior of the New York State School of Industrial and Labor Relations at Cornell University. He received his B.S. degree in economics from Washington Square College of Arts and Sciences, New York University, and his Ph.D. degree in sociology from the University of Wisconsin. He has served on the editorial board of *Administrative Science Quarterly* and is currently the book review editor of that journal. Bacharach is also the editor of an annual review, *Sociology of Organizations: Theory and Research*. He has published articles in *Administrative Science Quarterly, Journal of Personality and Social Psychology, Industrial and Labor Relations Review, Academy of Management Journal,* and *Social Forces,* among others. His current projects include an experimental investigation of power in bargaining, with Edward J. Lawler, under a grant from the National Science Foundation, and an investigation of school district governance and administration sponsored by the National Institute of Education.

Edward J. Lawler is currently an associate professor of sociology at the University of Iowa. He received his B.A. degree in sociology from California State University at Long Beach and his Ph.D. degree in sociology from the University of Wisconsin. Lawler was a visiting faculty member in the School of Industrial and Labor Relations at Cornell University during 1978-79. He has served on the editorial board of *Sociometry* (now *Social Psychology Quarterly*), and his articles have appeared in such journals as *Journal of Personality and Social Psychology, Social Forces, Journal of Conflict Resolution,* and *Industrial and Labor Relations Review.* In addition to his current investigation of power in bargaining with Bacharach, Lawler is doing research on revolutionary coalitions.

Power and Politics in Organizations

The Social Psychology of Conflict, Coalitions, and Bargaining

1

Toward a
Political Theory
of Organizations

▀▄

Organizations are neither the rational, harmonious entities cele-
brated in managerial theory nor the arenas of apocalyptic class
conflict projected by Marxists. Rather, it may be argued, a more
suitable notion lies somewhere between those two—a concept of
organizations as politically negotiated orders. Adopting this
view, we can observe organizational actors in their daily transactions perpetually bargaining, repeatedly forming and reforming
coalitions, and constantly availing themselves of influence tactics. Few organizational actors are the totally passive, apolitical
entities that are presented by industrial psychologists and
organizational sociologists. Survival in an organization is a political act. Corporations, universities, and voluntary associations are
arenas for daily political action.

　　This book is predicated on the assumption that organizational life is dominated by political interactions; politics in
organizations involve the tactical use of power to retain or obtain control of real or symbolic resources. In describing the

1

processes of organizations as political acts, we are not making a moral judgment; we simply are making an observation about a process. What we saw on the television screen during the Watergate hearings, for better or worse, told us more about organizational reality than all the theses and academic articles that have been published since 1972: The innermost workings of one of the largest and most complex bureaucracies in the world was exposed daily for our scrutiny. Machinations of this type—although not necessarily corrupt ones, like those—were, and are, a basic reality of organizational life.

At the time of the Nixon presidency, when rival coalitions within the federal government (for example, the FBI and the CIA) were frequently vying to outmaneuver each other in a series of tactical initiatives designed to gain control over various domains of organizational power, sociologists were emphasizing that the greater the size of the organization, the greater the propensity for the decentralization of authority. However, decentralization, like other organizational structures, does not occur with the inevitability of natural processes, such as photosynthesis; rather, it involves the conscious actions of organizational members. Organizational structures are emergent entities; that is, they are the result of the conscious political decisions of particular actors and interest groups.

Comparative sociological studies of organizations of the last fifteen years have, for the most part, adopted an apolitical view of organizations (for example, Blau and Schoenherr, 1971; Hage and Aiken, 1970; Pugh and others, 1968). This viewpoint may be attributed to a narrow interpretation of Max Weber's (1947) approach to organizations. Sociologists have spent a disproportionate amount of time trying to prove or disprove the plausibility of Weber's ideal construct of bureaucracy. It is safe to say that Weber remains the most cited organizational theorist; however, the narrowness of his impact is best exemplified by the fact that the pages of his work most frequently cited by organizational researchers are those few where he presents his ideal typical model of the organization.

Sociologists of organizations have, to date, failed to recognize that the Weberian perspective is based on a primary concern with group and individual action. While it is true that

Weber specified some of the primary dimensions of organizational structure, it is also true that he viewed organizational structure as emerging from the conscious political decisions of interest groups. For Weber, organizations are not simply rationally determined systems of interdependent structures; they are also systems in which political tension among interest groups can emerge and reemerge. Weber viewed organizations as "imperatively coordinated" systems. The comparative sociological studies of organizations have, for the most part, chosen to concentrate on the theme of coordination, with little or no emphasis on Weber's imperative dimension. That is, they have been preoccupied with the formal mechanisms of coordination without recognizing the power and the political negotiations that buttress these mechanisms. The work of Blau and Schoenherr (1971) best exemplifies this one-sided view of Weber. In effect, Blau and Schoenherr view Weber's work as providing the lead for examination of the interrelated attributes of formal organizations, and they have chosen to follow this lead. However, as Collins (1975) has recently pointed out, Weber's examination of organizations transcends this important, but nonetheless circumscribed, concern with formal coordination. The Weberian perspective also includes an emphasis on interest groups, tactics, and compliance. Indeed, much earlier, Etzioni (1961) contended that an examination of compliance relationships (that is, the power relationships among groups of actors within the organization) is essential to any exposition of the Weberian model. Blau, himself, in what we consider his most Weberian work, *Exchange and Power in Social Life* (1964), maintains that the examination of social power in exchange relationships will allow us to understand the emergent nature of social structure.

As Bacharach (1978) has observed, students working within the structural tradition of Blau and Schoenherr have been guided by two assumptions that inhibit the development of a political interpretation of intraorganizational dynamics. First, they have tended to cast organizations as normatively integrated systems, thereby ignoring political conflicts and other tensions. Second, they tend to view the organization as a holistic entity, and this view overlooks such organizational subunits as interest groups and coalitions, which are crucial to the development of a political perspective of intraorganizational behavior. Put another way, organizations are not inherently apolitical; instead, such a characterization may be an artifact of a given theoretical perspective, especially one that emphasizes normative integration and maintenance of the total organization.

Despite the structural tradition, some sociologists have been concerned with power in organizations. For example, Crozier (1964) and Selznick (1949), relying on the case study approach, contend that power is the central concept in the analysis of intraorganizational behavior. Crozier argues that the examination of power relationships has advanced little since the work of Machiavelli and Marx. Students of Weber, Michels, Lipset, Selznick, Dahl, and others may take exception to the specifics of Crozier's argument; nonetheless, there is an element of truth to Crozier's initial assertion that has yet to be challenged —namely, it is not *power* that has remained unexamined but rather the patterns of intraorganizational politics. Furthermore Crozier's own work has not addressed this issue. It has contributed to a new conceptualization of power, but it has had little or no impact on the conceptualization of politics within the organization.

Until now, sociological analyses of intraorganizational politics have been limited to a few case studies that resemble Crozier's work in many respects. Because of their design, these studies have failed to produce a theoretical framework conducive to a multiple-case analysis. The works of Allison (1971), Baldridge (1971), and Pettigrew (1973) offer insights into the subtle workings of organizational systems; however, because of the idiographic nature of their concerns, they are unable to develop fully a series of hypotheses that can be examined across a large number of organizations.

While some of the sociological literature (Aldrich, 1979; Karpik, 1972; Zald, 1970) is beginning to develop a macroinstitutional theory for analyzing organizational transactions in the political economy, no political perspective has been developed for analyzing the internal workings of organizations as political systems. Hence, what is currently needed in the field of intraorganizational research is a theory of intraorganizational politics. Such an understanding is the main task of this volume.

Our efforts are directed toward integrating the social psychology of politics with the structural analysis of organizations in order to develop the dimensions of intraorganizational politics. Our orientation is mainly built on theoretical and experimental work on the social psychology of power and politics. The concepts that have emerged from this research tradition have seldom been applied to actual organizational settings. The lack of impact of the social psychological tradition on organizational politics is best exemplified by Pettigrew's (1973, p. 23) observation: "Only political scientists appear to have collected extensive data with the concept of power in mind." Pettigrew, like many other organizational researchers, has chosen to ignore twenty years of social psychological research (for example, Tedeschi, 1970; Tedeschi, Schlenker, and Bonoma, 1973).

It should be noted that, in subscribing to a social psychological perspective of politics, we are not aligning ourselves with organizational or industrial psychologists. Their research, from the Hawthorne studies (Roethlisberger and Dickson, 1939) to date, has exhibited a narrow concern with issues of cooperation, cooptation, and control of workers. Organizational and industrial psychologists have ignored the political nature of organizations, while studying motivation, leadership, and so forth. Yet, if motivation, control, and leadership are problem areas in an organization, then the political reality underlying these issues must necessarily be one of struggle, conflict, and lack of consensus.

Even the more theoretical organizational psychologists, who set out to overcome some of the flaws inherent in the standard psychological approaches to organizations, fail to come to grips with the political reality of organizations. For example, in *The Social Psychology of Organizing* (1969), Weick focuses on the negotiation of order, yet he adheres to the implicit assumption that organizations are harmonious, cooperative systems. He places greater emphasis on the establishment of social order in a given environment than on the political conflict and negotiation intrinsic to a given order.

Running through the preceding discussion has been an

implicit criticism of the image of man that has informed
much of the work on organizations. This criticism merits elaboration. Many students of organizations have unquestioningly
subscribed to an oversocialized notion of people. The uncritical
acceptance of this notion fosters a one-sided view of organizations. If "the organization man," to invoke Whyte's (1956)
term, is presumed to be inherently cooperative, desirous of social approval, and eager not to disrupt the prevailing consensus,
then an organization's dominance over its members (as projected in much of the sociological and psychological research)
becomes more plausible. Likewise, the notion that relationships
between the organization and its members are essentially in conflict becomes more difficult to accept. To elaborate, once the
notion of an oversocialized man is espoused, the idea that organizations are systems of controversy and power conflict seems
alien.

For organizational analysis, the most relevant explication
of the oversocialized notion of man may be found in
Wrong's (1961) classic essay. Wrong maintains that, in implicitly
accepting the oversocialized conception, psychologists and
sociologists make parallel assumptions about people and their
behavior in social situations. According to Wrong, psychologists
assume that people today are motivated by a desire for normative approval, whereas sociologists assume that the social situation is governed by consensus. The industrial psychology literature (the literature on leadership, motivation, and satisfaction,
for example) assumes that behavior is motivated and controlled
by the normative quest for rewards and approval. In a parallel
vein, organizational sociologists in their concern with coordina-
tive mechanisms and structure, assume that people usually per-
form their work in organizational settings characterized by
consensus and cooperation. When these two traditions of organizational research fuse, they preclude the emergence of a
political perspective of organizations, for the psychologists' concern with the normative quest for rewards and approval and the
sociologists' concern with structural coordination and consensus
are mutually reinforcing. Such an orientation toward organizations is not likely to engender an interest in power politics and

conflict. With the exception of the recent works of Pfeffer (1978), the organizational design literature is the best example of the apolitical consequences of this fusion (Beer, 1976; Bennis, 1975; Burke, 1976; Friedlander and Brown, 1974; Nord, 1975).

The solution of the underlying epistemological dilemma confronting organizational theory and research is to bring action to the forefront of organizational analysis. An action perspective is concerned with discovering how people act in and on a given social setting. We need not begin by making any assumptions about the consensual nature of organizations but, rather, concern ourselves with deciphering the patterned relationships between actors' definitions of the situation and their consequent behavior. The action perspective may give rise to a phenomenological perspective on organizations. We, however, contend that an action perspective can serve another purpose: It provides a means for arraying the various concepts and themes from previous social psychological research that are germane to the development of a political theory of organizations. Taking an action perspective, social psychologists who are concerned with politics stress such issues as actors' definitions of the power situation and the tactical actions they undertake to bring about desired outcomes. For social psychologists, politics is a series of competitive tactical encounters. These encounters entail an assessment of the situation (that is, an evaluation of one's power vis-à-vis that of significant competitors), and a selection of countertactics by which to thwart the competitors' tactics. Parallel encounters occur in organizational settings.

If organizations are arenas of political conflict, then for the sake of analysis we need to specify what are the viable units of political action. Hirschman (1972) has suggested that individual organizational members are frequently confronted with dilemmas that require a choice between two options: exit and voice. That is, when facing an unsatisfactory situation in the organization, members have the option of alleviating their dissatisfaction by voicing their opinion or by exiting from the organization. Barry (1974) and Aldrich (1979) have pointed out that individuals can exit and remain silent, exit and be vocal, stay put and remain silent, or stay put and be vocal. From our perspective, voicing and staying put are manifestations of intra-organizational politics. For the majority of organizational members in contemporary society, exiting is a difficult option. The lack of flexibility in today's labor market militates against a high degree of interorganizational mobility. Furthermore, the longer the tenure of the individual in a given organization, the more likely it is that his or her skills will be organizationally specific. Hence, occupational mobility is viewed primarily as an intraorganizational phenomenon. Given these constraints, as length of their tenure increases, most individuals become locked into the organizations in which they work. Most, because of their invested costs in the organization, have an interest in voicing their opinions politically. Unless individuals belong to the organizational elite, it becomes difficult for them to voice their opinions politically without being vulnerable to either manipulation or outright coercion by management. In effect, when individuals engage in politics, there is a high risk of forced exit (dismissal). The only political recourse that most individuals have for their grievances is the group. The group becomes the viable unit for political action. It provides the maximum mobilization of power and some protection against retaliation. Put simply, the group is the viable unit because, as the adage holds, there is strength in numbers.

Building on the work of Dahrendorf (1959), we assert that three groups appear to be critical to the development of a political analysis of organizations: work groups, interest groups, and coalitions. Work groups may be based on departmental differences, differences in departmental work activity, or differences prescribed by the organizational hierarchy. Interest groups may be defined as groups of actors who are aware of the commonality of their goals and the commonality of their fate beyond simply their interdependence with regard to the conduct of work. A coalition is defined as a grouping of interest groups who are committed to achieving a common goal. They are based on the joint action of two or more interest groups against other interest groups. In this context, a political analysis must be concerned primarily with the nature of power across groupings in the organization and the specification of tactics and countertactics that groups employ. Our primary concern is to discover under what conditions interest groups will form coalitions and how coalitions relate to each other politically.

In emphasizing work groups, interest groups, and coalitions as units of analysis, we hope to accentuate the dynamic aspects of organizations. Many students of organizations implicitly or explicitly view behavior in organizations as predetermined and apolitical. Some arrive at this view because they hold to the assumption that, with the exception of the organizational elite, organizational members are indifferent in regard to organizational policy, distribution of organizational resources, and so forth. Others view behavior as predetermined because they accept the belief that reified structures shape and govern the behavior of organizational members. We, however, hold to the sociological adage that is maintained by Marx, Weber, and Durkheim: that individuals become political in groups and that groups are capable of effecting and often do effect structure. In turn, if we are to understand organizations as political systems we must come to grips with how, when, and why groups mobilize power. We are reintroducing political actors and the political processes through the use of work groups, interest groups, and coalitions in an attempt to present the politics of interacting groups as the middle ground between reductionism and reification. Whether the participation in or lack of political activity of such groups leads to pluralistic or elitist organizations is an empirical question we can begin to understand only after we have examined the principles governing political interaction in organizations.

2

Form of Power

▪▪

As indicated in the Preface, power is a critical element of a political analysis of organizations. Political scientists, sociologists, psychologists, and economists have been immersed in the debate over the nature and application of power to different social spheres. This debate has both a *conceptual* and an *empirical* dimension. On a conceptual level, there are innumerable theories, clarifications, and reclarifications. On an empirical level, the measurement of power in concrete circumstances is variable and often bears only a loose correspondence to any specific concept of power. In spite of extensive concern about power on both levels, there appears to be little consensus about the meaning of power or its application to concrete social circumstances.

To understand the debate about power, we must examine the epistemological assumptions underlying power constructs. We must further distinguish between the position taken by theorists of power and the position taken by their empirical counterparts. There is a conspicuous difference in orientation between those who theorize about power and those who conduct research. Although one might expect that researchers would approach power deductively by examining their theoretical formulations empirically, the reverse is usually the case: Researchers typically proceed in an inductive fashion, deriving their formulations of power from its empirical manifestations. In effect, researchers invoke power as an empirical label of some event or phenomenon, while its utility as a nomological construct is ignored. Most researchers ask how power manifests itself in concrete social settings, often without offering a nominal definition of power. For example, in the sociological research on communities and organizations, power is frequently defined in terms of the actor's response to the query: Do you participate in community decisions or do you participate in organizational decisions? The operation or measurement becomes the concept, thereby enabling researchers to skirt the theoretical and conceptual issues posed by power (Adler, 1947).

This empiricist/operationalist approach fosters apparently irreconcilable debates over the nature of power. Interpretive differences are frequently dismissed as misrepresentations of the empirical reality rather than being viewed as consequences of different constructs or approaches to power. For example, the debate between elitists and pluralists in political science has stagnated because, rather than admit that one group subscribes to a notion of power that results in a pluralistic interpretation of the political situation and the other group subscribes to a notion that results in an elitist interpretation, both groups have implicitly maintained that they hold a common conception of power but divergent interpretations of the empirical data.

Empirical students of power appear to assume, for the most part, that power is similarly viewed by other researchers, while theoreticians writing about power (Dahl, 1957; Bierstedt, 1950; Emerson, 1962; Blau, 1964; Thibaut and Kelley, 1959; and Etzioni, 1961) confront a different dilemma: They fail to integrate the insights of other theorists systematically. This produces the impression that various theorists hold conflicting notions of power rather than that they emphasize different and complementary dimensions of power. A review of this literature leads readers to question whether consensus is possible and whether the variety of concepts implies conflicting or complementary notions of power. The answers will become clear as we examine a few conceptual treatments of power.

Most conceptions of power are based on Weber's (1947) classic definition that power is the probability that a person can carry out his or her own will despite resistance. Nearly all theorists who have written about power would express agreement with this very broad definition; yet, there are subtle and not-so-subtle differences among their various perspectives. In a frequently quoted article, Bierstedt (1950) portrays power as force or the ability to apply sanctions. It is a *potential* and not to be confused with the actual use of force, that is, the application of sanctions. Furthermore, power is distinguished from influence: Power is inherently coercive and implies involuntary submission, whereas influence is persuasive and implies voluntary submission.

Dahl (1957) begins with Weber's basic idea, but his analysis differs in important ways from Bierstedt's. Dahl fuses the *potential* and *use* dimensions of power and also equates power with influence. To Dahl, power is viewed in terms of cause and effect, and the criteria for determining causation are virtually the same as those researchers apply to their data. Based on John Stuart Mill's method of difference, if party B does X when party A does Y but not when party A does Y', then A has power over B. The degree of power depends on the specific probabilities of B doing X (instead of X') when A does Y versus Y'. From Dahl's standpoint, power is exercised whenever one party affects the behavior of another, combining what Bierstedt calls force and influence. Furthermore, Dahl's conception implies that an unused potential is not power, because power implies successful use of the potential.

Wrong (1968) offers still another point of view, once again grounded in Weber's conception. The basic thrust of Wrong's approach is reflected in his distinction between potential power, actual power, and the potential for power. First of all, Wrong draws a sharp distinction between potential power and use of power (that is, "actual" power). To Wrong, power does not imply the use or successful use of the potential because the potential, itself, may be enough to alter the behavior of others. A party can have power without using it: The compliance of possible targets is often based on their *subjective* expectation that the potential can and will be used when necessary. The potential may thus make use unnecessary. Second, Wrong (1968) suggests that groups or individuals may control resources that can be developed into a base for power or can be left dormant and undeveloped. That is, some groups or individuals may have a potential for power through which they can acquire power in a particular situation or relationship. Overall, Wrong's analysis suggests that greater attention should be given to the subjective nature of power and the processes of power acquisition.

There are many other differences among the conceptualizations of Bierstedt, Dahl, and Wrong, and there are many other theoretical treatments revealing even further complexities (see Blau, 1964; Etzioni, 1961; French and Raven, 1959; Raven, 1974; Tedeschi and Bonoma, 1972; Thibaut and Kelley, 1959). This literature creates a rather fragmented picture, which makes the operationalist stance of the researchers understandable. Does this mean that the concept of power is worthy of pursuit or that we should dismiss the concept? Our position is that one of the key problems has been the theoretical stance taken toward the concept of power. From our standpoint, the concept is best understood as a sensitizing device.

Power as a Sensitizing Device

Typical treatments of power assume that power can and should be a precise, well-defined term. Precise concepts are, of course, generally more valuable than imprecise ones, and the social sciences are already burdened with enough ill-defined notions. However, the theory-construction literature of the last fifteen years or so reveals that ill-defined terms are sometimes critical to the theory-construction enterprise (see Hage, 1972; Gibbs, 1972; Reynolds, 1971; Stinchecombe, 1968; Zetterberg, 1965). The theory-construction literature distinguishes two general types of concepts: *primitive* and *derived* terms. The value of primitive terms is primarily heuristic. Such ideas sensitize us to a series of phenomena or issues without necessarily providing clear, precise ideas or hypotheses. Despite the inherent vagueness of primitive concepts, they often (1) reveal the complexity and multidimensionality of phenomena that might otherwise be treated in an oversimplified or unidimensional manner, (2) serve as integrative devices for analyzing seemingly disparate ideas, and (3) lead to more specific well-defined ideas. These more specific ideas are often called derived terms (Hage, 1972; Reynolds, 1971). Derived terms are at a lower level of abstraction, ostensibly allow more precise definitions, and facilitate concrete operationalization of ideas embedded in the primitive term. Alone, primitive terms are difficult to apply in any way other than a loose, sensitizing fashion.

In our opinion, power is inherently a primitive term, and this is a major reason for the current state of the power literature. Extant work on power usually attempts to impose on the concept a level of precision beyond that appropriate for a primitive term. Thus, we must ask not what *is* power, but to what phenomena does the notion of power sensitize us? When doing research, we must not ask how to measure power, but how to measure a more concrete phenomenon or idea to which the primitive term points.

Elaborating the implications of a primitive term, like power, is not easy. There are few explicit standards or guidelines in the field or in the theory-construction literature. However, using Simmel's (1950) ideas as a backdrop, it appears that we should distinguish the *form* and the *content* of the phenomenon in question. That is, any sensitizing construct should bring to the forefront the basic dimensions of form and content relevant to an application of the construct.

Form and Content

As a primitive term, power sensitizes us to certain forms and contents in a social relationship. *Form* refers broadly to the basic pattern or configuration of the phenomenon, such as the parameters within which action or interaction occurs. The form is a generic characterization of the phenomenon that tends to be present in any concrete, empirical case. Our prior discussion of Bierstedt, Dahl, and Wrong has implied several forms. For example, virtually all concepts of power include sanctions as an essential feature of a power relationship and assume some level of dependence or interdependence in the power relationship. Such forms can vary by degree across settings, but they are likely to be present in every empirical instance or representation of the phenomenon. In other words, the forms are, by definition, the most basic aspects of the phenomenon.

Content refers to dimensions that are not omnipresent in empirical representations. Content is idiosyncratic and specific to the situation. Dimensions of content vary not only in terms of degree but also in terms of presence. As an example, consider the concept of authority. This has been closely allied to power since Weber's work, and it typically plays a role in contemporary conceptualizations of power. Yet, not all power is authority and not all power relationships are authority relationships. Authority is a specific content within which power may be manifested, but it is by no means inevitable in a power relationship. Similarly, influence is a manifestation of power in a relationship. However, it may be present or absent from setting to setting. Authority and influence are issues of content, not form, and their salience varies from one power situation to another.

The remainder of this chapter deals with the formal aspects of power. We focus specifically on three dimensions: (1) the relational aspect of power, (2) the dependence aspect, and (3) the sanctioning aspect. Chapter Three will examine content issues and focus on authority and influence in organizational contexts.

Relational Aspect of Power

Based primarily on the Weberian tradition, sociologists often begin even macrosociological analyses with some assumptions about actors, the unit act, or, specifically, the interaction of subunits. *Interaction* is the ultimate cornerstone of most sociological analyses. Structural properties are typically conceptualized as the crystallization, institutionalization, or stabilization of interaction patterns. However, while sociologists stress interaction and its implications, they tend to neglect this orientation when doing actual analyses in macrosociological settings. The more they concern themselves with macroanalysis, the more distant they become from interaction as a focal point. The work of Talcott Parsons (1937; 1951) is the epitome of this tendency. Parsons began his sociological approach by placing strong emphasis on the context and elements of social interaction. As his work evolved, he became increasingly concerned with the organization of society. As a result of this shift in emphasis, structural characteristics ceased to be construed as crystallized interaction and instead assumed an empirical and conceptual reality themselves. Similarly, sociologists dealing with power assume it to be based on interaction but, more often than not, deal with it as a structural phenomenon. The best example of this tendency may be found in the work of Blau. In *Exchange and Power in Social Life* (1964), Blau adopts an interactive approach to power. Seven years later, in his volume with Schoenherr entitled *The Structure of Organizations* (1971), power is treated not as an interactive process of the organization but as one of its structural attributes.

An example of some noted definitions of power reveals that most theorists view power as a mode of interaction rather than as a structural characteristic that stands independent of and in opposition to the actors engaged in the interaction:

- Weber (1947): "Power is the probability that one actor within a social relationship will be in a position to carry out his own will, despite resistance, and regardless of the basis on which this probability rests."
- Blau (1964): "Power is the ability of persons as groups to impose their will on others despite resistance through deterrence either in the form of withholding regularly supplied rewards or in the form of punishment inasmuch as the former, as well as the latter, constitutes in effect negative sanction."

- Mechanic (1962): "Power is defined as a force that results in behavior that would not have occurred if the forces had not been present."
- Dahl (1957): "A has power over B to the extent that he can get B to do something that he would not otherwise do."
- Kaplan (1964): "[Power is] the ability of one person or group of persons to influence the behavior of others, that is, to change the probabilities that others will respond in certain ways to specified stimuli."
- Bierstedt (1950): "Power is latent force. . . . Power itself is the prior capacity which makes the application of force possible."

In most of the above definitions, power is placed in an interactive situation. All the definitions imply that the actors take each other into account, that one actor tries to direct the other, and that they are operating in a common situation. However, while power is defined within an interactionist perspective, this is not to say that power is restricted to an individualistic or interpersonal context. The foregoing definitions do not preclude the possibility of examining power as the interaction between structural units. Although power is used by individuals, in the organizational context it is used by individuals as members of specific organizational subgroups. Parsons' definition of power is an interactionist formulation but within a structural framework:

- Parsons (1956a, b): "Power we may define as the realistic capacity of a system-*unit* to actualize its interests within the context of system-*interaction* and in this sense exert influence on processes in the system."

What makes Parsons' definition different from most of the others is that it deals with the power of interacting parties embedded in larger structures—structures independent of the component actors. If we view the system as a composite of its parts (individuals), then indeed Parsons' definition is consistent with the other definitions. However, to the extent that Parsons views the system as independent of its parts, his definition differs from these other definitions with regard to the level of analysis, yet interaction is still a critical aspect of his notion of power.

There is a tendency in the sociological literature on organizations to anthropomorphize and reify elements of social structure. This is particularly true in dealing with power. Despite the interactionist emphasis of most definitions of power, it is easy to speak of such things as the power of the organization, the power of particular structures, the relationship of powerful and nonpowerful organizations, and so forth.

There are two problems in attaching the notion of power to macroentities. First, the resulting reification neglects the interactional dynamics inherent in the concept of power. Second, it distracts our attention from the manner in which these dynamics impinge on and are manifested in intraorganizational relations. Treating power as simply another macroorganizational characteristic results in the neglect of organizational politics. Organizational politics must be understood through an analysis of the power relations among conscious actors or groups of actors; an analysis that fails to do this tells little about the everyday political workings of the organization. Interaction is an essential ingredient.

The key point underlying the relational aspect of power is that, whatever the unit of analysis, we must attend to the interactional dynamics of power relationships. Once we begin to analyze the interactional aspects, a critical question is: Who are the key actors? The power of an organization vis-à-vis other organizations in its environment becomes a question of how key actors and groups within each organization compete for scarce resources. The power of the organization vis-à-vis its members becomes a question of how key actors or groups, such as organizational elites, interact with other subgroups within the organization. The power of different departments within an organization becomes a question of how different departments interact with each other and with those higher and lower in the organizational hierarchy (Hinings and others, 1974; Pfeffer, 1978). Thus, giving serious consideration to the relational aspect of power results in a significant shift in the way power in organizations is studied.

Dependence Aspect of Power

We approach the dependence aspect of power from the standpoint of social exchange theory (see Blau, 1964; Emerson, 1962, 1972b; Homans, 1974; Thibaut and Kelley, 1959). Social exchange provides a parsimonious way to examine social relationships; moreover, power is a central aspect of an exchange approach to social relationships, and dependence or interdependence constitutes the point of departure for analyzing power. In fact, nowhere has the dependence dimension of power been more systematically treated than in social exchange theory (see Blau, 1964; Emerson, 1962, 1972b; Thibaut and Kelley, 1959).

Dependence is what makes exchange an integral part of any social relationship. Without dependence, there is no reason for an exchange, because parties can operate and obtain outcomes in total isolation. Two assumptions in exchange theory are that dependence (or interdependence) is an inherent feature of social life and, therefore, that exchanges are intrinsic aspects of any social relationship. Dependence exists when an actor's outcomes are contingent not just on the actor's own behavior but also on what other actors do simultaneously and/or in response to the actor's behavior (Thibaut and Kelley, 1959). That is, dependence implies that an actor's outcomes are determined by the interrelationship between his or her behavior and the behavior of others. In this sense, there are few human experiences that do not occur in the context of dependence relations. One might even argue that the hermit living in the mountains, by choosing to ignore the outside world, is minimally dependent on it. The main point is that social exchange, however rudimentary or infrequent, is ultimately grounded in dependence.

Naturally, dependence is not a constant. It varies across relationships and settings, and it is this variable aspect of dependence that is of prime concern to social exchange theory. For example, in an organizational context, a given subgroup is likely to have relationships with many other individuals and groups within the organization. From the standpoint of social exchange theory, the nature and level of dependence between the particular subgroup and each other subgroup will determine

the position of the subgroup within the total organization. In
addition, the network of dependence should have a bearing on
the difficulty, frequency, and exact nature of the exchanges between the subgroup and each other subgroup.

The dependence aspect of power has been treated most
fully in the power-dependence theory of Emerson (1962,
1972b) and Blau (1964). Power-dependence theory suggests
that dependence is a foundation not only for social relationships in general but also for each actor's power in a relationship.
The implication, of course, is that power is an intrinsic aspect of
social relationships, even though it need not always be salient or
perceived as such by the actors. From the standpoint of power-
dependence theory, power is a function of dependence. More
specifically, the power of an actor is a function of the other
person's dependence on the actor. The greater the other's dependence on the actor, the greater the actor's power in the relationship. Similarly, the other's power is a function of the
actor's dependence on the other. The greater the actor's dependence on the other, the greater the other's power in the
social relationship.

Power-dependence theory further develops the specific
basis or dimensions of dependence. Dependence is based on (1)
the availability of alternative outcome sources (outcome alternatives), and (2) the degree of value attributed to the outcome
at stake (outcome value). Outcome alternatives refer to the
probability that an actor can obtain better outcomes from other
relationships. This concept is virtually identical to Thibaut and
Kelley's (1959) comparison level for alternatives (see Blau,
1964; Emerson, 1962, 1972b; Gergen, 1969; Homans, 1974).
The implication of the outcome alternatives dimension is that
power must be examined not simply in terms of a particular
relationship in isolation but in terms of the network of relationships that encompasses the particular relationship. For example,
if we return to our notion of an organizational subgroup embedded in a network of relationships with other subgroups, the
power of the subgroup in any one relation is determined partially by the nature and level of outcomes available from the
other relationships. The outcome alternatives dimension taps
this source of power.

The second dimension of dependence, outcome value, is generally treated as the importance of or need for the outcomes in the social relationship (Blau, 1964; Emerson, 1972b; Gergen, 1969). In other words, the theory indicates that actors will attach values or priorities to the various outcomes obtained from a given relationship. The greater the value attached to the outcomes in the relationship, the greater the power of the other; by the same token, the more value the other attaches to the outcomes, the greater the actor's own power in the relationship. The overall implication is that actors evaluate not only their alternatives to the current relationship but also the importance of the outcomes in question. The power of each party is a function of both these dimensions.

Like most conceptualizations of power, power-dependence theory relates its concerns to standard definitions of power. The most standard definition, of course, is Weber's. Based on power-dependence theory, the capability to overcome resistance is ultimately grounded in the dependence relationship. Given that power is a function of dependence, the ability of A to overcome B's resistance is based primarily on the value B attributes to the relationship and the alternative relationships available to B (B's dependence on A); the ability of B to overcome A's resistance is grounded in the value A attributes to the relationship and A's alternatives.

The link between dependence and the standard Weberian definition of power overlooks some important differences between power-dependence theory and most other conceptualizations of power (see Bierstedt, 1950; Dahl, 1957; Etzioni, 1961; French and Raven, 1959; Tedeschi and Bonoma, 1972; Wrong, 1968). First of all, most conceptualizations of power do not directly link power to dependence or explicitly ground the concept in basic assumptions about social relationships such as those provided by exchange theory. It seems clear that dependence is inherent in social life. A strong case can be made for treating dependence as a formal dimension of power and making power a central concern of almost any sociological analysis. If we take the basic assumptions of exchange theory seriously, power becomes the heart of the sociological enterprise.

A second distinguishing characteristic of a power-dependence framework is that it implies a distinction between the stakes actors have in a relationship and outcome control, the ability of each to manipulate the other's outcome (see Bacharach and Lawler, 1976, for an elaboration). The difference between stakes and outcome control is best illustrated by a comparison between dependence (that is, outcome alternatives and the value attributed to the outcomes) and punitive or coercive power. A coercive capability allows an actor to reduce the outcomes of another by directly administering punishments. A coercive potential gives an actor the prerogative of directly manipulating the outcomes of an opponent. In contrast, the dimensions of dependence reflect the stakes actors have in a relationship. Most theories and research on power emphasize the coercive aspects of power relationships and neglect the underlying stakes actors have in existing relationships. We will further examine this issue in Chapters Seven and Eight, where we develop the tactical implications of power-dependence theory and discuss the role of coercion in organizations.

A final advantage of power-dependence theory is that its "objective" features have subjective relevance for actors in conflict settings (see Bacharach and Lawler, 1976; Lawler and Bacharach, 1979). This is critical because the cognitive aspect of power relationships becomes important in any concrete setting. Actors seldom have complete, perfect information on the dimensions of dependence or other aspects of the power relationship. The use of power, therefore, is almost always based not just on the objective conditions of dependence but also on the judgments actors make about these conditions. The dimensions of dependence are the criteria by which actors synthesize and summarize the multitude of conditions underlying a power relationship. Actors may take ineffective or counterproductive actions in part because of a miscalculation of power capabilities; similarly they may receive more outcomes in a relationship than we would expect from the objective power conditions, because they manipulate and manage the impressions others have of their power. As a consequence, it is relevant to ask whether actors are likely to use their evaluations of dependence to make subjective judgments about power and its use.

Bacharach and Lawler conducted a series of experimental studies on the cognitive implications of power-dependence theory (Bacharach and Lawler, 1976, 1980; Lawler and Bacharach, 1976, 1979). These dealt with different cognitive processes in conflict settings. As a whole, the research affirms the notion that the evaluation of the level of dependence will provide a basis for (1) the actors' perceptions of their own and others' power, (2) the perceived likelihood of the others' using power, and (3) the evaluation and selection of multiple tactical options. In effect, there is evidence that the objective conditions specified in power-dependence theory do enable us to understand some basic cognitive issues in conflict. Bacharach and Lawler affirm that the objective conditions of dependence have subjective meaning to parties in a conflict setting.

Thus, we can say that power-dependence theory identifies the basic parameters that constrain a power relationship. These parameters are simultaneously a source of integration and conflict. The dimensions of dependence determine whether parties stay in a given relationship, attempt to change it by tactical action, increase the amount of distance in the relationship, or simply abandon it. However, as noted in our contrast between dependence and coercion, there is another aspect of power relationships that is only implicit in extant versions of power-dependence theory (Blau, 1964; Emerson, 1962, 1972a, b): the sanctioning aspect of power. Any power relationship contains sanctions or potential sanctions, and this is a critical element in most of the broader conceptualizations of power (for example Bierstedt, 1950; Dahl, 1957; Wrong, 1968).

Sanctioning Aspect of Power

The sanctioning aspect of power is manifested in the interaction of parties. It refers to the actual changes actors can and do make in each other's outcomes. While patterns of dependence are the parameters of the power relationship, the sanctioning aspect of power is a more integral part of the interaction process. It is the active component of the power relationship, referring to the direct manipulations of the other's outcomes.

Sanctions can consist of manipulations of rewards, punishments, or both. In any case, they are a significant part of the process through which parties actually affect one another.

The formal aspects of sanctions can be derived from the probabilities intrinsic to most definitions of power (see Dahl, 1957; Weber, 1947). The probability that one party will overcome the *resistance* of another implies the probability that one actor will apply sanctions and make the other yield to his or her wishes. Thus, two probability dimensions are relevant: the probability that an actor will apply sanctions, and the probability that sanctions will have the intended effect. On a formal level, any power relationship is likely to encompass both these probabilities. Under certain conditions, actors will be more or less likely to apply sanctions, and sanctions are more or less likely to be successful. The sanctioning aspect of power should be viewed in terms of these probabilities.

Some writers examine these probabilities and others do not. Dahl (1957), for example, indicates that the power of A over B is a function of the difference between the probability that B will engage in some behavior with the intervention of A and the probability that B will do so without the intervention of A. From this standpoint, a distinction between the probability of using sanctions and the probability of successful influence is inappropriate. Power is not power in Dahl's terms unless it is used and is used successfully. If a person or group does not use the available power, then power cannot be attributed to that person or group. Hence Dahl's analysis implies a fusion of the two probability dimensions we distinguished above.

Dahl's approach to the probability issue is inadequate for several reasons. First of all, it emphasizes power as an objective probability and neglects the subjective component of power relationships. This theme is developed in Gamson's (1974) analysis of power as a subjective probability and in a theory of power attribution offered by Schopler and Layton (1974). Dahl's objective probabilities are ultimately based on a comparison of a current situation with past circumstances. Given the ambiguity in the comparisons of different circumstances, such probabilities are inevitably the result of an inferential process through which actors transform and possibly distort the raw information on the comparability of the settings. In application, even Dahl's analysis must turn into an analysis of these subjective inferential processes (see Gamson, 1974).

Second, Dahl's approach is inadequate because actors may respond or comply in anticipation of sanctions rather than awaiting their actual application. As noted earlier, Wrong (1968) argues that power potential and use are, for this reason, distinct phenomena. A party with a substantial sanction potential or merely a reputation for power may have influence simply because others anticipate that party's wishes and act accordingly. This separation of power potential and power use is also one of the main themes of deterrence theory (Morgan, 1977; Schelling, 1960). From the standpoint of deterrence theory, it is the latent force exerted by a power potential that is most critical in many conflict relationships. Specifically, deterrence theory indicates that a mere potential for power can facilitate the compliance of others depending on the magnitude of the potential and the subjective probability of power use. From the standpoint of deterrence theory, power has failed if an actor must resort to its use. Thus, it may be inferred that, while the effects of power potential are analytically independent of the effects of power use, in descriptive terms they are highly similar.

Third, Dahl's approach is inadequate because the use of power need not yield success. In any concrete circumstance, an actor may use power against another and meet with failure rather than success. As a consequence, the theoretical and empirical criteria for identifying instances of power use should be distinct from the indicators of success. Dahl's analysis neglects important empirical issues regarding the tactics of power because he sees a circular relationship between power and influence: Power implies its use, use implies influence, and influence, by definition, implies power. Consistent with Wrong's (1968) treatment of power, we believe that power potential, power use, and the consequences of power potential or power use are distinct phenomena and must be treated as such on both a theoretical and an empirical level. As will become clear later, our approach to power heightens the importance of tactical issues.

In summary, sanctions are an inherent part of a power

relationship. While the specific ways in which the sanctions are manifested in a relationship vary with the social setting, we can treat sanctions in terms of two probability dimensions on a formal level: the probability of using sanctions and the probability of successful sanctions. Regardless of the specific content, power can be partially portrayed in terms of these formal probabilities.

Summary

This chapter has dealt with the basic forms underlying the concept of power—the recurrent aspects of any power relationships. Specifically, we proposed three formal dimensions of power: the relational aspect of it, the dependence aspect, and the sanctioning aspect. These formal aspects of power are plausible starting points for nearly any analysis of power. Our discussion suggests the following specific advice: Power must be embedded in the social relationship and not treated as an attribute of a single person, group, or organization. The relationship can and should be portrayed in terms of dependence. The patterns and degree of dependence are the basic parameters or context within which actors affect one another. Within the dependence relationship, actors confront the issue of when to use sanctions and whether sanctions will be effective with respect to the other party. Thus, a power analysis should further determine when the actors generally use power (the probability of use under different conditions) and when the use of power yields results (the probability of success under different conditions).

Now that we have analyzed the form of power, Chapter Three will focus on the content of power relationships—the more circumstantial aspects of power. Our analysis of content will stress dimensions of content that are particularly relevant to organizations.

3

Content of Power

While the form dimensions discussed in Chapter Two occur in almost all power relationships, those relationships do differ in content. Our basic tenet is that a distinction between *authority* and *influence* allows us to specify the differences in content within organizations. We maintain that the failure to explain and apply this distinction to organizational behavior supports the current apolitical analysis of organizational processes.

Influence and Authority

There is a good deal of confusion about the concepts of power, influence, and authority. Peabody (1964) notes that there have been three approaches to the conceptualization of authority and influence. Some authors tend to equate them; some tend to equate power with influence and assert that authority is a special case of power; and others see authority and influence as distinctly different dimensions (the position we

27

take here). While Peabody tends to subsume power in the organization under the all-encompassing label of authority, Lawrence and Lorsch (1967), in their presentation of a contingency model of organizations, tend to go to the other extreme, subsuming all organizational power under the label of influence. They draw a distinction between knowledge influence and position influence. Position influence is defined as the delegation of power to a particular position in the organization. Knowledge influence is based on the relevance of the information that is available to an individual. But, where Peabody speaks of authority, Lawrence and Lorsch speak of influence as the major base of power within organizations.

It should be noted that neither Peabody nor Lawrence and Lorsch treat power generally; rather they focus on either authority or influence and maintain that these two aspects of power are essential in an organizational analysis. Furthermore, these authors all tap the same dimension in their analyses: the basis of power. This suggests that an integration of their perspectives could be brought about by simply relabeling their terms—what Peabody calls *functional authority* and Lawrence and Lorsch call *knowledge influence* we would call *influence*; what Peabody has called *formal authority* and what Lawrence and Lorsch have called *position influence* we would call *authority*.

Thus, we are forced to superimpose the distinction between authority and influence on the work of Peabody and Lawrence and Lorsch. But a number of other social scientists explicitly make this distinction. Building on the work of Barnard (1938), Simon (1953) sees authority as the right to make decisions that affect the activities of others in the organization. The superior frames and transmits decisions with the expectation that, because they are normatively supported by organizational rules, the decisions will be accepted by subordinates. Accepting the right of the superior to make such decisions, subordinates feel obliged to comply with the decisions. The unique aspect of authority is that subordinates acquiesce without question and are willing to (1) suspend any intellectual or moral judgments about the appropriateness of the superior's directives, or (2) act as if they subscribed to the judgment of the superior even if, in fact, they personally find the directive distasteful, irrational, or morally suspect. As Bierstedt (1950) notes, authority implies involuntary submission. An individual has authority when he or she can obtain unquestioning obedience from subordinates. In contrast, influence implies that subordinates do not suspend their critical faculties or willingness to act on the basis of their own inclinations.

Taking a perspective akin to Simon's, Tannenbaum (1950, 1958) suggests that influence is intrinsic to functional differentiation, while authority is lodged in or allocated across hierarchical positions. Like Simon, Tannenbaum sees authority as implying uncritical acceptance by subordinates. Yet Tannenbaum is aware that a superior must often rely on or seriously consider information or advice from subordinates in order to arrive at the "best possible" decision. The provision of information by one level to another or by one person to another is influence, according to Tannenbaum. An individual exercises influence by offering advice, making suggestions, entering into discussions, persuading, and the like, but that individual does not make the final decision: He or she does not exercise authority. Influence, thus, consists of efforts to affect organizational decisions indirectly, while authority makes final decisions. It should be noted that Tannenbaum is making a distinction not simply in terms of the locus of decision making but also on the basis of the direction or flow of power. Authority usually flows downward, while influence may be multidirectional. People can influence colleagues, superiors, or subordinates; they exercise authority only if their positions give them the prerogative of making the final decision.

A similar conceptualization of authority and influence is presented by Gamson (1968). He draws a distinction between targets of social control and targets of influence. In a social system, persons in positions of authority function as the sources of social control. Authorities make and enforce the final decisions. The targets of control are the partisans or those affected by the outcome of the decisions. In organizations, these will tend to be the organizational members, although in some instances they will also be individuals outside the organization. Gamson treats the power possessed by the potential partisans as influence. Hence, those with authority are the recipients or targets of influence and initiators of social control, while the potential partisans are the agents or initiators of influence and the targets of social control. The major dimension by which authority is differentiated from influence is the direction in which it is activated. Parties at lower levels in the organizational hierarchy can have substantial influence, while those at higher levels have substantial authority but little influence.

Gamson's treatment not only draws attention to the direction of power but also sensitizes us to the potential tension between authority and influence. While authority may be a prime source of social control, influence is the dynamic aspect of power and may be the ultimate source of change. Those in authority typically want to restrict the influence of subordinates; subordinates typically want to use influence to restrict the exercise of authority by superiors. It should also be noted that, while authority is inherently an aspect of hierarchy, influence is not. The context of influence need not be superior-subordinate relations; in fact, influence is the mechanism through which divergent subgroups without authority over one another may compete for power within an organization.

The work of Tannenbaum and Gamson may be construed as a subtle transition from Weber's (1947) to Simmel's (1950) concept of power. In the Weberian framework, organizational theorists see power as a relational phenomenon in which one party constantly maintains control. These theorists are concerned with the subordinate only in terms of examining whether the subordinate accepts directives initiated by the superior or not. For example, in an expansion of the Weberian model, Etzioni (1961) is predominantly concerned with the nature of subordinate compliance, not with subordinate power. Simon's (1953) work again focuses on the nature of subordinate compliance, whether it is skeptical or obedient. Rarely do we find authors adopting Simmel's (1950) suggestion that in all power relations the subordinate has some degree of power.

Indeed, while authority is lodged in the superior, influence need not be. As Bacharach and Aiken (1976) have argued, authority is a dichotomous variable, while influence is a continuous variable. It makes little sense to speak of someone having *some* authority in a particular decision area, for a person either has or does not have the authority to make a particular decision. It is reasonable, however, to describe someone as having *some* influence. Comparative organizational studies that concentrate primarily on the decentralization of authority have failed to recognize the multidirectional nature of power relations and have overlooked the potential tension between different facets of power.

Bacharach and Aiken (1976) contend that the distinction between authority and influence becomes particularly important when considering the dilemma the decision-making process poses for the higher echelons in an organization. These theorists maintain that the dilemma stems from two potentially conflicting imperatives: the need for reliable information to facilitate decision making and the need to maintain formal control of decision making. To make the proper decisions, higher echelons must avail themselves of all possible sources of information. To achieve this objective, they must involve actors from all levels in the organization in the decision-making process. Despite the need for information, they may still be reluctant to permit this broad involvement to occur if it is going to undermine their formal control over the decision-making process. Decentralization of authority, while supplying the requisite information, presents a challenge to the decision maker's control and, therefore, is not by itself a viable solution to the dilemma. The dispersion of influence, however, does provide a way out of this dilemma, for higher echelons can obtain the necessary information without relinquishing their formal control. The dispersion of influence permits actors from all levels in the organization to make their expertise felt in specific decision areas, while final approval of their recommendations rests with the higher echelons.

Another way of casting this issue is to say that authority is a zero-sum game, whereas influence is not. A basic point of debate between Marxists and functionalists has, in fact, been whether power is a zero-sum phenomenon (that is, there is a finite amount, so that an increase for one party means a decrease for another) or non-zero-sum phenomenon (that is, there is an infinite amount, so that amounts for all may vary up and down). A well-known debate in this area occurred between the Marxist C. Wright Mills (1959) and the functionalist Talcott Parsons (1951, 1956a, b). Marxists tend to view power as zero-sum. They contend that any increase in the power of subordinates ostensibly implies a decrease in the power of superiors and vice versa. Functionalists (see Parsons, 1951, 1956a, b) typically treat power as the ability to mobilize the resources of a system. This conception implies that the total amount of power in the system is indefinite and variable over time. Consequently, an increase in the power of superiors may actually enhance the power of subordinates if the mobilization potential of subordinates in the organization is also increased. In light of our distinction between authority and influence, we argue that authority is zero-sum in nature: a party either does or does not have the right to make the final decisions in a given context; if one party has the right, another does not have it. Influence, on the other hand, can be seen as non-zero-sum in nature. The influence of different groups within an organization should vary across specific organizational conditions and decision areas. An increase in one subgroup's influence does not inevitably imply any change in another subgroup's influence. Thus, our conceptualization of power implies that it has both zero-sum (authority) and non-zero-sum (influence) manifestations. In our opinion, Marxists and functionalists are focusing on different aspects of power in organizations: Marxists stress authority relations, and functionalists emphasize influence process.

Now that we have introduced the distinction between authority and influence, linking it to prior theoretical work, we will elaborate the distinction. First, we relate the distinction to sources of power and bases of power in organizations. Second, we discuss three basic dimensions of authority relationships: scope, domain, and legitimacy. Third, we detail the primary spheres of decision making within formal organizations.

Bases and Sources of Power

French and Raven (1959) distinguish five major bases of power: coercion, rewards, expertise, legitimacy, and referent power. Later versions of the scheme add information as a sixth basis of power (Raven, 1974; Raven and Kruglanski, 1970). Coercion implies the threat of decreasing another's outcomes. Rewards imply the promise of increasing those outcomes. These bases are the sanctioning aspect of power that we elaborated on in Chapter Two. Expertise is formal or specialized knowledge about particular issues or activities within an organization. It is distinguishable from information, which consists of the access or opportunity actors have to gain information about the inner workings of the organization or about the relation of the organization to the environment. This information may or may not be related to the actor's level in the hierarchy of authority. As Mechanic (1962) has noted, even those at low levels (such as secretarial staff members) can accumulate and use informational resources in a manner that gives them much more power than one would expect from their formal positions in the organization. Expertise is tantamount to the basis of power available to lawyers, psychiatrists, accountants, and others who bring specialized knowledge with them to the organization. Information is diffuse, unspecialized, and obtained from actual experience within the organization, not brought into the organization from outside.

The other two bases of power, legitimacy and referent power, are distinctly different animals. Legitimacy is tantamount to what we have called authority—power based on rights of control and concomitant obligations to obey. Referent power is more interpersonal in nature than legitimacy. On the most general level, it means power based on identification with another. This is exemplified by the power of charismatic leaders who elicit deference and are accorded credibility by others.

While French and Raven provide an extensive repertoire of possible bases of power, they do not present a cogent theoretical framework. There is overlap between some of the categories (for instance, legitimacy and expertise, information and expertise); at least one category (referent power) appears as a catchall; and, most important, what is being controlled or used by the party with power is not clear in all cases. Much of the ambiguity in the French and Raven scheme results from their confusion of the bases of power with the sources of power.

A distinction must be made between *bases* of power and *sources* of power. This distinction has important implications for the authority-influence contrast. In dealing with the bases of power we are interested in what parties control that enables them to manipulate the behavior of others; in referring to the sources of power we are speaking of how parties come to control the bases of power. Given our contrast of bases and sources of power, Etzioni's (1961) work provides a somewhat better starting point. Unlike French and Raven, Etzioni appears to maintain a consistent focus on the bases of power. He identifies three forms of power, each relying on a different type of sanction. Coercive power rests on the ability to apply the threat of physical sanctions; remunerative power is based on the control of material resources and rewards; normative power is based on the control of symbolic rewards.

One additional basis for power needs to be added to Etzioni's three. In an organizational setting, access to information, that is, knowledge, also becomes a basis of power. When an actor in an organization controls unique information and when that information is needed to make a decision, the actor has power (Pettigrew, 1973). Drawing on the Etzioni and the French and Raven schemes, we can identify four primary bases of power: coercive, remunerative, normative, and knowledge. The coercive base of power is the control of punishment; the remunerative base is the control of rewards; the normative base is the control of symbols; and the knowledge base is the control of information. Any power relationship in an organization can encompass all of these bases, but each relationship may well be characterized by one of them rather than another.

Having identified the primary bases of power, we must now turn to the sources of power. There appear to be four:

1. *Office or structural position.* The office or structural position might provide a party access to various bases of power. Some positions might provide little information but substantial coercive resources, while others might give the occupant the capacity to manipulate symbols or mobilize internalized commitments to certain norms. The office or structural position should be treated as independent of the bases of power, given the diverse ways in which offices can constrain or facilitate the power bases.

2. *Personal characteristics.* The most marked personal characteristic that is a source of power is, of course, charisma. As Weber indicates, the charismatic leader has power by virtue of extraordinary and often mystical characteristics. However, relevant personal characteristics might also include verbal skill, ability to argue effectively for positions, or even physical attributes (for example, a physical disability of a veteran espousing a pro- or antiwar position). In the organizational literature, personal characteristics are typically treated under the construct *leadership.* Leadership encompasses the personal abilities and characteristics that key individuals have apart from their offices or other sources of power.

3. *Expertise.* As noted earlier, expertise refers to the specialized information actors bring to the organization. It is typically based on activities outside the organization, for example, education. We treat this as a source of power, rather than a basis of power in French and Raven's terms, because it seems to be a means by which a party comes to control specialized information rather than the control itself. Expertise is brought to bear on the particular concerns of a given organization at specific points in time. It provides a potential resource but must be further developed and applied to the organizational context before it takes on the characteristic of an intraorganizational power base.

4. *Opportunity.* This source of power is embedded in the informal structure of the organization. The idea comes from Mechanic's (1962) analysis of the power of the lower levels

in an organization (such as secretarial staff). The informal aspects of formal positions or informal positions that are not identified officially by the organization can provide an important source of power. Certain positions can provide access to a significant amount of information of importance to others, and there may be no formal rules regarding transmission or withholding of the information. Similarly, certain points in the production process are more critical than others; consequently, those who occupy these critical positions have greater capability of obstructing or doing damage to the productivity of an organization.

At this point, we have identified two types of power (authority and influence), four bases of power, and four sources of power. Table 1 presents the relationships among these aspects

Table 1. Relationships of Sources, Bases, and Types of Power

Source	Type	Bases
Structure	Authority	Coercion Remunerative Normative Knowledge
Personality	Influence	Normative Knowledge
Expertise	Influence	Normative Knowledge
Opportunity	Influence	Coercion Knowledge

of power and enables us to relate the sources and bases to the authority-influence distinction. One could argue that all the bases of power could be generated from each source in a given context. The table is a tentative attempt to identify the dominant bases of power provided by each of the sources.

The table helps to illustrate some of the contrasts between authority and influence. First, authority and influence rely on different sources of power. Authority is based solely on structural sources of power, whereas influence can be grounded in any of the other sources—personality, expertise, or opportunity. Second, the relevance of the four bases of power depends on the power source, and this also has important implications for the authority-influence contrast. In the case of authority, it is not possible to exclude any of the bases of power. In a given structural context, one or more of the power bases may be constrained or limited by the structure, but on a general theoretical level authority implies all four bases of power. Superiors typically control the resources used to reward or punish; their prerogatives are normatively sanctioned by the organizational rules; and their formal positions should give them exclusive knowledge over which they have substantial control. In sum, all four bases of power should characterize authority relations.

In the case of influence relationships, we can make some tentative judgments about the importance of different power bases. The dominant or most critical basis of power depends somewhat on the power source. Personal characteristics can make knowledge a viable power basis because such characteristics might enhance the credibility of the party's information. People are likely to attribute more credibility to information from a person who has a reputation for honesty or appears honest, who is similar to them in background, or who has special qualities with which they wish to be identified. These same qualities might enable a person to invoke and use informal norms to sway the targets of influence. The manner in which these bases of power flow from personality is illustrated in Weber's (1947) analysis of charismatic leaders.

Expertise and opportunity differ somewhat from personal characteristics. Expertise is obviously important primarily because it provides a knowledge basis. That knowledge basis is unavailable to those who have not had specialized training; those without expertise are, therefore, dependent on those with expertise for certain kinds of information. As noted earlier, opportunity is grounded in the informal aspects of an organization. A person's (or group's) place in the informal network can provide knowledge or information about the inner workings of the organization or a strategic location from which to apply coercion. Overall, the table implies that manipulation and control of knowledge are the key elements of influence processes. All three sources of influence—personality, expertise, and opportunity—provide this basis of power. Other bases of power may also flow from these sources, even ones not noted in the table, but the most critical basis appears to be knowledge.

Circumscribed and Uncircumscribed Power

Our discussion of Table 1 implies another important difference between authority and influence—the degree to which the power is circumscribed or uncircumscribed. Authority is clearly circumscribed power, since it is lodged in the formal structure of an organization. While authority typically provides access to a multitude of power bases, its structural source is also likely to constrain the use of power by superiors. Influence, on the other hand, has no clear boundaries that are formally recognized or sanctioned by the organization. It is inherently informal and, technically, unlimited. The authority position of a party can limit his or her influence by constraining the ability to present "favorable" personal characteristics, project or use expertise, or take advantage of informal opportunities. However, influence is uncircumscribed.

The degree to which power is circumscribed or uncircumscribed can be analyzed in terms of three dimensions: domain, scope, and legitimacy. The domain of authority refers to the number of units or individuals under the control of a superior (Kaplan, 1964). Note that the targets of control may be subgroups or individuals within an organization. The more subgroups or individuals under the formal jurisdiction of a given party with authority, the greater the domain of authority. The scope of a superior's power, by contrast, is the range of behaviors or activities controlled for each unit, whether individuals or groups. The greater the range of behaviors or activities controlled by a superior, the greater the scope of authority.

The scope and domain of authority are typically well specified and formally defined. Because authority is grounded in the formal structure of the organization, it is written into the unit's actual rules. Formalization implies that parameters such as scope and domain are relatively specific. The scope and domain of influence are typically unspecified and unclear. Its scope and domain are not established from the top but emerge from the day-to-day influence processes. Thus, we can expect greater ambiguity and variance over time in the scope and domain of influence.

Legitimacy of Authority

The third and most important dimension of authority is legitimacy. Whereas the scope and domain of authority are part of the formal rules underlying authority, legitimacy is a cognitive or perceptual phenomenon. As Weber (1947) indicates, legitimacy is a belief, that is, belief in the appropriateness of the authority structure. Judgments about that appropriateness might be based on moral values, normative ideals, or pragmatic or utilitarian criteria. In any case, legitimacy implies that subordinates accept not just the authority of a superior but also the rationale or justification (implicit or explicit) for attaching authority to certain positions and their occupants. The greater the legitimacy attributed to the structure by organizational members, the greater the compliance an organization can command from its members. Legitimacy means that subordinates are willing to work within the confines of the existing organizational structure and that all members of the organization (regardless of their level in the hierarchy) are willing to follow standard procedures for conducting organizational activities.

Since authority is the right to make the final decision, legitimacy refers specifically to beliefs about rights of decision making. The specific content of legitimacy depends on the issues at hand as well as the congruence of superiors' and subordinates' beliefs about legitimacy. A lack of congruent beliefs means an organization has a legitimacy problem.

On a broad level there are two basic types of legitimate authority: centralized and decentralized. Two variants of incongruence between superiors' and subordinates' beliefs can also be labeled: authority shirking and authority usurpation (Bacharach, 1978). These four types of authority relations are summarized:

A. Congruence (Legitimate Authority)
   1. Centralized: superiors and their subordinates concur that the right to make a final decision belongs to only the superior.
   2. Decentralized: superiors and subordinates concur that subordinates have the right to make final decisions.
B. Incongruence
   1. Shirking: superiors maintain that subordinates have the right to make final decisions but subordinates refuse to do so.
   2. Usurpation: superiors maintain that subordinates do not have the right to make final decisions, but subordinates maintain that they do have the right to make final decisions.

The two congruent authority relations are legitimized ones while the two incongruent ones imply nonlegitimized authority. The nonlegitimized types identify two basic legitimacy problems that organizations and their members confront.

Thus, authority has a cognitive and a structural foundation, and the ultimate test of legitimacy is the congruence of these cognitive and structural components. Such a test is not available for influence, primarily because influence processes do not have the official sanction of the organization. The legitimacy of an attempt to influence is much more ambiguous than that of an action taken on the basis of authority. Authority can provide a justification for directives or for compliance, but there is no comparable justification for influence. It is not even clear how we evaluate the legitimacy of influence cognitively. There is no formal test for the legitimacy of influence, because its informal relations are based more on personal characteristics than structure. As a result, influence is constrained by such matters as taste, morality, and expedience. People can defend and justify actions based on authority by specifying their source in the structure. Actions based on influence, however, are not amenable to such a defense.

The importance of legitimacy is further illustrated by legal cases in which bureaucrats are accused of misconduct. The bureaucrat will often hide behind the justification, "I was simply carrying out orders." The prosecution will, more often than not, contend that "orders" do not justify exceeding the bounds of legitimate authority. Occupants of authority positions sometimes make illegitimate demands on subordinates; carrying out such orders can be construed as a submission to the influence aspect of power, not a response to authority. The target of influence is likely to be seen as more responsible for compliance than the target of legitimate authority. Furthermore, in joining an organization, a person is implicitly agreeing to submit to authority but not necessarily to influence. A complete discussion of these issues would entail treatment of collective and individual responsibility, universal and organizational justice, and so forth. This analysis is simply designed to sensitize readers to some broader implications of the authority-influence distinction.

Flow of Power

Our treatment of dimensions of authority has necessarily implied that authority is essentially unidirectional. It typically flows from the top or higher levels downward. That is, it applies solely to superior-subordinate relationships and deals with the power of superiors over subordinates. Our treatment of power implies that subordinates can also exercise power, that power is actually multidirectional. Influence, of course, is the multidirectional aspect of power. It is the mode of power that both gives subordinates the capability of manipulating superiors and gives superiors the capability of getting more from their subordinates than is specified in the formal role obligations. Influence is two-directional in hierarchical relations, but it also applies to horizontal relations not lodged in an authority structure.

The organizational literature stresses the authority aspect of power. This is reflected in the long-standing concern with centralization and decentralization. From the standpoint of this literature, power flows down from the top of the organization. It is something allocated by a higher echelon to a lower echelon.

This unidirectional and managerial view of power is an integral element of rationalistic consensual models of organizations. The major gap in this approach is a failure to consider that power may also be *taken* by the lower echelon. The organizational literature places emphasis on power given by the top while neglecting the possibility that subordinates will take power beyond that given to them in the organizational structure. This additional side of power—the taking of power—must be a central concern of a political model of organizations. Individuals and subgroups within organizations are not passive recipients awaiting the downward trickle of power but rather active participants mobilizing power for their own ends. A political approach to organizations implies a multidirectional image of power, and this means an emphasis on influence apart from, as well as in the context of, the authority structure.

Dynamics of Change

It should be apparent that influence is the dynamic, tactical aspect of power relationships. Authority is the static, stable feature of organizations, whereas influence is the fulcrum of change. In fact, an argument can be made that influence processes are a primary source of adaptation and innovation. Informal influence processes enhance the discretion of organizational members, and more discretion, in turn, increases the organization's capacity to adapt internally and externally. We do not want to imply that authority relations do not change, only that they constitute a major source of resistance to any deviation or departure from standard procedures. In fact, influence relationships may be transformed into authority relationships. That is, influence relationships sometimes undergo institutionalization, acquire legitimacy, and reemerge as authority relationships. When examined over time, the relationship between authority and influence exhibits a distinctly dialectical pattern. To elaborate, those in positions of authority may be so entrenched that they are incapable of adapting to critical changes emanating from either the organization or its environment. Such an unyielding defense of the status quo is epitomized by the time-honored bureaucratic refrain "we have to go by the book."

Those so entrenched in authority become vulnerable to usurpation by actors in positions of influence. This inherent tension in organizational power relationships brings to the forefront a theme long ignored in organizational research, namely, that organizations like other social systems may be viewed as systems of circulating elites (Michels, 1959; Mosca, 1939; and Pareto, 1935). The conditions that precipitate circulation and the mechanisms by which it occurs remain empirical questions warranting further investigation.

Decision Areas

While the distinction between authority and influence is helpful to us in trying to understand organizational dynamics, it is important to recognize that power relations come to the fore with reference to specific issues at particular points in time. Many of the points that we make in this book have to be modified when examined in terms of specific decisions. For example, Bacharach and Aiken (1976) draw a distinction between work decisions and strategic decisions. Work decisions pertain to the specific manner in which a task is carried out within the organization. Strategic decisions are concerned with broad organizational policies. Work decisions include such issues as work methods and work assignments, while strategic decisions include issues of personnel, public relations, and budget. In terms of the present discussion, authority and influence relationships need not be consistent across all decisions. In fact Bacharach and Aiken (1976) have illustrated that the factors that constrain influence in work decisions vary somewhat from those that constrain influence in strategic decisions. Therefore, in any empirical application of the issues raised in this volume, we need to be sensitive to the type of the organizational decision being examined.

Summary

This chapter has focused on the content dimensions of power relationships. Two major content dimensions were identified: authority and influence. There are several points of contrast between them:

1. Authority is the static, structural aspect of power in organizations; influence is the dynamic, tactical element.
2. Authority is the formal aspect of power; influence is the informal aspect.
3. Authority refers to the formally sanctioned right to make final decisions; influence is not sanctioned by the organization and is, therefore, not a matter of organizational rights.
4. Authority implies involuntary submission by subordinates; influence implies voluntary submission and does not necessarily entail a superior-subordinate relationship.
5. Authority flows downward, and it is unidirectional; influence is multidirectional and can flow upward, downward, or horizontally.
6. The source of authority is solely structural; the source of influence may be personal characteristics, expertise, or opportunity.
7. Authority is circumscribed, that is, the domain, scope, and legitimacy of the power are specifically and clearly delimited; influence is uncircumscribed, that is, its domain, scope, and legitimacy are typically ambiguous.

Overall, the distinction between authority and influence heightens our awareness of power in organizational settings and provides the starting point for a political analysis of organizations.

When power is discussed in terms of authority and influence, it becomes apparent that organizational politics, for the most part, take place within the realm of influence. Drawing on this distinction, three aspects of organizational politics require further examination: (1) how the authority structure affects coalition processes, (2) how interest groups in the organization form coalitions, and (3) how these coalitions bargain within the organization. The rest of this volume will address these issues.

4

Authority Structure and Coalition Formation

◤◤

The major purpose in this chapter is to develop some very basic ideas and principles for linking coalitions to the authority structure. Recall that coalitions refer to joint action by two or more interest groups against another subgroup in an organizational context. The authority structure constitutes the formal dimension of stratification in organizations, while the informal dimension emerges from the influence processes. We will focus here on the formal aspect of the stratification system, that is, authority. Chapter Five places coalitions more explicitly in the influence processes within organizations.

Social psychological work on coalitions (see Caplow, 1968; Gamson, 1964; Komorita and Chertkoff, 1973; Lawler and Youngs, 1975; Murnighan, 1978; Stryker, 1972) provides a rich, untapped source of ideas relevant to an organizational analysis. These ideas are embedded in abstract, formal treatments of coalition action that can provide reference points for organizational analyses.

Social psychological theory on coalitions dovetails rather nicely with organizational analyses of coalitions. In fact, the social psychological tradition essentially begins where organizational analysis tends to stop. Based on organizational work, our task is to link the stratification of subgroups to coalition formation, and this is precisely where social psychological theory becomes most relevant. Its major thrust has been to predict and explain why some coalitions develop and others do not, based on the distribution of resources across actors in the situation. The most basic proposition guiding social psychological work is that the distribution of resources will determine which coalition forms in a multiple-party setting.

As might be expected, the social psychological tradition treats the terms *resources* and *distribution of resources* in a very abstract, artificial manner. Formal resources are not distinguished from informal ones, and little reference is made to the concrete resources in real world situations. In brief, a resource is some commodity that is exchangeable or that leads to some divisible payoff. Despite this abstract and simple definition, the literature treats the distribution of resources as tantamount to a formal stratification system. The specific content of the resources can be quite variable; the point is that, whatever the specific resources, stratification along some formal dimension (for example, authority) remains the ultimate foundation for coalition action. As a consequence, social psychological theory provides an excellent starting point for linking the formal stratification or hierarchy of an organization to coalition processes.

A complete, detailed review of coalition theory and research is beyond the scope of this volume, and such reviews can be found elsewhere (see Caplow, 1968; Gamson, 1964; Murnighan, 1978; Stryker, 1972; Vinacke, 1969). We will focus on *major* coalition *theories* in the social psychological tradition. We have excluded strictly game theory models (cf. Rapoport, 1966), because these typically bear less on the questions we are concerned with and because the most relevant notions from game theory have been incorporated into the social psychological theories. Also, for the sake of simplicity, we will use three-party contexts to illustrate the implications of the theories for organizations. The theories have comparable implications for larger units, and concrete applications to particular organizations often require designations of more than three basic subgroups. However, three-party contexts are sufficient to develop the basic implications of the theories, and, for purposes of illustration, we will assume that three of the basic subgroups in any organization are upper levels of management, middle levels of management, and lower levels of the organization (workers).

In his analysis of triads, Caplow (1956, 1968) has identified eight types of resource distributions. Most social psychological work has stressed one or more of these structures. Labeling the three parties A, B, and C, respectively, the eight structures can be portrayed as follows:

1. $A = B = C$
2. $A > B, B = C, A < (B + C)$
3. $A > B, B = C, A = (B + C)$
4. $B = C, A > (B + C)$
5. $A > B > C, A < (B + C)$
6. $A > B > C, A > (B + C)$
7. $A > B > C, A = (B + C)$
8. $A = (B + C), B = C$

Thus, in stratification system 5, A has more resources than B, B has more resources than C, and a coalition between B and C would control more resources than A. Contrast this with distribution 6, where A has more than B, B more than C, but a coalition between B and C would not control more resources than A. The major difference between these two situations is that in 5 a coalition places A in a subordinate power position, while in 6 a coalition is still inferior to A in terms of the resources controlled.

These resource distributions can be construed as basic types of stratification systems. However, a close examination of them suggests that many are rare or nonexistent in organizational contexts. For example, we have defined A as the upper level of management, B as the middle level, and C as the workers; for these categories, it is hard to visualize organizations with formal stratification systems analogous to 1 and 8; furthermore, while 3 and 7 are plausible, they appear less interesting or relevant than 2, 4, 5, and 6. Applied to organizations, the four of primary relevance are those presented in Table 2. The formal structure of an organization tends to approximate one of these

Table 2. Four Types of Stratification Systems

Pattern of Stratification	Type of Stratification
1. A > B > C, A > (B + C)	Centralized authority; Developed middle level of management
2. B = C, A > (B + C)	Centralized authority; Undeveloped middle level of management
3. A > B, B = C, A < (B + C)	Decentralized authority; Undeveloped middle level of management
4. A > B > C, A < (B + C)	Decentralized authority; Developed middle level of management

stratification systems. In all four structures, A is highest on the authority dimension. Structures 1 and 2 represent contexts where authority is highly concentrated at the top. The only difference between these two structures is the degree to which middle levels of management are well developed and have significantly higher resources than the lower levels of employees. Structures 3 and 4 constitute less centralized stratification systems, where coalitions between middle and lower levels can undermine the authority of the upper level. These structures are analogous to decentralized systems of authority. Subsequent sections of this chapter will focus on these four structures, two centralized ones (1 and 2) and two decentralized ones (3 and 4).

Coalition Theories

Five major coalition theories are relevant to our concerns: Caplow's (1968) power theory of coalitions, Gamson's (1961a, b, 1964) minimum resource theory, Komorita and Chertkoff's (1973) bargaining theory, Komorita's (1974) weighted probability model, and ideological-distance models (DeSwann, 1970, 1973; Leiserson, 1970). Each of these theories is concerned with how actors choose among alternative coalition opportunities. Given that three or more actors have two or more coalition options, what coalitions are most likely to form? While each theory uses the distribution of resources as a major basis for predicting coalition formation, their predictions diverge in ways that are important to organizational analyses. Before we consider each theory, we will further elaborate the common context that the theories are attempting to understand.

The theories begin with the assumption that parties are trying to maximize their gain and that the distribution of resources is a criterion for estimating the gain from alternative coalition options. However, the theories place additional rather strong constraints on the settings of interest. Specifically, the theories (with some minor variations) are primarily designed for the following context:

1. Each party in the organization represents a distinct organizational entity in competition with other entities for scarce resources. Examples include three or more nations competing in international markets, three or more political parties competing for votes or political patronage in a legislative context, and three unions competing for members. The competitive aspects of the relationship are stressed in these situations, and coalition theories have consequently neglected or deemphasized the position of the competing parties in a larger social system. There have been few theories and little research on coalitions within stratified social entities such as organizations (for exceptions, Caplow, 1968, chap. 5; Lawler, 1975a, b; Lawler, Youngs, and Lesh, 1978; Webster and Smith, 1978).

2. Coalitions have either a 100 percent or zero probability of success ("winning the game"). The theories predict that coalitions that cannot obtain the scarce outcomes at stake will not form, and that actors will choose among coalitions with a 100 percent chance of success on the basis of their expected gain. The implication is that the basic problem faced by parties is not the success of the coalition but rather the ability of a party to negotiate a satisfactory agreement with one or more prospective allies.

3. The payoff accrued by winning coalitions (those with

100 percent probability of success) is constant across all winning coalitions. That is, different coalitions do not yield different magnitudes of collective payoff to be divided among members of the coalition. In a political convention, for example, this assumption indicates that the total payoff received by the winning coalition will be constant regardless of which coalition musters the necessary votes. The implication of this assumption is that the gain from alternative coalition options depends totally on how the coalition's payoff is distributed to its members.

4. The winning coalition's payoff is divisible in an unrestricted manner among its members. That is, the structure of the setting does not inherently restrict the manner in which allies divide their collective benefit. Members of the coalition technically have the freedom to negotiate virtually any division of the collective payoff. This means that estimates of gain underlying and preceding coalition choices are based on actors' assumptions about the result of the bargaining process.

5. No party in the context has *dictatorial power,* that is, no party can win or obtain the scarce outcomes without a coalition. The only way for any party to obtain the outcomes is through a coalition. This means that the major issue is not *whether* coalitions form in a given setting but simply *which* coalition will form, given various possible winning coalitions.

6. No party has *veto power* (if a party *must* be included in any coalition in order for that coalition to win, that party has veto power: see Gamson, 1964; Michener and others, 1975b). In general, the social psychological research focuses on resource distributions that do not confer veto power on any party. Veto power tends to occur where some coalitions are disallowed or have a zero probability of success. The implication of this assumption is that virtually any coalition in the context can be a winning coalition (all coalitions have a 100 percent chance of success).

The overall implication of these context assumptions is that the coalition theories were not specifically designed for application to organizations. The six assumptions noted above are essentially the scope conditions of the theories, and it is clear that their applicability to any concrete organizational setting can vary substantially. However, some of the assumptions are more important than others, and some can be relaxed without doing damage to the basic thrust of the theories. It is best to interpret these scope conditions in a loose manner (unless, of course, one is attempting to test the theories). Despite these rather constraining scope conditions, the coalition theories still provide indispensable heuristic devices for an organizational analysis. We will return to some of these scope conditions later in this chapter as we draw out the implications of the theories for an organizational analysis.

Caplow's Power Theory of Coalitions

Caplow's (1956) theory is based on one assumption: parties will prefer the coalition that maximizes the *number* of others they have control over. Specifically, actors will consider their power *within* a prospective coalition as well as the power the coalition provides them over others *outside* the coalition. In evaluating these dimensions of power, internal and external to the coalition, they will stress not the degree of power difference between themselves and others but the number of others who will occupy positions subordinate to themselves. This will become clearer if we analyze the specific predictions derived from this assumption.

Caplow's theory predicts whether coalitions will form in each of the four resource distributions of primary interest. The predictions are indicated in Table 3. In structures 1 and 2, party A can maintain power without a coalition, and there is no reason for B and C to coalesce, because such a coalition has a zero

Table 3. Predictions of Caplow's Power Theory

Structure	Predicted Coalition
1. A > B > C, A > (B + C)	None
2. B = C, A > (B + C)	None
3. A > B, B = C, A < (B + C)	BC
4. A > B > C, A < (B + C)	BC or AC

chance of success. Consequently, Caplow's theory predicts no coalition in these "top heavy" structures.

The primary focus of Caplow's theory is on structures 3 and 4. Consider structure 3 first. Here, if B or C forms a coalition with A, B or C will have an inferior position within the coalition but the coalition will control the one party outside it. A BC coalition, however, allows these two parties to avoid an inferior position within the coalition while also permitting control over the one party outside the coalition. Thus, in terms of the two power dimensions (internal and external to the coalition), Caplow predicts a BC coalition. It enables both B and C to maximize their power in the situation.

In distribution 4, a BC coalition is more advantageous to party B than the alternative, an AB coalition. Party B has an inferior position within the AB coalition but a superior position within the BC coalition. In both, it gains control of the outside party. Thus, B should prefer a BC coalition. Party C's alternatives, however, the AC and BC coalitions, are not distinguishable: In both, C has an inferior position within the coalition and gains control over one party outside it. If the theory took account of the power difference between the parties in the AC and the BC coalitions, it might predict a BC coalition in this situation as well. However, given C's ambivalence regarding the BC and AC coalitions, the theory predicts that either an AC or a BC coalition will form.

Caplow's theory has two broad implications for organizations. First, the comparison between structures 1 and 2 (centralized authority) and structures 3 and 4 (decentralized authority) suggests that a concentration of authority at the top engenders more stability regardless of the authority relationship between the two lower-power parties. That is, top heavy organizations should be less subject to coalition politics. Second, in the case of organizations with less concentration of authority, not only will coalition action be more likely but also the type of coalition formed will vary with the relationship of the parties in a subordinate position. Where the subordinates have relatively equal power, the organization faces the prospect of a *revolutionary* coalition. A revolutionary coalition broadly refers to joint action by two or more subordinates against a superior (see

Caplow, 1968; Lawler, 1975a). In this sense, the BC coalition is revolutionary in the organizational context. In contrast, through an AC coalition unequal power between the subordinates provides those at the top with the opportunity to coopt those at the bottom.

Gamson's Minimum Resource Theory

Gamson (1961a, b) treats the distribution of resources not as an indicator of power, or the number of others over whom a party can gain control, but as a determinant of the payoff distribution within a coalition. The theory assumes that parties will attempt to form the coalition from which they expect the largest payoff. It further assumes that payoff estimates will be based on equity considerations. In other words, parties will expect an equitable division of a coalition's payoff, and they will choose the coalition in which equity gives them the greatest payoff. The distribution of resources is important because it ostensibly constitutes the inputs from which members will determine the appropriate (the equitable) payoff allocation. The predictions of the theory are derived from the following postulate: Any party will demand, and expect others to demand, a share of the payoff proportional to that party's resource contribution to the coalition. The specific predictions for coalition formation in the four structures we are analyzing are set forth in Table 4.

Table 4. Predictions of Gamson's Minimum Resource Theory

Structure	Predicted Coalition
1. $A > B > C, A > (B + C)$	None
2. $B = C, A > (B + C)$	None
3. $A > B, B = C, A < (B + C)$	BC
4. $A > B > C, A < (B + C)$	BC

Like Caplow's theory, minimum resource theory predicts no coalitions in structures 1 and 2, because A will tend to "go it alone," and a BC coalition is futile. In structures 3 and 4, Gamson's theory offers a different explanation for the prediction of a BC coalition in structure 3 and a different prediction for structure 4 from Caplow's theory. In structure 3, Gamson's theory predicts a BC coalition because both B and C would expect greater payoffs from this coalition than from AB or AC coalitions. Using the equity criterion, Gamson's theory indicates that B and C would equally divide the coalition's payoff because they contribute equally to the coalition. However, B or C would expect less than half of the payoff in a coalition with A. Turning to structure 4, Gamson's theory suggests that A and B would both prefer to coalesce with C. A would expect a greater share of the payoff in a coalition with C than in a coalition with B because the difference in resource contributions to the coalition would be greater in an AC coalition. For similar reasons, B would also prefer to coalesce with C. The critical difference between the Caplow and the Gamson theories is in C's preferences. Whereas Caplow argues that C will be ambivalent, Gamson indicates that C will prefer B, since C expects a greater share of the payoff (under equity criteria) in an alliance with B. Given the reciprocal preferences of B and C for one another, the theory predicts a BC coalition.

Considered together, the Caplow and Gamson theories have a number of important implications for organizations. First, both theories suggest that "top heavy" organizations are less vulnerable to coalition formation. Second, in less centralized organizations, both theories suggest that a hierarchy of authority or differentiation of resources promotes tendencies toward coalitions by subordinates against upper levels of management. Such coalitions can pose significant control problems for organizations. However, consistent with our heuristic use of these theories, the foregoing implications should be conceptualized as merely tendencies, which are often modified or undermined by organizational structure and processes. The question of how organizations deal with these issues is as important as the truth or falsity of the predictions. We will return to these implications later as we modify the ideas encompassed in the theories to fit the realities of organizational life more closely.

The Caplow and Gamson theories neglect a number of issues that are addressed in subsequent theories. In the first place, the theories of Caplow and Gamson apply primarily to a static situation: The game ends once the coalition is formed. Neither theory pays sufficient attention to coalition dynamics over time within an ongoing relationship, although Caplow (1968) makes some effort in this direction in his later work. Briefly, these theories can best account for particular coalition alignments at given points in time or can identify the most stable alignments within short time intervals. They do not deal with the countercoalition and retaliatory processes that typically occur when the coalition and outsiders have a continuing relationship over time. Obviously, these processes are particularly relevant to the analysis of organizations, in which there clearly are long-term relationships. A recent theory by Komorita and Chertkoff (1973), called the *bargaining theory,* takes a small but important step toward incorporating these dynamics into coalition theory.

A second problem with the Caplow and Gamson theories is that they do not deal with the issue of coalition size. The theories can and do predict coalitions of different sizes when we apply them to groups larger than three, and Riker's (1962) famous size principle bears a rather close relationship to minimum resource theory. However, the size of the coalition may affect coalition processes independently of the resource distribution, since larger coalitions may be more difficult to mobilize and hold together over time. A theory by Komorita (1974) constitutes the most recent attempt to incorporate the size issue into coalition theory.

Finally, the Caplow and Gamson theories assume that coalition action is governed solely by utilitarian considerations; they thereby neglect the role of ideological compatibility. This is reflected in the failure of the theories to consider AB coalitions as plausible options. In an organizational context, A and B may indeed coalesce because of ideological compatibility and a shared interest in keeping workers or those at lower levels in their place. Furthermore, some research documents the importance of ideology to coalition formation (see Druckman, 1977;

Leiserson, 1970), and some even suggests that ideological or attitudinal compatibility is more important than utilitarian issues in coalition decision making (Lawler and Youngs, 1975). Political science approaches have typically emphasized ideological compatibility as a criterion for coalition decisions.

Bargaining Theory of Coalitions

The bargaining theory of coalitions is an explicit extension of Gamson's minimum resource theory (Chertkoff, 1970; Komorita and Chertkoff, 1973). Like Gamson's theory, the bargaining theory is concerned primarily with the allocation of payoff within coalitions. It, too, is grounded in the assumption that parties will estimate payoffs from the initial distribution of resources. It differs from Gamson's theory in that the bargaining theory (1) posits that payoff expectations are based on the midpoint between equality and equity, and (2) distinguishes coalition formation at the beginning or early stages of conflict from that at later stages (Komorita and Chertkoff, 1973). We can use structure 4 ($A > B > C$, $A < [B + C]$) to compare the bargaining theory of coalitions to Gamson's minimum resource theory.

Assume that the relative resources of three social entities, A, B, and C are 4, 3, and 2 respectively. In other words, A controls resources that reach a level of 4 on some hypothetical continuum, B controls 3, and C controls 2. To put it another way, the parties control resources in a ratio of 4:3:2. In the context of this resource distribution, any coalition will win, no party has veto power (no party is absolutely necessary to any winning coalition), and no party has dictatorial power (no party alone can win against an opposing coalition). The scope conditions outlined at the beginning of this section are, therefore, fully satisfied. In this situation, Gamson's theory predicts that parties will expect the payoffs shown in Table 5 from their coalition options. Using Gamson's equity criterion, it is obvious that both B and C would expect the greatest payoff from the BC coalition. However, this prediction is based on the assumption that both parties to a coalition will use the equity criterion

Table 5. Expected Payoff Shares for Each Party in Each Coalition
(Minimum Resource Theory)

	Coalition with A	Coalition with B	Coalition with C
A's expected payoff	—	57%	67%
B's expected payoff	43%	—	60%
C's expected payoff	33%	40%	—

and, therefore, that the negotiations are relatively cut-and-dried.

In contrast, the bargaining theory of coalitions stipulates that both parties will not adopt an equity criterion when making payoff estimates. Instead, self-interest will determine the criterion selected. Specifically, the bargaining theory assumes that the stronger party (the party with greater resources) entering a prospective coalition will adopt the equity criterion, while the weaker party (the one with lower resources) will adopt the equality criterion. The stronger party will initially propose an equitable split of the coalition's payoff, and the weaker party will initially propose an equal split. These divergent initial proposals are each grounded in the criterion most consistent with the party's own interest. The consequence, of course, is a conflict of interest through which the payoff division becomes a more negotiable item than in Gamson's minimum resource theory. Clearly, the only way the conflict of interest can be resolved (and, hence, the coalition formed) is through actual bargaining.

The Komorita and Chertkoff theory suggests that the solution to the bargaining problem is to "split the difference." In other words, the theory assumes that prospective allies will recognize their conflicting interests, anticipate the divergent equity and equality criteria, and expect a division of the payoff at the midpoint between the equity and the equality divisions. In contrast to Gamson's expected payoffs, therefore, the bargaining theory predicts those shown in Table 6.

In our specific example, in which A, B, and C have a 4, 3, and 2 resource distribution, the bargaining theory would predict the same coalition as Gamson's minimum resource theory: BC.

Table 6. Expected Payoff Shares for Each Party in Each Coalition
(Bargaining Theory)

	Coalition with A	Coalition with B	Coalition with C
A's expected payoff	—	53.5%	58.5%
B's expected payoff	46.5%	—	55%
C's expected payoff	41.5%	45%	—

However, the rationale for this prediction and the predicted payoff divisions are different. Furthermore, in larger settings, the coalitions predicted by the theories are also likely to be different. For example, consider a four-party (A, B, C, D) situation where the resource distribution is 8, 4, 3, 2 and where a total of 9 resources is necessary to win. Minimum resource theory predicts a BCD coalition, which could be construed as revolutionary in an organizational context. The bargaining theory, on the other hand, would predict an AD coalition, which could be construed as cooptive in a formal organization. The reader can verify these predictions by calculating the expected payoffs from Gamson's equity criterion and the midpoint between equity and equality in the bargaining theory. Thus, the minimum resource and bargaining theories can have very different implications in specific organizational settings.

Aside from its greater emphasis on bargaining, the bargaining theory improves on Gamson's theory in one other important respect: It envisions a setting in which the parties who develop a coalition have a continuing relationship with those excluded from the coalition. Clearly this is relevant to an organizational context, in which not only the initial formation of a coalition but also its stability or instability over time is critical. The bargaining theory assumes that the excluded parties will not be satisfied with their position once the opposing coalition is formed. They will attempt to break apart the coalition by weakening their own payoff demands. A stronger party will express a willingness to accept less than equity, and a weaker party will ask for less than equality. Thus, the midpoint between equity and equality may be the foundation for both the initial coalition and its subsequent demise. To maintain the coalition over time, the parties may have to renegotiate the pay-off division periodically, because excluded third parties are likely to offer coalition members more than those members are currently receiving from the coalition.

Excluded parties essentially constitute a temptation for members of a coalition. The theory posits that:

1. Excluded parties will be willing to make more concessions in coalition negotiations than an already included party.
2. This inclination of the excluded parties to concede will increase over time. The longer the time, the greater the concessions.
3. The temptation of a coalition member to defect is a positive function of the difference between that member's share in the current coalition and the maximum to be expected from an alternative coalition. A coalition is likely to have long-run stability only when the maximum expectation from alternative coalitions is equal to or less than the payoff currently received within the coalition. Consequently, agreements over time within a given coalition will evolve toward payoff divisions that minimize the difference between payoffs within a coalition and the maximum expectation from alternatives.

The maximum expectation (from alternatives) is not unlimited—it is constrained by equity and equality criteria. The theory further assumes that only offers within the equity-equality range will be credible to the parties. A stronger party who offers to take less than equality will be refused, just as an offer by a weaker party to accept less than equity will be refused. The reason is that coalitions with payoff divisions outside this range will be inherently unstable—they are particularly vulnerable to bifurcation by outside parties. The maximum expectation of the disadvantaged party would invariably be greater than the outcome from within the coalition. Overall, the theory indicates that, after the initial period of coalitional action, it is the alternatives available to coalition members that determine future distributions of the coalition payoff.

If we consider the four resource structures previously

used to contrast Gamson's theory with Caplow's, the bargaining theory predicts the same coalitions as Gamson's theory. However, the long-term developmental aspect of the bargaining theory suggests an important difference between structures 3 and 4. With regard to structure 3, the BC coalition should constitute a relatively permanent coalition, since the equal split within the coalition enables both members to obtain as much as either could possibly expect from an alternative coalition with A (equality). It would be difficult, if not impossible, for A to break apart this coalition; A would have to offer a payoff distribution outside the equity-equality range. Turning to structure 4, the BC coalition as originally constituted should be unstable. Given the midpoint of equity and equality as an initial resolution, C would have some temptation to leave the coalition over time. C's maximum expectation is a fifty-fifty split in a coalition with A; unless and until B makes enough concessions to yield a fifty-fifty split of the coalition's payoff, the BC coalition will be unstable. Short of those concessions by B, A can break apart the coalition by offering an equal split to C. Thus, in comparing structures 3 and 4, the bargaining theory indicates that the stability of a BC coalition depends on the relative resources brought to the coalition by B and C.

The implications of the bargaining theory of coalitions for an organizational analysis go beyond those of the Caplow and Gamson theories. This theory supports an image of organizations in continuous flux due to coalition and countercoalition processes. Furthermore, the theory indicates that a stratification system (structure 4) that is quite common to organizations also happens to be the least stable of the structures we have identified as our primary concern. The bargaining theory, therefore, provides an important additional step toward a coalition theory for organizational analyses.

Nevertheless, the theory is not completely adequate. It still neglects issues such as coalition size and ideological compatibility (which we will consider in the next two sections). More important, it does not really come to grips with countercoalition processes for two major reasons. First, countercoalition processes can include not only attempts to break apart an existing coalition but also the formation of opposing coalitions and other forms of retaliation, such as coercion and repression. Excluded parties may blunt the effects of the coalition by mobilizing a coalition among themselves or by levying some kind of punishment on coalition members. The bargaining theory is concerned only with attempts to break apart the coalition and only with very specific mechanisms for doing this: making offers that are more attractive to one or more of the coalition members. Second, an oversimplified and rather constrained image of bargaining underlies this theory. Despite its focus on bargaining, the theory tends to neglect the actual bargaining process and stress the outcome or result of bargaining (that is, the midpoint between equity and equality). The split-the-difference rule is seductive in that it provides a simple "solution" grounded in the vast body of game theory notions (compare Nash, 1953; Rapoport, 1966). Yet, the empirical value of this rule in concrete contexts is open to serious question (see Bowl by and Schriver, 1978; Hamermesh, 1976), in part because it leads to a neglect of the actual bargaining process. The most basic problem is that the bargaining theory of Komorita and Chertkoff (1973), like game theory models, assumes that parties have information that they are not likely to have in real world contexts. We return to these issues of countercoalition process in Chapters Five and Six. We will move well beyond the bargaining theory of coalitions in those chapters.

Size of the Coalition

When there are more than three parties in a setting, the size of prospective coalitions is a consideration. The size of the coalition has been a central issue in political science approaches to coalitions at least since Riker (1962) formulated his famous size principle. We will focus on a more recent variant of this idea: Komorita's (1974) weighted probability model.

The weighted probability model extends and supplements the bargaining theory of coalitions by stressing the *number* of coalition alternatives available to the parties. This theory stipulates that the distribution of resources is important, not as an input according to which parties divide payoffs, but only because it gives parties coalition alternatives that have different numbers of members. We must carefully separate the implications of this theory for coalition formation and for the division of payoffs within coalitions.

With regard to coalition formation, the theory assumes that parties will prefer smaller to larger coalitions. Larger coalitions tend to be more difficult to mobilize initially and to maintain over time than smaller coalitions. Larger coalitions pose greater problems of coordination at initial stages of formation and may have to resolve more complex, cross-cutting conflicts of interest among prospective members. Coalitional agreements among a multitude of parties are likely to be more fragile and subject to greater disruption over time. For these reasons, the theory predicts that parties will prefer smaller to larger coalitions, all other things being equal. More specifically, consistent with Riker's (1962) size principle, parties will form coalitions that are just large enough to win and will resist the inclusion of excess members.

Supplementing this size principle, the weighted probability model indicates that parties will use the *number* of alternatives available to each member as the (input) criterion for the payoff demands and expectations of that member. The division of payoff will ostensibly be proportional to the number of alternatives available to each party. For example, if B has twice as many alternatives as C, then the theory expects B to receive twice as much of the coalition's payoff. Applying this idea to our four resource structures, the theory diverges in important ways from the other theories. In contrast to the minimum resource and the bargaining theories, the weighted probability model does not predict the BC coalition in structures 3 and 4. In both structures, B and C have one coalition alternative (a coalition with A) and, therefore, the BC coalition should make an equal split of the payoff regardless of the resource structure. Now examine the AB and AC coalitions in these structures. Since the number of alternatives is the criterion for payoffs, the theory predicts an equal split in these coalitions as well. This means that parties would expect the same level of payoff from each coalition, and the theory predicts that each coalition (AB, AC, and BC) is equally likely to form. (In structures 1 and 2, the theory, like the other theories, predicts no coalition.)

The weighted probability model can be useful to an organizational analysis in a number of ways. First, it treats the issue of coalition size, which can begin to deal with the multitude of coalition alternatives that might be available in an organizational context. Second, its focus on the number of alternatives enables the theory to apply to situations in which certain coalitions are essentially not feasible or allowed due to the formal structure of the organization. The other theories tend to focus on situations in which the only limitation on coalition formation is utilitarian—will it win or not? When other factors restrict the formation of certain coalitions, the weighted probability model merely adjusts the number of alternatives for the parties whose coalitions are restricted and incorporates that information into the predictions. The basic problem with the theory is that it cannot distinguish between coalitions of the same size. In this sense, the implications of this theory supplement rather than supersede those of the other theories.

Ideological Distance Models

All the theories we have discussed so far are grounded in the social psychological tradition. Clearly, this tradition tends to focus solely on utilitarian features of coalition action. All the theories are ultimately based on the assumption that parties will select the coalition with the greatest payoff, and virtually all attempt to exclude nonutilitarian variables or to interpret seemingly nonutilitarian issues in terms of utility. Consequently, there is a glaring gap in these theories: the failure to consider attitudinal or ideological issues.

The importance of this gap is suggested in a study by Lawler and Youngs (1975). They used a political convention context to compare the effects of three variables on the choice of coalition: the expected payoff, ideological similarity, and the probability of the coalition's ultimate success. The results of the study indicate that all three variables affect coalition formation, but that attitudinal or ideological similarity is more important than the expected payoff from the prospective coalition. The study further indicates that expected payoff and ideological similarity are not completely independent. Ideological similarity has utilitarian and nonutilitarian implications for parties. This study and other research (see Druckman, 1977; Leiserson, 1970) suggest that the gap in the social psychological tradition is, indeed, important and that the most complete theory would incorporate both ideological and utilitarian issues.

Political science models of coalition formation have made some progress in this direction (see Murnighan, 1978, for a review). Although these models suffer from many of the same defects as the social psychological models, they still have important implications for our organizational analysis. The major difference between the social psychology and the political science models is that the latter place greater emphasis on ideological or policy issues. These models tend to rest on two basic assumptions: (1) Parties' beliefs, attitudes, policy orientations, and the like can be placed on an ideological dimension—typically a unidimensional ideological scale; and (2) in forming coalitions, parties will minimize the range or diversity of ideologies represented (Axelrod, 1970; DeSwann, 1970, 1973; Leiserson, 1970; Murnighan, 1978).

The appropriate ideological scale can vary substantially from context to context. In a political convention or legislative context, the most relevant dimensions may be left to right or conservative to liberal. In the politics of bureaucratic organizations, the ideological dimensions might include worker participation, strategies for changing the environment, recruitment and promotion policies, or even the priority given to different work activities (for example, teaching versus research in a university). The type of organization would probably significantly affect the ideological dimensions relevant to coalition formation. However, regardless of the specific dimensions, the basic assumption of ideological distance models is that parties make coalition decisions on the basis of both ideology and utility.

An extensive review of the political science models is beyond the scope of our endeavor (see Murnighan, 1978, for a review). Our purpose is to examine the basic implications of incorporating ideological distance into coalition theories. To illustrate the ideological distance approach, consider a situation in which there are five parties (A, B, C, D, and E) with resources equal to 5, 4, 3, 2, and 1, respectively. A total of 6 resources is required to win, meaning that any coalition containing six or more resources can win (if formed before any of the other coalitions that can exceed the minimum of six). Assume that the parties are arranged from left to right on an ideological dimension with equal ideological distance between each adjacent pair. In this situation, all of the coalitions except for DE, CE, BE, and CD are winning ones. All the theories, whether from a political science or a social psychological tradition, would predict coalitions falling into this subset.

The predictions of an ideological distance model would depend on the nature of the additional assumptions and the relationship posited between ideology and utility. If we simply assume that parties prefer to coalesce with those adjacent to them on the ideological dimension, we could narrow the predicted subset to those coalitions that string together parties who are adjacent on the ideological dimension, such as AB, BCD, ABCD, and so forth. Each of these coalitions ties together adjacent parties without leaving substantial ideological gaps in the coalition, such as those in AC, ADE, and several others (Leiserson, 1970). A more stringent assumption is that parties will minimize the overall ideological distance within the coalition. For example, the distance in the ABCD coalition is from A to D; in the ABC coalition, it is from A to C; and so forth. With this assumption, we could narrow the prediction to an AB or BC coalition because these are the winning coalitions with the least ideological distance within the coalition. Another approach would be to combine the ideological distance criterion with the notion that smaller coalitions are preferred to larger ones (Komorita's [1974] weighted probability model). While the size notion itself suggests only that two-party coalitions are more likely than three-party coalitions, in combination with the ideological distance notion, the AC coalition would be excluded in favor of the AB or BC coalitions, because the latter contain a smaller distance than the AC coalition. We might also employ minimum resource theory to add the restriction that coalitions containing the slightest excess of resources over the decision point (that is, six) will be most likely under identical ideological distance conditions. Since a BC coalition fits this minimum resource criterion better than AB, BC would be the prediction. Alone, minimum resource theory would predict the CDE coalition.

The point is that ideological distance can be useful in contrast to or in combination with the other theories we have examined. It is noteworthy, in terms of organizational contexts, that none of the social psychology theories viewed an AB coalition as a viable option. If, for purposes of illustration, we conceptualize A as the upper levels of management and B as the middle levels of management, then we must consider AB coalitions as not only more viable but also more frequent than the strictly utilitarian coalition theories predict. The ideological distance approach is the only one that has suggested AB as a plausible possibility, and, of course, ideology may be the key basis on which upper and middle levels of management form and maintain alliances against workers. In the next section, we will further analyze the implications of the theories for organizations.

Coalitions in Organizational Contexts

From the preceding discussion, it is undoubtedly clear that the theories of coalitions were not designed for an organizational analysis. The theories provide a set of basic predictions embedded in a very abstract, content-free, idealized model. By virtue of their abstract, formal character, such theories provide important reference points with which to compare particular social contexts. Yet, it is important to keep in mind that the theories provide only an idealized image identifying coalition tendencies inherent in a given context. Applied to organizations, therefore, these theories propose a relationship between the formal hierarchy of authority and the tendency of different subgroups to coalesce; however, we would expect particular organizational contexts to modify or even eliminate some of these tendencies. In fact, among the key empirical questions raised by our discussion are: How, to what extent, and when do organizations depart from the basic processes identified in these theories?

Aside from their use as an idealization, the theories may provide a source of preliminary ideas from which to generate a theory of *organizational* coalitions. We noted earlier that the theories make rather stringent assumptions that do not apply to typical organizational contexts, and we briefly treated the implications for organizations as we reviewed the various theories. Now we will examine the theories critically and illustrate how we might use them as more than an idealization in an organizational analysis. Specifically, we will identify the assumptions or scope conditions that make it difficult to apply the theories concretely, and then we will illustrate how a weakening of the stringent assumptions underlying the theories can facilitate a more thorough treatment of coalition processes in the context of centralized and decentralized authority. Consistent with the rest of this chapter, our focus remains on the link between the formal aspects of power (that is, authority structure) and coalition tendencies.

Applied to an organizational context, the coalition theories are subject to two basic criticisms, both of which relate to their assumptions or scope conditions. First, all the theories conceptualize winning or losing as a zero-sum issue. A coalition is either a winning one or a losing one, and only winning coalitions will be mobilized. The implication, of course, is that no coalitions will form under structures 1 and 2, the highly centralized authority structures. As compelling as this reasoning may be, nonwinning coalitions (as defined by the theories) do seem to occur quite frequently. The reason is that winning is a matter of degree in any concrete context, not a finite dichotomy. Nonwinning coalitions may narrow the power differences between losing and winning groups and, thereby, reduce the immediate costs of losing on a given issue at a given point in time. Furthermore, in an ongoing relationship, the formation of a losing coalition might be the initial step in creating a future win-

ning one. In sum, there is substantial reason to view nonwinning
coalitions as viable tactical alternatives. In organizational contexts, minimizing losses through such coalitions may be as important to parties as winning in the strict sense. The overall
implication is that an application of the ideas in the theories to
organizational contexts is facilitated by weakening the assumption that only winning coalitions will form. The corollary notion that dictatorial power will eliminate coalition action must
also be weakened.

The second criticism is that the theories assume that parties have complete and perfect information on matters such as
the level of resources controlled by each party, the ideological
position of each party, and the utility of the coalition. Such
assumptions are indispensable to the creation of idealized
models, but they have little relation to concrete conflict settings
within or outside organizational contexts. Parties in real world
conflict settings rarely have the level of certainty about each
other (or even themselves, for that matter) that is commonly
assumed by these theories. On the contrary, it is ambiguity of
information that characterizes most conflict settings.

The implication of the second criticism is that we must
conceptualize utility, the probability of a coalition actually winning, the resource distribution, and other factors as *subjective*
phenomena. The total payoff available to winning coalitions is
not a fixed, constant, objectively obvious matter but rather a
matter subject to the interpretation of the parties involved. The
probability of coalition success is not given by the setting but
inferred by parties based on often subtle cues and information.
The resources and, hence, resource contributions of parties to a
prospective coalition are ambiguous and negotiable items. Thus,
we need a theoretical scheme for analyzing how parties evaluate
and synthesize diverse information to arrive at judgments about
the utilitarian and other aspects of prospective coalitions. A
starting point is provided by *subjective-expected-utility theory*.
The implications of this more subjectively oriented approach to
utility will be detailed in Chapter Five.

In light of the two criticisms of formal coalition theories,
we need to reconsider the implications of these theories for cen-

tralized and decentralized authority structures. Our discussion here is related primarily to the first criticism. The second criticism has much broader implications that are primarily relevant to Chapter Five.

Centralized Authority

To apply the theories to centralized authority structures, we will stay with our example of an organization with subgroups falling into three hierarchal levels: upper (U), middle (M), and lower (L). This system of stratification is most consistent with the structures we identified as 1 and 4 earlier in this chapter. Structure 1 can be construed as centralized authority and structure 4 as decentalized authority. First we will consider centralized authority, where the resources are distributed as follows: $U > M > L$, $U > (M + L)$. (The resources, in this case, are the formal perquisites of *authority,* rather than the informal aspects of power that we subsume under the rubric *influence.*)

Applied to an organizational context, the coalition options in this structure can be construed as a choice between conservative, revolutionary, and reform coalitions (see Caplow, 1968). The UM coalition is a *conservative* one, because it is consistent with the organizational hierarchy. It involves higher-level subgroups coalescing against lower-level subgroups, and it essentially affirms the existing hierarchy of authority. The ML coalition can be loosely termed *revolutionary.* While such a coalition does not qualitatively change the authority structure, it weakens the existing hierarchy of authority by pitting subordinates (M + L) against the upper levels of the organization. The last alternative, a UL coalition, might be termed a *reformist* one (Caplow labels it an *improper* coalition). It affirms part of the authority structure and weakens other aspects of it: Given the superior position of U within and outside the coalition, it buttresses U's authority position in the organization and could be a means for U to co-opt L; however, the authority of M is weakened.

In this context, the ML coalition is a nonwinning one, in that it does not qualitatively alter or overturn the authority structure. Nevertheless, the potential power of an ML coalition may still pose a threat to U. Such a coalition could obstruct the decision-making processes of U, reduce the compliance of M and L to U's directives, and generally make it difficult for U to control various activities within the organization. In fact, even periodic or relatively infrequent coalitions between M and L could present significant problems for U, depending on the timing of the coalitions and the issues over which M and L coalesce. As a consequence, U may be inclined to coalesce with M or L in an attempt to forestall periodic ML coalitions. The tendency of U toward such coalitions should depend on the level of threat posed by the prospective ML coalition; the level of threat, in turn, should be a function of the power difference between U and the ML coalition. Specifically, we posit the following hypothesis:

Hypothesis 1. The smaller the power difference between U and the prospective ML coalition, the greater the inclination of U to form a coalition with M or L.

Furthermore, L should view the prospective ML coalition more positively under conditions of relatively small power difference. Hence:

Hypothesis 2. The smaller the power difference between U and the prospective ML coalition, the greater the inclination of L to form an ML coalition.

These propositions indicate that the inclinations of U and L will vary with the power differences. In the case of M, the situation is more complex. While a decrease in the power difference between U and the ML coalition may incline M toward an ML coalition, M has more to lose than L from such a non-winning coalition. Furthermore, subgroups in the middle levels are likely to feel greater ideological affinity with subgroups at upper levels of the organization. As a result, we would expect M to be ambivalent about an ML coalition but certainly tempted to mobilize such an alliance where the power differences between U and the ML coalition are slight. The middle level of the organization can be construed as the battleground for conflict between U and L. That is, the conflict between U and L is often over the allegiance of subgroups within the middle level of the organization.

Hypotheses 1 and 2 indicate the inclinations of U and L without predicting which of these alternative coalitions is most likely to form. Overall, we would expect a *conservative* coalition in Caplow's (1968) terms—that is, UM. This prediction is based on both utility and ideology. The basic problem for U is to strengthen its power position in the face of a prospective ML coalition. A coalition with either M or L could serve this utilitarian purpose, as U would remain in a superior position within and outside both coalitions. However, since there is closer ideological affinity between U and M than between U and L, we would expect U to prefer M. From M's point of view, a coalition with U would ostensibly strengthen M's bargaining position with U, avoid the potential costs of a nonwinning ML coalition, and be most consistent with M's ideological proclivities. All other things being equal, therefore, the most likely coalition is the conservative one.

This very general prediction is likely to be modified somewhat by the structure of the setting. Our discussion of hypotheses 1 and 2 indicates that, as the power difference between U and the ML coalition decreases, the ML coalition becomes more tempting to M. This is one condition that could reduce the likelihood of the predicted UM coalition. The power differences among U, M, and L can also facilitate or weaken the likelihood of the predicted coalition. If a powerful middle level of management poses a threat to U, U might be inclined toward a *reformist* coalition (UL) at key points in the decision-making process. Such a coalition might enhance U's ability to obtain compliance and other rewards from L while offsetting the power of M within the organization. Thus:

Hypothesis 3. As the power difference between U and M decreases, a UL coalition becomes more likely.

We can derive a rationale for this proposition from our prior treatment of coalition theories—even though those theories would not predict any coalition under centralized authority. A relatively small difference in power between U and M not only implies that M poses a greater threat to U within the organization but also suggests that a UM coalition will be more costly to U. Assuming that parties use equity (minimum resource theory) or the midpoint between equity and equality (the bargaining theory of coalitions) as the basis for dividing the coalition payoff, U would have to give up more of the payoff to a stronger M in order to mobilize or maintain a UM coalition. Facing a relatively strong subgroup within the middle level of the authority structure, U may find it cheaper to weaken M's position through a UL coalition. Thus, theories on the division of payoff (see Gamson, 1961b; Komorita and Chertkoff, 1973) can still be helpful even if we weaken the assumptions on which they are based.

Our discussion of centralized authority thus indicates that prior coalition theories neglect some important political processes in organizations, because they conceptualize winning coalitions in zero-sum terms. Nonwinning coalitions or coalitions defined as unnecessary by those theories are apparently critical to the day-to-day political activities of organizations. Winning coalitions imply qualitative changes in the structure of authority, that is, the formal distribution of resources. Nonwinning coalitions imply shifts in power relationships within the existing formal ranking of power. In other words, nonwinning coalitions assume a given ranking and simply alter the *relative* power of parties within this ranking. Such coalitions are essential elements of the influence processes that take place in particular authority structures.

Overall, our discussion points to the fact that coalitions need not take over or qualitatively change the authority structure in order to influence organizational decision making. Prior coalition theory and research stressed the role of coalitions in changing the formal resource structure and neglected the bearing of coalitions on influence processes within a structure, a topic that is developed further in Chapter Five.

Decentralized Authority

One of the characteristics distinguishing decentralized authority from centralized authority is the potential for subordinates to overcome or transform the authority lodged at the top of the organization. For comparative purposes, we will consider structure 4, a hierarchy of authority identical to the one in the prior section (U > M > L), except that in this case an ML coalition is more powerful than U (U < [M + L]).

In this decentralized structure, all the possible coalitions are winning ones, and the coalition theories make various relatively clear predictions, summarized in Table 7. Minimum re-

Table 7. Coalitions Predicted by Different Theories
for Structure 4

Theory	Predicted Coalitions
Gamson's minimum resource theory	ML
Caplow's power theory	UL or ML
The bargaining theory	ML
Weighted probability model	UM, ML, or UL
Ideological distance models	UM or ML

source theory and the bargaining theory of coalitions predict a coalition between middle and lower levels in the organization, based on the expected division of payoff. Caplow predicts either ML or UL, based primarily on the control the coalition provides over other actors in the situation. The weighted probability model predicts that any of the three coalition options may form and that there will be an equal split of the coalition's outcomes, since all parties have an equal number of alternatives. Finally, the ideological distance approach, based on the assumption that parties will minimize the range of policy orientations within a coalition, hypothesizes either UM or ML—although, if we assume that M is closer to U on the ideological dimension than to L, UM is somewhat more likely than ML. Thus, different theories portray the specific coalition tendencies in a somewhat different manner under decentralized authority conditions. Despite these differences, the coalition theories imply a relatively fluid and unstable coalition structure over time.

Whereas these theories suggest that coalition action is intrinsic only to decentralized systems, we have argued in the preceding section of this chapter that such action is also inherent in centralized structures. This raises an important question: Do coalition dynamics differ under centralized and decentralized authority? Taking the broader implications of coalition theories and our treatment of decentralized authority, we can point to a number of important differences.

In decentralized systems, coalitions are likely to address broader, more basic issues, since the very nature of the authority structure is at stake. In centralized systems, coalitions tend to engender changes in power relationships within the existing authority structure, and such coalitions are likely to address more specific, time-bound issues. We would also expect coalitions in decentralized structures to be of short duration because of the countercoalition processes unleashed by a given coalition. Given the nature of the authority structure and the issues, excluded parties are more likely to continue the fight under decentralized authority. Finally, under centralized authority, coalition *action* may be irregular or infrequent, but a given coalition might remain stable over a long duration. That is, a coalition may remain dormant for long periods of time and be activated only on occasion. In the case of decentralized authority, we would expect more persistent coalition *action* and less stable coalition structures.

The effects of centralization on coalition processes within an organization are summarized by the following interrelated hypotheses:

Hypothesis 4. The greater the centralization of authority, the lower the frequency of coalition action.

Hypothesis 5. The greater the centralization of authority, the lower the frequency of countercoalition action.

Hypothesis 6. The greater the centralization of authority, the lower the scope or breadth of issues raised and fought for by coalition action.

Hypothesis 7. The greater the centralization of authority, the greater the stability of a given structure of coalitions.

Our criticism of the winning coalition assumption underlying coalition theories can also apply to decentralized systems.

If there are more than four basic parties in a decentralized system, there are likely to be nonwinning coalitions as well as winning ones. While formal coalition theories would exclude the nonwinning ones, we see these as viable alternatives here too. Again, we must emphasize that the coalition theories are relevant primarily to the formal conditions of coalition action, that is, the effect of the authority structure on coalitions that engender qualitative changes in that structure. The theories are less relevant in dealing with influence-based coalitions or in examining the multitude of conditions underlying the mobilization of coalitions (see Lawler, 1975a; Lawler, Youngs, and Lesh, 1978; Lawler and Thompson, 1979). The inability of these theories to explain why nonwinning coalitions can and do form in organizational contexts is only one indicator of this gap in the previous literature. Now that we have used prior coalition theory to embed coalitions in the authority structure of the organization, Chapter Five will treat coalitions as a central element within the influence processes of organizations.

Summary

This chapter used theories of coalitions to examine the relationship between the authority structure and coalition activity within organizations. Five major theories were analyzed: Caplow's power theory of coalitions, Gamson's minimum resource theory, the bargaining theory of coalitions, the weighted probability model, and ideological distance approaches. Grounded primarily in social psychological literature, these theories were not specifically designed for an organizational analysis. They provide idealized, content-free models that can serve as reference points for an organizational analysis. We have demonstrated important implications these theories have for the manner in which the formal stratification system in an organization (the hierarchy of authority) affects the formation of coalitions.

The most general implications are that (1) the hierarchy of authority unleashes tendencies toward coalitions by subordinates against the upper levels of management, and (2) centralized or top-heavy organizations are less vulnerable to coalition processes than less centralized or decentralized organizations. These general implications are elaborated, extended, and modified in different ways by different theories. For example, the bargaining theory of coalitions places greater emphasis than the other theories on coalition and countercoalition processes within ongoing relationships. This theory explicitly leads to an image of organizations in continuous flux due to coalition processes. Caplow's power theory and Gamson's minimum resource theory provide a more static image of coalition structure. The weighted probability model indicates that subgroups will attempt to minimize the size of coalitions and that this can undermine the tendencies toward coalition formation. Ideological distance models suggest that subgroups will consider not only utilitarian issues when forming coalitions but also the disparities among potential members in policy preferences, attitudes, and the like. These ideological issues can also obstruct the coalition formation tendencies. Overall, coalition theories provide a starting point for an organizational analysis. Applied to organizations, the major issues posed by the theories are as important as, if not more important than, the truth of the specific predictions in the theories. The task of any concrete organizational analysis is to determine how the tendencies articulated in the theories are modified or buttressed by organizational structure and processes.

A complete analysis of coalition processes within organizations requires that we move beyond these theories, primarily because of the stringent assumptions that underlie them. The coalition theories assume that nonwinning coalitions will not form, yet we can point to strong theoretical reasons for expecting such coalitions to form periodically. In fact, the history of organizations sometimes appears to be a virtual graveyard of nonwinning coalitions. To assume that only winning coalitions will form is to place a disproportionate faith in the ability of interest groups to perceive and respond to the objective nature of their context. The most basic problem is that the theories simply assume that interest groups will have more information about themselves and others than is feasible in an organization.

The subjective or cognitive nature of coalition decision making is neglected in these theories. For example, utilities are ultimately grounded in subjective estimates; the success probabilities attached to different coalitions are likely to have a strong subjective component; and, in considering the influence, rather than the authority, dimension of organizations, the resources or resource distribution tends to be ambiguous and a key topic for subjective judgments.

Because of their stringent assumptions, the coalition theories have a rather narrow scope, leading to an incomplete analysis of coalitions in organizations. The theories are most critical to an understanding of the way coalitions are grounded in the formal stratification system. Even if we focus on the formal aspects and foundation of coalitional action, a weakening of the assumptions facilitates a more thorough treatment of centralized and decentralized authority. If we attempt to extend the theories to the influence processes or informal aspects of the stratification, we find more glaring gaps in application of the theories. To deal with the informal dimension of coalition action, we need a more robust and dynamic approach. First of all, we must emphasize the subjective foundation of coalition decisions and deal with the issue of how interest groups estimate utilities, probabilities of success, and other factors. Second, the resources and distribution of resources in the influence sphere are different from those in the authority structure; resources endemic to influence processes are also more fluid and less fixed than those attached to the authority structure. Third, coalitions in organizations are not *necessary to the parties* in the same sense that they are necessary under the constraining conditions of the coalition theories. The implication of this is that we must deal more explicitly with the question of *when* and *why* interest groups are inclined to form coalitions in the first place. Fourth, the coalition theories neglect or inadequately treat the bargaining processes between coalitions once they are formed. The focus of the theories is on the bargaining processes that lead to the formation of coalitions, and even here the conceptualization of bargaining is seriously limited. Chapter Five will address the first three gaps or issues: the subjective nature of utilities, the resources at stake in influence processes in organizations, and the mobilization of interest groups into coalitions. Chapters Six and Seven deal with the last issue: intercoalition bargaining.

5

Interest Group
Versus
Coalition Politics

▄▀

In Chapter One we asserted that interest groups and coalitions dominate politics in organizations. All organizations are networks of interest groups, whether professional groupings, work groups, or other divisions. In turn, organizational politics involve the efforts of interest groups to influence decisions that affect their positions in the organization. In each political struggle, interest groups must decide whether to pursue their political goals in isolation from other interest groups or to form a coalition of interest groups in their pursuit of a common goal. A distinction may thus be drawn between organizations dominated by interest group politics and organizations dominated by coalition politics. This chapter presents the conditions that either facilitate the emergence of coalitions or reinforce the maintenance of interest group politics.

Subjective-Expected-Utility Theory

To understand the analytical dimensions of an interest group's decision to mobilize a coalition of interest groups or not, we will rely on subjective-expected-utility theory (Tedeschi, Schlenker, and Bonoma, 1973). This theory directly addresses the issue of when a course of action will be perceived as having utility for the party about to take it. In terms of our analysis, it sensitizes us to the conditions that increase or decrease the probability that a specific interest group will engage in organizational politics as part of a coalition rather than as an interest group.

Subjective-expected-utility theory is based on two primary assumptions. First, it assumes that in any relationship parties attempt to maximize their gain. In other words, an interest group will attempt to maximize its own gain without regard to the gain or lack of gain of other interest groups. A maximizing gain orientation must be distinguished from a maximizing difference (competitive) orientation, in which interest groups attempt to maximize the difference in gains between themselves and other interest groups. In a maximizing difference situation, interest groups view all resources in zero-sum terms and assume that the increase in gain to one interest group is at the expense of gains to other interest groups. A cooperative orientation is also distinguishable. In that view interest groups consciously attempt to maximize their joint gain; gains are viewed in terms of the sum of the gains to the interest groups. In a maximizing difference situation the gain of one interest group is negatively related to the gain of another interest group; in a cooperative situation, the gain is positively correlated. But the reality of the organizational life is such that interest groups are encouraged to cooperate and compete at the same time. In organizations, interest groups exist in a mixed-motive setting.

Built into the maximizing gain approach is the assumption that interest groups operate, for the most part, in a live-and-let-live world. As long as their gain is maximized, they care little about the gain of others. They cooperate when needed and compete when needed. For the analysis of organizations such an orientation seems particularly appropriate. On the one hand, no particular interest group is interested in the total annihilation of another because, in the long run, the operation of the organization depends on the existence of various subgroups. On the

other hand, interest groups will not go out of their way to cooperate on every issue with every other interest group for the sake
of organizational harmony and the gain of the total organization. Some issues ordinarily push an interest group closer to
cooperation or competition; however, we are assuming that
interest groups generally exist somewhere between cooperation
and competition. In terms of resources this means that interest
groups generally will view resources as being neither zero-sum
nor infinite.

The second assumption of subjective-expected-utility theory is that parties will subjectively attach utility to different
lines of action by estimating the magnitude of outcomes attached to each option and weighting these magnitude estimates
by the probability of achieving the outcomes. In other words,
parties will synthesize and summarize the meaning of key aspects of the situation and the potential relationship in terms of
outcome magnitude and outcome probability estimates. The
choice of option is not based simply on magnitude but rather
on a function of magnitude multiplied by probability (Lawler
and Bacharach, 1979; Tedeschi, Schlenker, and Bonoma, 1973).

In organizational contexts, subjective-expected-utility
theory implies that actors compare the magnitude of working
within a coalition of interest groups and working outside such a
coalition. If, for example, the resource involved is a pay increase, the magnitude may be viewed as the pay increase expected if an interest group operates within a coalition versus the
pay increase expected if the interest group works outside the
coalition. The probability factor is the probability of achieving
the magnitude expected as a member of a coalition versus the
probability of achieving the magnitude expected when operating as an individual interest group.

Interest groups will form a coalition when the magnitude
of outcomes expected as part of a coalition multiplied by the
probability of achieving these outcomes as a coalition exceeds
the magnitude of outcomes expected when operating as a single
interest group multiplied by the probability of achieving these
outcomes as a single interest group. Returning to the case of an
increase in salary, let us say that the expected increase in salary

that can be achieved by a coalition of interest groups is $10, and the increase that can be achieved by a single interest group is also $10. However, let us hypothesize that the probability that the goal can be achieved by the coalition is .7 and the probability that the goal can be achieved by a single interest group is .5. Multiplying magnitude by probability for each option, we have 7.0 versus 5.0, making net expected utility of joining a coalition of interest groups 2.0. Obviously, numerous combinations of magnitudes and probabilities may exist. For some situations, the utility of joining a coalition may be insignificant if not negative. This, of course, depends on the specific situation. What we are demonstrating here is the analytic procedure that interest groups may carry out in deciding whether or not to join coalitions, couched in terms of expected utility.

Resources at Stake

In the context of subjective-expected-utility theory, magnitude is viewed as the amount of potential resources that can be controlled by an emerging coalition. Clearly, any interest group trying to decide whether or not to form a coalition will first evaluate the magnitude of resources it controls compared to the magnitude of resources controlled by opposing interest groups. This evaluation is obviously done with an eye to the magnitude of total resources in the organization. Consequently, we must also consider the total amount of resources that the organization distributes to interest groups and coalitions. The theory of subjective expected utility does not explicitly deal with this but it does have implications for how parties evaluate the resources in relation to the total resources within the organization.

Considering the total resources of the organization, we can begin with a very simple hypothesis:

Hypothesis 8. The greater the resource scarcity within an organization, the greater the likelihood that interest groups will coalesce with other interest groups.

Underlying this hypothesis are two assumptions. First, it is assumed that the more scarce a resource is, the more it will be perceived in zero-sum terms by an interest group. Thus, when a resource is scarce, interest groups tend to view the situation in terms of exclusive control of that resource. If one party gains control of the resource, another party is less likely to have control of that resource. Clearly, this proposition is strongly grounded in only one model of resources, the finite model. That model assumes that there are a fixed number of individuals and an exhaustible resource base; this increases the competitive atmosphere among interest groups. Our assumption is that, given resource scarcity, interest groups may choose to decrease the competition by forming a coalition. When there is an infinite amount of a resource, no coalition will be formed because each interest group will have access to more than enough of the desired resource.

Our second assumption is that, in the face of a scarcity of resources, it is also essential for an interest group to maintain the resources it already controls. In combination, these two assumptions lead to the conclusion that the closer resources approach a zero-sum situation, the more likely it is that interest groups will form coalitions to protect or enhance their position at the expense of those outside the coalition.

Three other broad hypotheses may be derived from the first:

Hypothesis 9. The greater the proportion of total organizational resources controlled by a given interest group, the lower the likelihood that that interest group will join a coalition.

Hypothesis 10. The greater the proportion of total organizational resources controlled by a prospective coalition of interest groups, the greater the likelihood that any interest group will join that coalition.

Hypothesis 11. When the proportion of total organizational resources controlled by a potential coalition exceeds the proportion of total organizational resources controlled by a single interest group, the likelihood increases that that interest group will join the coalition.

In our discussion resources refer to the knowledge and

technology needed for the production of the final commodity.
For organizational interest groups the control of resources is
not an end in itself, but rather the foundation for the amount
of influence a particular interest group will have in the decision-
making process. Therefore, embedded in the above hypotheses
about resources are three hypotheses concerning influence.

Hypothesis 12. The greater the proportion of total organizational resources controlled by a given interest group, the
more influence that interest group will have in the decision-making process and the lower the likelihood that
that interest group will join a coalition of interest groups.

In the context of organizations, an interest group that is
critical to the production process, for example, one that has
control of a key technology and is not easily replaceable, is
likely to be very influential in organizational decisions. Even if
such a group does not have authority, those who do may pay
close attention to it when making specific decisions. High resource control, therefore, implies high influence, which in turn
increases the magnitude of the group's effect on the outcome of
organizational decisions. Such an interest group is not likely to
coalesce easily, which would mean sharing its influence with
other interest groups. Hence:

Hypothesis 13. The greater the proportion of total organizational resources controlled by a prospective coalition of
interest groups, the greater the potential influence of that
coalition in decision making and the greater the likelihood that any interest group will join the coalition.

The more resources are pooled in a coalition, the greater
the control that coalition can exert in the decision-making
process and the more influence it will have in any organizational
decisions. A remaining question is: At what point will interest
groups join the emerging coalition?

Hypothesis 14. When the proportion of total organizational resources controlled by the potential coalition exceeds the
proportion of total organizational resources controlled by
an interest group, the coalition will have greater influence

in decision making than the interest group. At this point the likelihood increases that the interest group will join the coalition.

Clearly, in these hypotheses, we are explicating an untested but basic assumption of prior research on coalitions: that the magnitude of available resources affects influence and bears on the subjective utilities attached to the formation of coalitions. Our propositions are closely related. They suggest that it is the comparison of interest group resources and influence with coalition resources and influence that is critical in determining the likelihood of coalition formation. This, of course, is consistent with subjective-expected-utility theory: The absolute level of utility attached to a given option is not important; rather, it is the compared utilities of alternative options (joining the coalition or not joining). In turn, the decision to join or not join the coalition is based on the connection between resources and influence.

Our argument implies that control of the resources of production is inherently related to influence in organizational decision making. The final link in this chain is that an increase of influence in decision making will increase the magnitude of positive outcomes available to an interest group or coalition. Therefore, a coalition that seeks to sustain itself must continuously demonstrate to its composite interest groups its capacity for achieving outcomes that would have been unattainable for the individual interest groups.

Some of the dynamics of internal organizational politics should become obvious at this point. Coalitions of interest groups will approach authorities and try to influence their final decisions. The coalition's influence is based on the composite contributions to production made by its component interest groups. Authorities in turn may or may not concede to the demands of the coalition. Whether they do or do not concede to the demands, that is, whether they provide the coalition with the magnitude of outcome that it had expected, is the measure of a winning or losing coalition. As we said before, most coalition theory assumes that a losing coalition will not mobilize; however, organizational realities make losing coalitions very real possibilities. One reason is that, while our hypotheses suggest a perfect fit among resources, control, influence, and outcomes in organizations, such a fit is not likely to occur. The pivotal issue is again the notion of influence. While in all likelihood the influence basis, that is, the proportion of resources controlled, is relatively stable, the demands made by individual interest groups or coalitions to authorities may vary dramatically and may not be in direct proportion to their controlled resources. For example, when a group or coalition wants to change work hours or work methods, its control of a high proportion of production may give it enough influence to affect the decision of authorities. If it wants to change the nature of the product produced, its control over the production process may be of minimum influence. In point of fact, the basis of influence may not be as wide in scope as the outcomes requested from authorities. In turn, the relationship between resource control, influence, and outcome may well be issue-specific.

One distinction among issues is whether they are long-term or short-term. The organizational authorities may need to resolve some decision issues immediately. This increases the probability that concessions will be made to a coalition of interest groups that is exerting its influence. The authorities may feel no need for immediate resolution of other issues, and it is unlikely that they will make any concessions. These factors will be more closely examined in Chapter Six on bargaining but must be kept in mind here as modifiers of the above hypotheses.

Technology and Work Processes

In recent years a great deal of emphasis has been placed on the notion of uncertainty in the work process. Uncertainty has been presented as a construct antithetical to bureaucratic, patterned work activities. Technology, environment, and other factors are viewed not as sources of predictable work behavior but rather as potential sources of uncertainty in the production process. Perrow's (1967) discussion of technology is one of the better examples of the operationalization of the notion of uncertainty in terms of how work is conducted. Workers confront raw material that they must remold into the appropriate commodity. Technology is the knowledge of procedures that enables workers to change a raw material into a recognizable commodity. Organizational technology may be viewed, according to Perrow, along two dimensions: the degree of variability of stimuli (variations in the raw material), and the degree to which search procedures are analyzable (the degree to which the techniques for dealing with the raw material are well established). He speaks of four types of technology: (1) craft technology, where there are few variations in the stimuli and an unanalyzable search process; (2) nonroutine technology, where there are many variations in the stimuli and an unanalyzable search process; (3) routine technology, where there are few variations in the stimuli and an analyzable search process; and (4) engineering technology, where there are many variations in the stimuli and an analyzable search process. While Perrow presents this scheme as a mode of categorizing technology in terms of its level of uncertainty, the scheme may be politicized if we make the assumption that the more uncertain the technology (the greater the variations in the stimuli and the less analyzable the search process), the greater the uncertainty of the workers in the production process. When technology is nonroutine, knowledge of the production process becomes difficult to transfer. It becomes the idiosyncratic knowledge of the worker rather than the formal, transferable knowledge of the organization as a whole. If knowledge is viewed as a resource, then we may talk about the greater resource wealth of workers under conditions of nonroutine technology than of routine technology.

In terms of the perennial politics of organizations, interest groups that are involved in nonroutine technology may not need to join in a coalition because their resource base may be sufficient to give them the type of influence they need to assure that any organizational decisions reflect their demands. On the other hand, interest groups involved in routine work activities may have minimum knowledge resources, and their attempts at influence are likely to fall short of their demands. Whatever knowledge resources are encompassed in their jobs will have to be pooled with the knowledge resources controlled by other

interest groups, if they are to have their desired impact on organizational decisions. This leads us to the following hypothesis:

Hypothesis 15. The more routine the technology of an organization, the greater the frequency with which coalitions of
interest groups will emerge.

Interest group politics, that is, the attempts of individual
interest groups to influence decision making, are therefore
likely to occur in nonroutine occupations. A parallel to this
may be seen if we analyze the political activities of professionals
versus nonprofessionals in organizations. Professionalization by
definition implies that workers bring knowledge and training to
the work setting. Although the organization may transfer some
specialized knowledge to professional workers, for the most
part their knowledge comes from sources external to the organization. They are in sole control of the majority of knowledge
they bring to bear on their work. The added strength of professional workers is that they can redefine their work situation to
reinforce the importance of the knowledge they bring to it.
Nonprofessional workers gain the majority of their knowledge
from the organization and have minimum impact on specifying
the knowledge needed for carrying out their work. Obviously,
nonprofessional workers do develop a certain level of expertise
from experience in the work place. However, we would expect
interest groups composed of nonprofessional workers to engage
in coalition politics while professional workers would engage in
interest group politics. The appeal of unions to nonprofessional
versus professional workers may be seen in these terms rather
than the simple status terms in which it is often couched in
theories about the early failure of the labor movement to
organize professional workers. It is interesting to note that, as
the number of professionally skilled employees has increased
and as their knowledge has become more transferable, these
groups also engage more frequently in coalition politics.

A number of writers have previously shown the relationship between routinization and power in decision making (Pugh
and others, 1969); others have already shown the relationship
between professionalization and influence in decision making

(Hage and Aiken, 1969). However, what these authors have failed to specify is how workers assure their impact on decision making. The theorists primarily view power as authority, rather than influence; therefore, they see the allocation of power to workers as a rational process that occurs from the top. The argument is that, under conditions of uncertainty, if authority to make specific decisions is not allocated to workers, the production process will be slowed down by the constant checking and rechecking between subordinates and superiors. To assure the smooth operation of the production process, power is therefore allocated to subordinates. While this may be true in regard to on-line work decisions, workers' demands often exceed this narrow focus, as we noted previously. It is not as clear that uncertainty will automatically result in workers having a say in such issues as personnel, policy, and budgeting. In these instances, the workers must take power, that is, consciously exert their influence on authorities. If they are successful, power is being exerted from the bottom up.

In our discussion of power we accentuated the fact that the unidirectional concept of power (from the top down) has depoliticized the analysis of organizations. The workers' control of uncertainty must be made clear to their superiors, that is, the control of uncertainty must become a clear basis for influence, an identifiable exchange commodity. Coalitions become the bargaining mechanisms that transfer the basis of influence (that is, knowledge) into exchangeable commodities. Some groups, such as highly professional workers dealing with nonroutine and engineering technology, have such abundant control of knowledge resources that they do not need coalitions for this purpose. Other groups, such as those composed of nonprofessional workers dealing with routine work, need to merge into interest groups and coalitions to transform their knowledge into influence and their influence into an impact on policy outcomes.

Boundary Spanning and the Environment

The knowledge resources that workers have may not be constant over time. They may vary depending on the particular situation in which the organization finds itself. In terms of cur-

rent organizational theory, this translates into a concern with
the organizational environment. The influence of an organization's environment on the internal nature of the organization
has been examined by a number of theorists in recent years
(Aiken and Bacharach, 1978; Aldrich, 1979; Dill, 1958, 1962;
Duncan, 1972; Karpik, 1978; Lawrence and Lorsch, 1967).
Each of these theorists has posited a relationship between the
uncertainty in the environment and the internal processes and
structure within the organization. Environmental uncertainty is
normally conceptualized as the degree to which the environment is unpredictable. Determining this operationally involves a
minimum of two dimensions: the complexity of the environment and its stability. For example, taking clients as one element of the environment, environmental complexity would be
measured by counting the number of different clients served,
while environmental stability would be measured in terms of
the change in the clients served over time. The more complex
and unstable the environment, the greater the uncertainty. It
should be clear that uncertainty is not an element of the environment but rather a statement about the organization's relationship to the environment. By saying that an organization's
environment is uncertain, we are simply maintaining that an
organization must continuously adapt and readjust in order to
accomplish its mission.

      The workers who are involved in the organization's rela-
tions with its environment often find themselves carrying out
unpredictable tasks. The activities of workers in an uncertain
environment are nonroutine. This is especially true of workers
whose primary task is contact with the environment, those
called *boundary spanners* (Aldrich and Herker, 1977). Recent
empirical work (Bacharach and Aiken, 1980) has shown that
workers with a high rate of boundary-spanning activity tend to
describe their work as nonroutine. Obviously, higher rates of
boundary-spanning activity occur in an uncertain environment.
The implication is that workers engaging in boundary-spanning
activity in an uncertain environment will have a high level of
knowledge resources. Using our previous logic, we may expect
that the interest groups composed of such boundary spanners

will not engage in coalition politics, because the magnitude of their knowledge resources inevitably gives them some influence on decision outcomes. In a highly certain environment, the activities of boundary spanners may become routine and provide minimum knowledge resource control, therefore decreasing the boundary spanners' direct influence in decision making. They are then more likely to engage in coalition politics. Boundary-spanning activity alone will not predict the emergence of interest group politics as opposed to coalition politics, but the interaction of boundary-spanning activity and an uncertain environment will.

Hypothesis 16. The more uncertain the environment, the greater the likelihood that boundary spanners will engage in interest group politics rather than coalition politics.

Thus, to understand coalitions it is not sufficient to examine the internal work dynamics of the organization; rather, we must also take into account the organization's relation to its environment and the role of interest groups in this relationship. The work process must be placed in this context if we are to get a total picture of the resources controlled by various interest groups and the relationship between this resource control and the likelihood that the groups will or will not form coalitions.

Conflict of Interest

So far we have concerned ourselves solely with the group's resource base as a factor affecting the formation of a coalition. A second component must also be considered, that is, the convergence or lack of convergence of interests among the interest groups that will compose the coalition. In terms of our earlier review of the coalition literature, this is the ideological component of coalition formation. It is especially germane to calculating the probability that the specified outcome that an interest group desires can be achieved by coalescing with other interest groups. Specifically, an interest group contemplating joining a coalition will weigh the implications of pooling resources and concomitantly weigh the commonality of interest.

Incongruent interests affect the probability that a coalition will not form in pursuit of a specific goal. Put simply, machinists and engineers may decide that their joint pooling of knowledge resources will enhance their bargaining position vis-à-vis management; however, they may realize at the same time that their divergent interests will make their coalition fragile.

Both macrosociological work on revolts (Dahrendorf, 1959) and social psychological theory and research on coalitions (Gamson, 1967; Thibaut and Kelley, 1959) have found that parties must have sufficiently common interests to organize or mobilize action and to maintain harmony within a coalition once it is formed (Lawler and Thompson, 1979; Lawler, Youngs, and Lesh, 1978). Thus, potential allies are likely to evaluate both the subjective utility of a given coalition and the compatibility of their interests. Parties should attempt to maximize the utility they will gain by forming a coalition and to minimize the potential conflict within the prospective alliance.

Hypothesis 17. The greater the potential conflict of interest, the less viable the coalition option.

In an organizational setting the discussion of different interests reduces itself to two interrelated components: the particular ideology of group members and the functional goals of group members. Ideology implies the normative framework in which group members work. It is the set of political and social beliefs the parties hold in common that provides a primary milieu for sustaining any social network. Such an orientation is brought from society into the organization by individual members. That is, it appears that social differences, political differences, and so forth do not end at the organization's boundaries. The degree to which an organization can harmonize such differences through recruitment and selection patterns may vary, but in most organizations we maintain that the harmonizing capacity is slight. A tendency to ignore this point has isolated organizational analysis from societal analysis and has contributed to the relatively homogeneous picture of organizations in the organization literature. Rather than seeing organizations as arenas in which the social and ideological differences of society are manifested, organizations are cast as all-powerful socializing mechanisms capable of diminishing these differences. While the image of the institutionalized "organization man" may be a potent statement about alienation, it may exaggerate the dichotomy between the work world and the nonwork world, presenting organizations as harmonious and portraying ideological and social differences as arising outside the work arena.

The second factor that must be considered is the functional goals of specific groups in the organization. A functional goal is the pragmatic result sought by the specific group. For example, in the area of overtime, sales personnel may have different specific goals from production personnel. On the issue of division of labor, engineers may have a different set of priorities from machinists. The source of functional goals, unlike ideologies, is the workplace.

In trying to predict when work groups will operate as interest groups or as members of coalitions we need to consider the convergence of their interests, that is, the convergence of both functional goals and ideologies across work groups. Table 8 presents the results of convergence and nonconvergence of

Table 8. The Relationship of Ideology and Functional Goals
to Organizational Politics

| Ideology | Functional Goals | |
	Convergent	Nonconvergent
Convergent	1. Coalition politics	2. Issue-specific outcomes
Nonconvergent	3. Issue-specific outcomes	4. Interest group politics

interests. The table can be summarized in terms of three hypotheses:

Hypothesis 18. When functional goals and ideologies converge across work groups, such groups are likely to engage in coalition politics.

Hypothesis 19. When there is a lack of convergence of both functional goals and ideologies across work groups, such groups are likely to engage in interest group politics.

Hypothesis 20. When there is a lack of convergence of either functional goals or ideologies, whether the work groups engage in coalition politics or interest group politics will depend on the specific issue at hand.

Convergent versus nonconvergent interests imply a cooperative versus a noncooperative situation. For a coalition to operate successfully, it must achieve a minimum degree of cohesion. Clearly, there will never be a perfect fit between the interests of one group and the interests of another. What condition 1 in Table 9 is implying is that, on the whole, the commonalities will be greater than the differences. Condition 4 implies just the opposite. Conflict among work groups must be overcome if they are to form a cooperative coalition rather than operating as individual interest groups. When there is an inherent divergence of functional goals or ideologies among interest groups (conditions 2 and 3), the ability to overcome the differences and to form a coalition will depend on the issue at hand.

Two aspects of the issue must be considered when evaluating whether that issue will produce coalition politics or interest group politics: the scope of the issue and the time period between emergence of the issue and the point at which final action must be taken. With regard to scope, the following hypothesis seems warranted:

Hypothesis 21. The more general the issue, the greater the likelihood that groups with divergent interests will engage in interest group politics rather than coalition politics.

When a very specific, time-bound issue is at stake, subgroups with conflicting interests might compartmentalize their areas of conflict, ignore them for purposes of their immediate relationship, and form a temporary coalition. However, an issue with a wider scope is more likely to accentuate the ideological and goal differences among work groups, reinforcing the tendency toward interest group politics rather than coalition politics. As an illustration, machinists and engineers may have divergent functional goals or ideologies. For the sake of a very specific work issue, such as the number of reels of wire that can be turned out per hour, they may concur and coalesce in order to assure a specific change in policy. The specific issue allows them to form a short-lived coalition that disintegrates once their demands are met. In the case of a broader policy issue, however, such as personnel policy, it is unlikely that they will find common grounds that override their goal or ideological differences. Even if such common grounds were found, it is unlikely that they could sustain the type of long-term coalition that is necessary for the continual monitoring of such broad policy issues.

Aside from scope, the time allowed for resolution of the issue is important. In a short time period, work groups are unlikely to be able to overcome potential conflicts of interest from divergent goals or ideologies and weld together in a common cause. Thus, the following hypothesis is warranted:

Hypothesis 22. The shorter the time period between emergence of an issue and the point at which final action is necessary, the greater the likelihood that work groups will engage in interest group politics rather than coalitional politics.

In hypotheses 20 and 21, we are assuming a commonality of either ideology or functional goals among the work groups (conditions 2 and 3 of Table 9). If neither type of convergence is present, all issues will be handled in terms of interest group politics (condition 4); if both are present, all interests will be handled in terms of coalition politics (condition 1).

In this context we now need to consider how the nature of the organization can constrain the interests its members have in decision outcomes. The constraint on ideology, as we have asserted before, depends on the organizational recruitment and selection processes. Two ideal constructs may be differentiated. Some organizations may operate as Weber (1947) envisioned, applying bureaucratic rules to the recruitment process. Weber argues that this results in the recruitment of technically competent personnel regardless of their ideological or political positions. On the other hand, an organization may subscribe to a model that envisions recruitment as a conscious effort to homogenize the beliefs and ideologies of all its members. Further-

more, beyond the recruitment process, some organizations engage in a conscious socialization process to superimpose a common organizational ideology over beliefs held by workers before
joining the organization. If the homogenizing efforts are totally
successful, then there is likely to be little political action outside formal authority relationships in the organization. However, if the organization remains politically and ideologically
neutral in its recruitment, then the potential for the emergence
of political pressure groups will exist. This perspective is somewhat at odds with Weber's interpretation of the same process.
Weber maintains that neutrality in recruitment depoliticizes
organizations. We are maintaining that neutrality in recruitment
politicizes organizations. Our different interpretation is a function of our different concerns. Weber is primarily concerned
with political patrimony. When he speaks of the need for political and ideological neutrality in recruitment, his concern is with
restricting the participation of external political groups in the
workings of an organization. Specifically, in the public sector,
Weber is concerned that political parties with specific constituencies do not consciously place their personnel in key positions
of administrative bureaucracies. We, on the other hand, see
political and ideological infiltration of organizations as occur-
ring much more subtly and much more on an individual basis.
Each member brings into the organization myriad political and
social beliefs, whether that person is a member of a particular
external party or social group or not. Guarding against the lack
of institutional patrimony will in no way depoliticize the internal workings of an organization. Contemporary concerns with
psychological, social, and political attitudes of individual re-
cruits are much more germane to this point. Organizations,
through a barrage of filtering mechanisms, try to assure that the
individuals' attitudes are consistent with the organization's phil-
osophy. However, even if organizations succeed in filtering out
very basic ideological differences, the sheer fact that contemporary organizations recruit different types of personnel for
various positions inevitably means that they are likely to get
variations in interests among workers. Simply stated, no matter
how stringent the organization's barriers to divergent interests,

and no matter how thorough its socialization mechanism, it cannot expect its members to leave their social identities, their socioeconomic backgrounds, their class identifications, and their political attitudes at home. To the degree that different beliefs are a source of some political tension in the organization, the only guarantee against politics is total automation.

While the organization's constraint on the ideologies of members is relatively ambiguous, its constraint on their functional interests is more directly located in the organizational structure. The two structural dimensions that are critical in this regard are differentiation (that is, role specialization) and segmentation (that is, departmentalization).

These two dimensions define to a significant degree the subgroups in the organization. They can be called the morphological confines that dictate the baseline from which any political grouping will emerge (Bacharach, 1978). Ostensibly segmentation and differentiation of work in the organization are done to enhance the efficiency of production. However, a latent function of these apparently rational managerial decisions is to define the functional goals of organizational actors.

Differentiation is a division of labor in terms of the specific task to be accomplished. It is the role-specific component of the rational management and administration of work. A high level of differentiation implies that the function of the role is limited. More importantly, the functional goals that any actor has while occupying this role are restricted in scope to the immediate task. Segmentation is the clustered division of labor. It is the division of labor into groups of tasks and roles. Segmentation has the effect of homogenizing workers' goals. It brings together workers with role-specific activities and possibly radically different work activities and places them beneath the umbrella of the departmental goal.

Inherently, there is an important tension between differentiation and segmentation. Often this means that individual actors are caught between two potentially merging groups. Take the case of a departmental secretary. On the one hand he or she is a member of the department and is concerned with the departmental mission. On the other hand, he or she holds much in

common with secretaries throughout the organization. In terms
of ideal constructs, two work groups can emerge on the basis of
this distinction: a differentiated work group and a segmented
work group. A differentiated work group will, by definition, cut
across departmental groupings while a segmented work group
will be departmental. In the decision process, the unit that will
become the basis for an interest group (that is, the unit that will
be most active) will depend on the issue at hand. For example,
in a public sector bureaucracy at times of budget allocations,
the segmented work groups are likely to become more vocal.
However, if the issue is overtime, then the differentiated work
groups are likely to become more important.

Will these two types of work groups engage in interest
group politics or coalitional politics? That is, once an issue has
arisen, will interest groups based on either role differentiation
or segmentation choose to coalesce with other interest groups,
and, if so, what other interest groups will they choose? Table 9
presents four types of possible coalitions.

Table 9. Type of Coalition by Type of Work Group

	Differentiated Group	Segmented Group
Differentiated Group	1. Role coalition	2. Mixed
Segmented Group	3. Mixed	4. Departmental coalition

The most common coalitions to emerge are obviously 1
and 4. Most labor issues are dealt with by role coalitions; most
management issues are dealt with through departmental coalitions. The mixed coalitions, while rarer, emerge in various
forms. Most often they emerge as what may be called *coattail
coalitions*. For example, a specific sales department may, for its
own reasons, choose to support the demands of a coalition of
machinists and engineers. On a different issue, the machinists
may choose to support demands of the sales and marketing departments. Which one of these coalitions will be formed is
determined by each group's calculation of subjective expected
utility and the resource to be gained, as described earlier in this

chapter, and by the ideological distance between groups, as discussed above.

Lines of Communication

Communication opportunity is obviously essential to the formation of coalitions. In an organizational context, however, it is not necessarily the presence or absence of communication lines that is important, but the degree of regulated formal and informal communication among representatives of different subgroups. An organization that constrains communication lines or rigidly enforces specific communication structures will limit the ability of some subgroups to coalesce while enhancing the ability of others to mobilize joint action. Regardless of whether the communication is formal (sanctioned by the organization) or informal, the following propositions are hypothesized:

Hypothesis 23. The lower the number of communication lines among different interest groups (or among segments within these interest groups), the greater the difficulty of coalition mobilization.

Hypothesis 24. The lower the frequency of communication using existing lines of communication, the greater the difficulty of coalition mobilization.

Hypothesis 25. The greater the organizational constraint on the development of new lines of communication, the greater the difficulty of coalition mobilization.

Communication is also important in conjunction with conflicts of interest. Resolution of interest conflicts requires both the opportunity to communicate and negotiate with potential allies and the actual use of communication channels. Therefore, the greater the opportunities to communicate, the lower the inhibiting effect of a conflict of interest. However, research on communication in bargaining and conflict settings indicates that hypothesis 25 requires further specification. The social psychological research suggests that communication opportunities do not have a consistent effect on conflict resolution; communication can have positive, negative, or no effect, depending on the social context (Rubin and Brown, 1975; Deutsch and Krauss, 1962; Krauss and Deutsch, 1966; Marwell and Schmitt, 1975). Some key conditions are the degree of conflict and the complexity of the conflict issue. The greater the degree of conflict or difficulty of conflict resolution, the lower the likelihood that conflicting parties will use the communication channels at all and the greater the likelihood that any communication that does occur will exacerbate rather than ameliorate the conflict. The implications of these findings are:

Hypothesis 26. Increasing the opportunities to communicate will have no effect or will actually increase conflict when there is a high, rather than low, conflict of interest between interest groups.

Hypothesis 27. Increasing communication opportunities will have no effect or will actually increase conflict when interest groups are in conflict over highly complex issues.

Communication is important in resolving conflicts only when there is not a severe conflict of interest and when the conflict issues dividing two or more interest groups are not too complex. The implication of these propositions is that an organization can inhibit conflict between subgroups with rather severe conflicting interests by separating or isolating them from one another.

Next we need to take into account the different patterns of communication that can emerge in an organization and the implication of these different patterns for the political dynamics of organizations. Communication in organizational analysis is most often distinguished by its direction. Katz and Kahn (1966) distinguish upward, downward, and lateral communications, and they specify the function of each. Downward communication serves five basic functions: exchange of job directives; specification of job rationale; exchange of information about organizational procedures and practices; feedback; and indoctrination to goals. Lateral communication is viewed as primarily a mode of enhancing task coordination, although Katz and Kahn also see it as furnishing emotional and social support to individuals. Katz and Kahn (1966) reduce upward communication to four basic types: workers' comments on themselves, their own performance and their problems; comments about others and their problems; comments on organizational practices and policies; and information on what needs to be done and can be done. Katz and Kahn's analysis of communication, while important, tends to be constricted by their functional orientation. That is, their primary concern is the specification of the aspects of communication that enhance efficiency from a managerial perspective. Because they view organizations as rational systems of interdependent parts, they fail to specify communication as an important political task.

Supplementary political interpretations may be given to each of the patterns discussed by Katz and Kahn. For example, from a political perspective downward communication may be conceptualized as attempts to generalize upward communication. This might be called information absorption, that is, efforts by members higher in the organization to absorb knowledge from the lower echelons. In terms of organizational politics, downward communication may be viewed as the efforts by superiors to assimilate the knowledge resources that are available to subordinates. Indeed, politically, downward communication may be seen not simply as a mode of sanctioning but also as a conscious effort at cooptation. In an organization where the primary political struggles are hierarchical, downward communication may be seen as an effort to short-circuit the potential political activities of subordinates.

Lateral communication may be seen as a prerequisite to the formation of peer group coalitions. Upward communication may be seen as an effort to influence or an attempt to form a cross-level coalition; however, if we believe that those who communicate frequently with their superiors will come to identify with their superiors, then such communication may be interpreted as an attempt to increase role domain through contact and communication with the higher echelon.

Katz and Kahn attribute importance to the individual actor as a communicator. For us the individual actor is important as a member or representative of a specific interest group. An analysis of the collective aspects of communication requires that we accentuate the intergroup nature of the communication.

Retaliatory Capacities

Whenever an interest group is deciding whether to join a coalition, it must consider the capacity of countercoalitions to retaliate. By joining a coalition, an interest group takes an active, political position in opposition to other interest groups or coalitions. This increase in its activity and visibility opens the coalition to potential retaliation by opposing coalitions. We will begin with the following hypothesis:

Hypothesis 28. The greater the retaliatory capacity of a countercoalition, the greater the difficulty of mobilizing a coalition between two interest groups with respect to a specific issue.

In evaluating the retaliatory capacity of a countercoalition, an interest group must consider that the formation of a coalition to pursue one issue may yield benefit at the time, but it may simultaneously reinforce countercoalitions, in turn, negating the influence of the newly formed coalition over future issues. A coalition's dependence on a countercoalition gives the countercoalition the capacity to retaliate in response to the coalition's influence attempts. These points may be stated as two hypotheses:

Hypothesis 29. The greater the power of potential countercoalitions over given interest groups and the greater the probability that such countercoalitions will mobilize in response to losing on the current issue, the greater the difficulty of mobilizing those interest groups to coalesce over the current issue.

Hypothesis 30. The greater the dependence of coalesced interest groups on groups that will lose to the coalition on an issue, the greater the difficulty of coalition formation over that issue.

Two interrelated conditions appear to aid a coalition in blunting or blocking future retaliation by countercoalitions. First, permanent coalitions are more likely to provide some defense in the future than temporary coalitions. In a temporary coalition, participating interest groups are left to their own resources after the immediate issue is past, and they must be prepared to deal on their own with retaliation from losers. An ongoing coalition is more likely not only to provide influence over the immediate issue but also to reduce the probability of future retaliation. Coalitions that are permanent or long-term, or that have an unspecified duration, or that have multiple issue concerns provide defense and protection for their member interest groups. Such defensive dimensions are particularly essential for interest groups that have the most to gain from a coalition because they also have the most to lose when not under the protection of the coalition. These interest groups have the least power outside of the coalition. Second, coalitions can also forestall retaliation by expanding the coalition to include more interest groups. This will increase the power of the coalition and possibly involve the co-optation of potential opponents (see Lawler, Youngs, and Lesh, 1978; Lawler and Thompson, 1979). In sum:

Hypothesis 31. In the face of potential retaliation, long-term coalitions with broad general goals or cooperative agreements, implying mutual defense of each participating member, will be more likely to form than more limited coalitions.

Hypothesis 32. Over time, coalitions that are successful are likely to expand to include a greater number of interest groups.

The tendency toward expansion is due to the coalition's need to increase its defensive and offensive capacities and also the need of unattached interest groups to become part of the power base. This suggests, contrary to much of coalition theory (Komorita and Chertkoff, 1973; Riker, 1962), that coalitions may become larger than is necessary to influence the immediate issue, in order to assure and maintain their long-term power positions. Finally:

Hypothesis 33. Long-term coalitions will accentuate intercoalition differences while homogenizing intracoalition differences.

Long-term coalitions typically require the development of broad areas of interest commonality and resolution of residual or underlying conflicts among coalition members. In attempting to achieve this commonality among its component interest groups, the coalition may need to dramatize its differences with other coalitions or with excluded interest groups. This suggests that organizations that have long-term coalitions are also likely to have well-defined lines of conflict.

Summary

In this chapter we have attempted to specify the conditions that will lead interest groups in organizations either to merge into a coalition of interest groups or to engage in individual interest group politics. The primary criterion is the subjective utility an interest group expects to gain from forming a coalition versus the subjective utility it expects to gain from engaging in individual interest group politics. We examined how such issues as boundary spanning, environment, conflict of interest, lines of communication, and retaliatory capacity affect the interest group's decision to form or not to form a coalition. Chapter Six will examine the bargaining processes in which coalitions engage.

6

Conflict as Bargaining

Coalitions essentially partition organization members into distinct groups on the basis of common interests. While coalitions bind the members with the most common interests together, they also pit those with the most divergent interests in opposition to one another. Coalitions create and define the parameters of conflict by crystallizing the different interests of subgroups. In any organization, there are likely to be numerous differences among members and subgroups, and it is coalitions that highlight and make salient the most critical differences. In this sense, coalitions are not just the principal units of political action but also the mechanisms for establishing and defining the political game. The political game, in turn, is manifested in bargaining between coalitions.

Conflict between intraorganizational coalitions takes the form of bargaining. Chapters Four and Five were concerned with *intra*coalition bargaining—specifically, with the conditions underlying the formation of coalitions. Bargaining was treated as a means of mobilizing interest groups into coalitions, and we viewed coalitions as the outcome of this bargaining process. However, coalitions are not ends in themselves; they are strategic devices to improve the power position of component interest groups vis-à-vis others with regard to some issue or set of issues. Thus, coalition mobilization gives rise to *inter*coalition bargaining. The goals underlying coalition formation require the maintenance of a strong coalition and bargaining with opposing coalitions. The bargaining in this case is not designed to develop a new coalition but to use the existing coalition to advantage. This intercoalition bargaining is the essence of conflict in organizations. Coalitions define and crystallize the different interests, and intercoalition bargaining is the concrete manifestation of conflict. In this sense, bargaining and conflict in organizations are indistinguishable phenomena.

Our fusion of conflict and bargaining becomes more understandable if we use some basic notions of game theory to examine alternative images of organizations. Using the jargon of game theory (see, for example, Rapoport, 1966), most organizational theory implicitly or explicitly assumes that intraorganizational relationships are *positive-sum* in nature, that is, the outcomes of interacting individuals or subgroups within organizations are positively correlated. A positive-sum view implies that cooperation or some variant of cooperation is the dominant, and most rational, mode of behavior. Conflict is likely to be attributed to irrationality or failure of the organizational structure to fully develop and institutionalize the inherently cooperative elements in the organization. At the other pole, radical critiques of organizational theory and research, typically informed by a Marxist perspective, assume that organizational relationships inherently reduce to class relationships and are zero-sum in nature, that is, the outcomes of subgroups are negatively correlated. In a zero-sum relationship, cooperation can be established and maintained only by domination, oppression, cooptation, false consciousness, and the like.

Bargaining has little place in these two models. A positive-sum situation, being inherently cooperative, requires little negotiation. Conflicts can be resolved by education or communication, because through such activities opposing parties

recognize their common interests and see the deleterious consequences of conflict for both. Given a positive-sum relationship,
who needs bargaining? In contrast, zero-sum relationships may
be altered in a non-zero-sum direction through negotiation, but
theorists in this tradition tend to view such relationships as
technically unresolvable. The only issue is: Who dominates or
can muster the greatest power? There is simply little common
ground for bargaining. Actors are in the position of either domi-
nating others or being dominated by them.

It is probably apparent by now that we adopt a course
between these two extremes. The coalition metaphor in the
prior chapters does not deny that there are positive-sum and
zero-sum elements within nearly any intraorganizational relationship, whether between individuals, interest groups, or coalitions. However, our coalition imagery does assume that these
elements are typically not the dominant ones governing the
interaction of subgroups. Instead, the coalition model implies
that intraorganizational relations are mixed motive. A mixed
motive situation encompasses elements from both positive-sum
and zero-sum situations. In other words, parties are simultaneously confronted with incentives to cooperate and incentives to
compete. Such situations encompass greater complexity and uncertainty than either positive-sum or zero-sum situations.

Bargaining is a central element of any mixed motive setting. Given simultaneous incentives to cooperate and compete,
mixed motive relationships are inherently unstable and inevitably involve some distrust. In this context, bargaining is the
primary means for keeping the conflict within acceptable
bounds and avoiding a complete bifurcation of the relationship.
Through bargaining, parties "resolve" the competition versus
cooperation dilemma, maintain or improve their positions, and
protect themselves from other groups or individuals. However, a
mixed motive situation further implies that any resolution of
the conflict is likely to be temporary, with the danger of conflict emerging repeatedly over time. Bargaining is a never-ending
aspect of mixed motive contexts. Thus, we expect persistent
bargaining over time, and there appears to be no way to separate or distinguish conflict from bargaining in organizations.

This chapter analyzes the basic elements of bargaining

within organizations. The first section analyzes the nature of bargaining relationships, using some basic dimensions from Schelling (1960) and Walton and McKersie (1965). The second section treats the major focus of social psychological work: the tactical dimension of bargaining. The last section examines the constituent-representative dimension of bargaining.

Nature of Bargaining Relationships

Bargaining is the give-and-take that occurs when two or more interdependent parties experience a conflict of interest. The degree of interdependence or conflict of interest can vary considerably across social settings. The point is that some minimal level of each is necessary to engender or maintain a bargaining relationship.

Bargaining is the action component of conflict. The central elements of bargaining are the tactical moves and countermoves by which parties attempt to achieve dual, often conflicting, objectives: to resolve the conflict, but to do it in a way that is advantageous to their own interests (see Druckman, 1977; Morley and Stephanson, 1977; Rubin and Brown, 1975). The dilemma is that parties wish to give as little as possible and take as much as possible, yet conflict resolution may necessitate more giving and less taking than they expect or desire. Resolution of the current issue or problem may also affect future bargaining and bear on the long-term maintenance of good relations.

By now, it is undoubtedly obvious that we view bargaining processes as ubiquitous aspects of complex organizations. The specific nature or form of bargaining can vary almost infinitely across different sectors, subgroups, issues, and other factors within a given organization. For example, bargaining may be tacit and involve little direct communication between parties, or it may be explicit and involve substantial contact, or it may lie somewhere between these two extremes. Bargaining may also be informal or formal. Informal bargaining usually is not officially recognized or sanctioned. Formal bargaining implies not only official sanctioning but also that parties accord recognition and legitimacy to one another and to the bargaining relationship.

Given the variability of bargaining in organizational contexts, our first task is to identify the basic dimensions of any bargaining relationship. In order to understand the tactical action that constitutes the essence of bargaining, we must have some sense of the relational context within which that tactical action takes place. As a first step in this direction, we contend that there are two basic dimensions. First, bargaining may be distributive or integrative in nature (Pruitt and Lewis, 1977; Walton and McKersie, 1965). This dimension of bargaining relationships deals primarily with the qualitative nature of the relationship. Second, as suggested by Schelling's (1960) writings on bargaining, bargaining relationships may be tacit or explicit. This dimension deals with the mode of bargaining. After discussing these dimensions, we will construct a typology of bargaining relationships that interrelates the integrative-distributive and tacit-explicit dimensions.

The integrative-distributive distinction is grounded in Walton and McKersie's (1965) work on labor-management collective bargaining. In distributive bargaining, the outcomes of parties are negatively correlated, but failure to reach agreement may involve substantial costs. Applied to union-management relations, Walton and McKersie argue that this type of bargaining typically occurs in negotiations over economic issues, such as pay. On a more general level, the critical aspect of distributive bargaining is that the parties are dealing with finite resources. Given finite resources, an increase in benefit to one party necessarily means a comparable decrease in that benefit to the other party. The conflict of interest, therefore, is quite evident. Overall, distributive bargaining implies an outcome structure that integrates a key element of zero-sum contexts (that is, negatively correlated outcomes) with an incentive to reach agreement (that is, the costs of continued, unabated conflict), thereby creating a mixed motive setting with relatively high conflict potential.

In integrative bargaining, there are important positive-sum elements underlying the relationship, despite its overall

mixed motive character. The task for bargainers, therefore, becomes not simply to bargain aggressively in their own interests
but also to engage in joint problem solving that will illuminate
the common ground between them. Integrative bargaining is
most likely to occur when the positive-sum elements are salient
to the parties—specifically, when parties recognize a mutually
troublesome issue that does not involve a precise division or
allocation of finite resources. As implied by the labels, distributive bargaining means that the most pressing problem is how to
distribute some benefit or cost among two or more parties; integrative bargaining means that the critical problem is finding a
way to maximize the benefit of both parties, to assure that the
conflict does not have deleterious consequences for both. If an
allocative or distributive problem remains, integrative bargaining
might lead to an expansion in the total pie, since resources in
this case are not strictly finite.

Walton and McKersie (1965) recognize that the distinction between integrative and distributive bargaining is a loose
one. The extreme versions of each type represent poles of a
hypothetical continuum, while most (if not all) real world bargaining tends to fall somewhere between those poles. In other
words, there are both integrative and distributive aspects in
most bargaining, and any attempt to classify concrete bargaining cases on this basis must be made as a matter of degree.

The integrative aspects of bargaining appear to be more
salient and prominent in intracoalition than in intercoalition
bargaining. The reason is that the mobilization of a coalition by
two or more interest groups presupposes that there is some
underlying common interest. This common interest typically
lies in the threat posed by other coalitions or subgroups within
the organization. Depending on the strength of the common
interest, intracoalition bargaining can gravitate more or less
toward joint problem solving. In extreme cases, the integrative
elements of such bargaining may become so strong that intracoalition processes do not even give the appearance of bargaining. This is one reason why prior coalition theory either neglected the bargaining processes underlying coalition formation

or dealt with bargaining in a very restricted sense (see the bargaining theory of coalitions by Komorita and Chertkoff, 1973).

Our focus in this chapter, of course, is on intercoalition bargaining. Here the distributive elements of the bargaining are likely to be more salient and pose a greater obstacle to conflict resolution. There is not necessarily much common ground underlying intercoalition bargaining beyond the interest of the coalitions to mitigate or resolve their conflict. As noted earlier, the purpose of intercoalition bargaining is not to form a coalition against other subgroups or coalitions but to deal with conflict between two or more distinct coalitions. As a consequence, intercoalition bargaining is likely to involve more severe conflict and have more dangerous implications for the organization.

Intercoalition bargaining can still contain both integrative and distributive elements, so it is important to consider the organizational conditions that heighten or weaken the tendencies toward one or the other type of bargaining. It should be clear from the discussion so far that the greater the integrative elements of bargaining, the greater the ease and effectiveness of conflict resolution. In organizational contexts, several structural conditions affect the ratio of integrative to distributive elements. For example, the finiteness of the resources exchanged by coalitions within the organization should have an important bearing on the nature of the bargaining relationship. As resources become more finite, there should be an increase in the likelihood of distributive bargaining. The pressures of the environment on the organization may also be manifested in intercoalition bargaining. External pressure should bind disparate coalitions together just as a common threat within the organization can weld two or more interest groups into a coalition. Finally, since the costs of continued conflict can reduce the severity of the conflict, the consequence of intercoalition conflict for the organization as a whole can affect the nature of the bargaining relationship. If the conflict will have negative effects on the functioning of the organization or its survival, coalitions that are highly dependent on the organization would be inclined more toward integrative bargaining. To summarize, we suggest the following hypotheses:

Hypothesis 34. The more finite the resources within the inter-coalition relationship, the greater the probability of distributive bargaining between conflicting coalitions.

Hypothesis 35. The greater the external pressure on the organization, the greater the probability of integrative bargaining between conflicting coalitions.

Hypothesis 36. The greater the dependence of the coalitions on the organization, the greater the probability of integrative bargaining between conflicting coalitions.

On a more general level, these hypotheses imply that three categories of phenomena will affect the bargaining relationship of two or more coalitions: (1) the existing relationship of the coalitions, that is, the resources that underlie and are at stake in the relationship; (2) the relationship of the organization to its environment; and (3) the relationship between the coalitions and the larger organization. On a more specific level, the hypotheses indicate that coalitions will engage in distributive bargaining to the extent that (1) the organization has limited resources to allocate to component interest groups and coalitions; (2) the organization has considerable control over, and experiences minimal threat from, the environment; and (3) the coalitions are not highly dependent on the organization. As these conditions change, there should be an increase in integrative bargaining.

To summarize, the integrative-distributive distinction deals with the qualitative nature of the bargaining relationship. A distributive relationship implies a more severe conflict of interest than an integrative relationship; hence, the problems of conflict resolution should be greater in distributive contexts. Furthermore, the bargaining relationship is likely to be linked to major structural dimensions of the larger organization. Next, we will turn to the mode of bargaining, that is, the tacit-explicit dimension of bargaining relationships.

The literature on bargaining emphasizes the formal, explicit, or conscious manifestation of bargaining (see Druckman, 1977; Rubin and Brown, 1975; Stahl, 1972; Young, 1975). Specifically, the give-and-take is conceptualized as an explicit exchange of offers and counteroffers, as action consciously designed to find a mutually acceptable solution to the conflict. While collective bargaining and international negotiations often fit this conceptualization, many instances of less explicit or less conscious bargaining are excluded by this approach. It is especially important to consider more subtle forms of negotiation when dealing with intraorganizational relations, because coalitions in this context may be hesitant to admit or confront conflict. Instead, they may try to handle issues in a less visible way. Intraorganizational relations provide a context within which highly explicit bargaining is likely to exist side-by-side with less explicit bargaining.

The conditions that affect the explicitness of the bargaining can be elaborated by considering Schelling's (1960) contrast between explicit and tacit bargaining. Explicit bargaining is essentially what nations, corporations, and unions do when they sit at the bargaining table, that is, they exchange offers and counteroffers. In such settings, the parties have relatively open lines of communication, define the relationship as a bargaining one, and consent to consider compromise. In this context, the most critical aspect of the give-and-take is concession behavior (the nature of the offers and counteroffers). Tacit bargaining, on the other hand, implies that the parties have obstructed communication lines and may not even define the relationship as a bargaining one or be conscious of the fact that they are in a bargaining relationship. At a minimum, tacit bargaining implies that the parties do not publicly acknowledge the bargaining relationship. The give-and-take involves few explicit offers or counteroffers; instead, parties attempt to outmaneuver and manipulate each other, often using subtle influence tactics or rewards and punishments. Tacit bargaining often precedes and is transformed into explicit bargaining.

Given this distinction, it is important to consider how or when bargaining is likely to become more explicit and formal. This is an extremely important question, because the labor-management literature assumes that an explicit, formal bargaining relationship provides the most effective way both to reduce immediate conflicts and to maintain harmonious relations over time while keeping conflict within acceptable or manageable bounds. From this standpoint, one of the key problems of conflict resolution is getting parties to recognize each other as legitimate and enter a formal, explicit bargaining relationship. Yet, the explicitness and formality of the bargaining vary substantially across sectors within an organization. For example, committees that contain representatives of different subgroups or coalitions can be construed as bargaining settings, but there is substantial variation in the degree to which parties treat such settings as arenas for explicit bargaining.

Unfortunately, there is little literature on the establishment of explicit bargaining relationships outside of research on unionization. However, Schelling's (1960) distinction between tacit and explicit bargaining does suggest a number of basic conditions that facilitate or are necessary for explicit bargaining, and these provide a worthwhile starting point.

Lines of Communication. Explicit bargaining implies free-flowing communication, typically face-to-face, allowing coalitions to examine, discuss, debate, and make proposals regarding all areas or issues in the conflict. Tacit bargaining implies that either the opportunities to communicate are constrained by the social setting or the existing opportunities are used ineffectively (to communicate aggression rather than conciliation).

The effect of communication on conflict resolution is not a simple matter. The common sense notion that getting the parties to communicate will eventually resolve the conflict is not clearly supported by the social psychological literature (see Rubin and Brown, 1975, pp. 91-119). Specifically, that research indicates that the mere opportunity to communicate does not have a consistent effect on conflict resolution. Sometimes parties use lines of communication to express hostility, instead of conciliation, or simply do not use the lines of communication at all (Deutsch and Krauss, 1962). Furthermore, open lines of communication may be more effective as a preventive than as a corrective measure. Marwell and Schmitt (1975) found that there was little conflict in a mixed motive setting when communication was possible from the beginning to the end of the experiment; when the communication was delayed or was possible only after conflict developed, it did not restore full cooperation. Once conflict is established, therefore, an expansion in communication opportunity is insufficient to produce conciliation.

Overall, it is the content of the communication, not the opportunity to communicate, that is critical. To the extent that coalitions use lines of communication to transmit conciliatory messages, those lines will enhance conflict resolution; if the lines of communication are used for messages of aggression, communication may exacerbate the conflict. In sum, lines of communication are a necessary, but not a sufficient, condition for explicit bargaining. An increase in explicit bargaining requires opportunity plus conciliatory use.

Potential for Compromise. Explicit bargaining implies that the issues underlying the conflict allow some room for compromise. In other words, there are intermediate positions or agreements that lie somewhere on a continuum between the preferred positions of the two coalitions. Tacit bargaining is more likely when there are undeveloped or relatively few intermediate positions, in part because coalitions are likely to perceive the situation as a win or lose choice. To the extent that coalitions can and do identify a range of intermediate positions, explicit bargaining becomes a more attractive alternative. Thus, explicit bargaining should increase with the number of viable intermediate positions between complete winning and complete losing.

Mutual Consent. The transformation of tacit to explicit bargaining requires the opening of lines of communication, a willingness to use the communication lines to search for the solution, and the ability to transform or redefine dichotomous win-lose issues into continuums with a number of intermediate positions. These conditions set the stage for an increase in the explicitness of bargaining, but fully developed explicit bargaining also requires a shift in the orientation of the parties. Specifically, it requires that coalitions consent to treat the relationship publicly as a bargaining one and consider the possibility of making concessions.

The conditions that give rise to explicit bargaining make it apparent why explicit bargaining should be a more effective mode of conflict resolution than tacit bargaining. As noted earlier, merely getting to the bargaining table is often a significant problem for coalitions in conflict. Some of the most basic obstacles to conflict resolution are related to the tacit-explicit distinction. Issues allowing few intermediate positions, the failure to develop or use communication lines, lack of willingness to recognize the claims of the opposing coalition, or unwillingness to make concessions will render it difficult for coalitions to establish an explicit bargaining relationship.

Furthermore, agreements established through explicit rather than tacit bargaining are likely to be more stable. Tacit agreements are likely to be more ambiguous, nonbinding, and unenforceable in a strict sense. Such agreements can be broken with relative impunity and typically require more trust than is likely to be present under conditions of tacit bargaining. On the other hand, agreements from explicit bargaining tend to be more specific and unambiguous. Unlike tacit agreements, explicit ones are likely to include some safeguards against a breach by either party. These safeguards may be a part of the formal agreement itself or a function of the public character of the negotiations and agreement.

The general implications of our discussion for organizations are summarized by the following hypotheses:

Hypothesis 37. Bargaining in the context of formal well-developed lines of communication will be more explicit than bargaining in the context of informal, undeveloped lines of communication.

Hypothesis 38. The more explicit the bargaining, the more stable the agreement reached by two (or more) coalitions.

Overall, these propositions indicate that the communication structure of an organization can facilitate or inhibit the ability of conflicting coalitions to resolve their conflicts. The communication structure affects the manner in which coalitions deal with their conflicting interests, that is, the mode of bargaining. By establishing formal, legitimized patterns of communication between some coalitions, the organizational structure facilitates relatively stable solutions to conflicts between these coalitions. Conflict will not be less likely to occur among coalitions with developed communication lines; but, when it does occur, it is likely to be less severe, last a shorter period of time, and be resolved more effectively. Thus, the foregoing hypotheses lead to the following one:

Hypothesis 39. Conflict between coalitions with formal, developed lines of communication will be less severe, less persistent, and less likely to recur over the same issue than conflict between coalitions with undeveloped lines of communication.

The most general factors underlying hypotheses 37-39 are the quality and quantity of the information flow between conflicting coalitions. In the last analysis, bargaining can be construed as a game of information exchange and manipulation. Parties will certainly attempt to manipulate the information flow and thereby bluff the opposing coalition into yielding more than it otherwise would. Despite the manipulative nature of this information flow, however, bargaining does enable the parties to infer each other's intentions, aspirations, orientations, and so forth. The information obtained from the other is never complete or completely accurate, but the quality of the inferences drawn is likely to depend, in part, on the amount of information a party can gather about the other. Consequently, explicit bargaining grounded in well-developed communication lines should provide each party more and better information with which to make tactical judgments. This should engender more effective agreements.

We have analyzed two basic dimensions of bargaining: integrative-distributive and tacit-explicit. The integrative-distributive dimension deals with the qualitative nature of the relationship; the tacit-explicit distinction deals with the mode of bargaining. We have treated these dimensions separately so far; we must now consider their relationship. The implications of tacit versus explicit bargaining depend on whether the context is an integrative or distributive one; and the bearing of an integrative or distributive context depends, to some extent, on whether the mode of bargaining is tacit or explicit.

Combining the dimensions leads to four types of bargaining relationships (see Table 10). Each relationship differs in its

Table 10. Types of Bargaining Relationships

Qualitative Nature	Mode of Bargaining	
	Tacit	Explicit
Integrative	Informal cooperative bargaining	Formal cooperative bargaining
Distributive	Informal competitive bargaining	Formal competitive bargaining

potential for conflict and conflict resolution. Tacit integrative bargaining implies informal cooperation. It is exemplified by a situation in which strong underlying common interests between the coalitions are combined with minimal opportunities for explicit bargaining. Explicit integrative relationships, in turn, imply formal cooperation, that is, cooperation induced, sanctioned, and regulated by the organization. Tacit distributive bargaining involves informal competition that is not officially sanctioned by the organization. Explicit distributive bargaining is competitive bargaining officially sanctioned and regulated by the organization. Any organization should contain these four types of bargaining relationships. The relative prominence of the four and their specific locations in the organization's activities will determine the character of intraorganizational conflict.

The four types of bargaining relationships have divergent implications for the resolution of conflict between coalitions in an organization. Conflict resolution should be easiest when coalitions have an explicit integrative bargaining relationship and most difficult when coalitions have a tacit distributive relationship. In the former situation, the integrative foundation of the relationship exerts pressure toward conflict resolution, and the structuring of the bargaining in explicit terms reinforces this tendency toward resolution. In a tacit distributive relationship, the distributive element implies a high level of disagreement between the coalitions while the tacit element connotes the lack of a structural mechanism for conflict resolution. In other words, organizations with structures that induce explicit integrative relations among their component coalitions will face less serious problems of conflict resolution than those with structures that induce or permit the emergence of tacit distributive relationships.

Within the other categories of our typology the tendencies toward conflict resolution should fall between the above extremes. In a tacit integrative relationship, coalitions are oriented toward resolving mutual problems and reaching agreements but, at the same time, are somewhat inhibited by the unstructured nature of the bargaining relationship. In an explicit distributive relationship, the structural mechanisms of explicit bargaining facilitate conflict resolution while the distributive foundation of the relationship poses an important obstacle to resolution. Overall, it is clear that these intermediate conditions in our typology imply basic incongruities in the bargaining relationship. One dimension of the bargaining relationship exerts pressure toward conflict resolution, while the other inhibits conflict resolution.

In conclusion, the nature of the bargaining relationship between coalitions in an organization should depend on the organizational structure. Various aspects of the structure can increase or decrease the tendency toward conflict resolution by altering the qualitative nature of the relationship (the integrative-distributive dimension) or the mode of bargaining (the tacit-explicit dimension). For example, the formalization of an organization may create a greater tendency toward explicit bargaining; finite resources may enhance the distributive elements in the relationship. It should be noted, however, that global aspects of the organization are important only insofar as they are manifested in the particular relationships between particular coalitions. An increase in formalization may establish conditions for explicit bargaining between some coalitions and undermine them for others. The overall level of formalization within an organization is not as important as the content and nature of specified relations between specific subgroups or coalitions. Similarly, the resources relevant to different coalitions within an organization may vary in finiteness across different sectors of the organization. Our typology emphasizes, once again, the need for subgroup analyses of organizations.

Tactical Dimension of Bargaining

Across different types of bargaining relationships, the key dimension of the actual bargaining process is the use of *tactics*. Tactics are the behavioral mechanisms and patterns that coalitions use to influence each other and achieve a satisfactory conclusion to a conflict encounter. On a specific level we would expect the behavior of parties to differ across the four types of bargaining relationships; but on a general level the tactical dimensions underlying these divergent behaviors are identical. It is these commonalities or basic dimensions of tactical action that are our primary concern in this section.

Parties in a bargaining relationship face a delicate tactical issue. Given uncertainty and incomplete information about each other's goals, aspirations, and intentions, they are faced with the task of gaining information about the other's situation while giving little information about their own. Bargaining should be viewed as an information-manipulation game in which parties fake, bluff, lie, and so forth, in an attempt to create certain impressions, to test or evaluate the impressions given by the opposing coalition, and, most important, to assess the resolve or commitment of the opponent. This view places strong emphasis on the cognitive aspects of bargaining.

While this image of bargaining appears to have substantial credibility, it is surprising how little attention has been given to the cognitive features of bargaining. Most approaches to bargaining reduce it to a rule-governed process that specifies a priori where an agreement or solution lies. The literature on coalition formation, covered in Chapter Four, is an example. Most theories assume that coalition bargaining will be governed by the equity norm, the equality norm, or some combination. Such theories further assume that actors can acquire information on each other's inputs and outputs and make relatively good, consensually based estimates of where the equity point lies. Unfortunately, such conditions are seldom met in organizations. First of all, conflicting parties do not have complete information about each other's inputs and outputs. Secondly, bargaining nearly always involves heteromorphic exchange, that is, the exchange of qualitatively different commodities. This means that the equivalence of the exchange is inherently indeterminate, and coalitions are likely to disagree with each other regarding the location and criteria for evaluating equity. At best, equity theory provides a very rough, imperfect foundation for predicting the outcome of conflicts in organizations. In the context of limited information and heteromorphic exchange, the bargaining process becomes the major determinant of the bargaining outcome.

A second perspective that tends to adopt a rule-governed approach is game theory (compare Rapoport, 1966, 1970). The rules in game theory differ on the surface from those in equity theory, but determinant game theory solutions often posit agreements that just happen to represent the equity point (compare Nash, 1953; Rapoport, 1966; Stahl, 1972). However, game theory approaches are debilitated even more than equity approaches by relatively stringent assumptions. Eschewing substance, game theory stresses the logic of the game (Rapoport, 1970) and develops mathematical models that identify how parties would act *if they were rational.* The basic thrust of game theory models is to use the actors' utility functions to deduce a solution to a bargaining problem. This orientation is expressed rather well by Rapoport (1970, p. 11): "In the context of game theory, the players are not endowed with any psychological characteristics except those that may be reflected in the description of the game itself, for example, what each of the outcomes is worth to each of the players. Therefore, the desirable properties of the proposed solution cannot depend on any personal characteristics of the players beyond the utilities ascribed to the outcomes *which are assumed to be known.* For instance, a solution cannot depend on . . . the particular *stances they may assume in bargaining (for example, taking a tough or conciliatory posture or the like).*" (Emphasis added.)

The solutions offered by the game theory can vary with

the exact nature of the assumptions made about actors' utility functions. However, regardless of the particular solution or whether the solution is determinate (that is, a precise solution point) or indeterminate (that is, a solution set or range), the solutions are essentially predetermined by rational actors' utilities. Bargaining, therefore, becomes a process whereby actors simply converge on the optimal solution or solution set (Harsanyi, 1977; Rapoport, 1966; Stahl, 1972; Von Neumann and Morgenstern, 1947; Young, 1975).

This volume is concerned with the social psychology aspects of bargaining that are generally neglected or assumed away by game theory (for brief comparisons of social psychological and game theory approaches, see Boulding, 1978, p. 345; Chertkoff and Esser, 1976; Druckman, 1977, pp. 21-24; Stahl, 1972, pp. 18-19; Tedeschi, Schlenker, and Bonoma, 1973, chap. 5). Game theorists are typically concerned with situations in which parties have complete information on each other's payoffs at a variety of potential solution points. The precise nature of this complete information assumption varies somewhat across different game theory models, yet some variant of complete or perfect information remains a key premise underlying nearly all game theory models (for reviews, see Harsanyi, 1977; Stahl, 1972; Young, 1975). On the other hand, social psychological approaches are more suitable to an organizational analysis, because relations within organizations are unlikely to provide coalitions with such information. Given the ambiguity that characterizes organizational relations, coalitions can only infer the preferences of the opposing coalitions from the actual process of negotiation, and such inferences are inherently tenuous, because deception and manipulation are intrinsic aspects of the political game.

In addition, while game theory would examine how the actual solution (agreement) arrived at by the actors compares with the optimal one (for rational actors) predicted by formal models, the present volume is concerned with the maneuvering and influence processes that lead a party to yield more or less. One of the key elements of this influence process is bargaining stance or posture, an element that Rapoport indicated (in the passage we quoted) could not form the basis for game theory solutions. Bargaining stance or posture is one of the prime means that parties use to manipulate information and interpret each other's intentions, orientations, and aspirations in the context of ambiguous information on payoffs, subjective utilities, and other factors. In sum, the focus of this book departs from game theory and falls squarely in the social psychological tradition reflected in a number of recent reviews (see Chertkoff and Esser, 1976; Druckman, 1977; Hamner and Yukl, 1977; Rubin and Brown, 1975; Tedeschi, Schlenker, and Bonoma, 1973, chap. 5). It is the social psychological tradition that is crucial to an understanding of bargaining between coalitions in an organizational context.

If, as the equity theory and game theory approaches imply, the outcome or result of bargaining is governed by a priori rules (such as equity), the bargaining process is important only with respect to how these rules are applied to the specific issues by the bargainers, and bargaining tactics are of relatively little importance. The only purpose of tactical action would be to prevent a divergence from equity by one side or to retaliate against the other for attempting to force an inequitable settlement. Tactics become merely protective mechanisms for assuring that the equilibrium point specified by equity or game theory is achieved, maintained, or at least approximated in the bargaining. This equilibrium point is essentially the reference point for making tactical decisions.

An alternative approach is implied by Siegel and Fouraker's (1960) level-of-aspiration theory. This theory makes no assumptions about an equilibrium point and cannot be used as a means to specify a determinate solution. It implicitly assumes that the outcome of a bargaining encounter is indeterminate, primarily because of the limited information available to the parties and their willingness to use deception and manipulation. In brief, level-of-aspiration theory emphasizes the impression-management aspects of bargaining.

Based on level-of-aspiration theory, the key point to which coalitions will direct their impression-management tactics is each other's *aspirations*. Each coalition in a bargaining setting has an aspiration level, that is, a goal or set of goals about the ultimate agreement; and each coalition will adopt a concession tactic or level based on its aspirations. The most basic assumption of the theory is that each coalition's aspiration level will be inversely related to its concession level: Higher aspirations will produce tougher bargaining. The theory suggests that tactically a coalition can extract more concessions from an opponent by manipulating the opponent's aspirations; and a key way to do this is by creating the impression that it has very high aspirations itself and is irrevocably committed to them. Figure 1 delineates the dynamics underlying this impression management

Figure 1. Relationship of Aspirations and Concessions

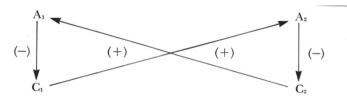

process. In the diagram, A_1 and C_1 represent the aspiration and concession levels of coalition 1; A_2 and C_2 represent the aspirations and concessions of coalition 2. The basic assumptions are that each party's aspirations (A_1 or A_2) will determine their own concessions (C_1 or C_2). The tactical implications are indicated by the links between each party's concessions and the opponent's aspirations, for example, the effect of C_1 on A_2. The key implication is that the tactics (concessions) of each coalition can convey high aspirations for itself and reduce the aspiration level of the other. That is, the effect of one coalition's *aspirations* on the other's *aspirations* is affected by the coalition's concession behavior; similarly, the effect of one coalition's *concessions* on the other's *concessions* is affected by the other's aspiration levels. Based on the theory, it "pays to be tough."

To summarize, level-of-aspiration theory stipulates that a bargainer's concessions will affect the opponent's aspirations, which, in turn, will determine the opponent's concessions. Soft tactics in the bargaining, therefore, will raise the opponent's aspiration level and reduce the opponent's yielding, while tough tactics will decrease the opponent's level of aspiration and, thereby, increase the opponent's yielding. The theory recommends a tough stance in bargaining. The best overall stance is to make no or only very small concessions or conciliatory gestures early in the bargaining or until the opponent stops making concessions. Then, relatively small, infrequent conciliatory actions will ostensibly prevent a deadlock while inducing the greatest yield from the opponent (see Esser and Komorita, 1975; Hamner, 1974; Siegel and Fouraker, 1960).

It is probably evident that the theory is concerned primarily with concession behavior and emphasizes the inferences parties are likely to draw from different patterns or types of concession tactics. However, tactical behavior is not limited to concession behavior; any verbal or nonverbal behavior can convey greater or lesser toughness. The specific behaviors that connote toughness will vary with the context and the type of bargaining relationship. The important point is that tactics of bargaining can be arrayed on a tough-soft continuum. Furthermore, regardless of whether coalitions group their tactics together or use them singly, and regardless of the nature of the tactic, level-of-aspiration theory indicates that behavior that conveys greater toughness is more likely to increase or maximize the yielding by an opposing coalition.

The basic problem with level-of-aspiration theory is the potential for an impasse. Toughness may indeed work, that is, produce an agreement that distinctly favors the coalition with the tougher posture, but it can also backfire and exacerbate the conflict. There are two interrelated reasons for this. First, as many theorists and researchers in the bargaining field note, bargaining often implies an expectation of reciprocal yielding. To the extent that parties recognize the rights of each other and consent to consider compromise, some reciprocity is likely to be not only expected but also demanded. The salience and strength of these reciprocity expectations should be closely related to the explicitness of the bargaining; specifically, greater explicitness should produce more pressure to reciprocate concessions. The failure to live up to these expectations, or a substantial departure from them, should heighten the opponent's inclination to meet toughness with toughness. Second, if toughness appears too aggressive, it is likely to arouse a loss of face issue. Yielding in response to excessive toughness is tantamount to accepting an inferior status and conveying a willingness to demean oneself; that is, conciliation in response to toughness could produce a loss of face. To avert a loss of face or restore already lost face, a coalition may counter excessive toughness with toughness.

Social psychological research tends to document the risks of following the advice of level-of-aspiration theory strictly. While substantial research indicates that toughness does extract more concessions than softer strategies (Bartos, 1970, 1972; Chertkoff and Conley, 1967; Komorita and Brenner, 1968; Liebert and others, 1968; Pruitt and Drews, 1969; Siegel and Fouraker, 1960; Yukl, 1974a, b), other research indicates that the most effective strategy is a tough but conciliatory one (Esser and Komorita, 1975; Hamner, 1974). In a review of this literature, Chertkoff and Esser (1976) indicate that bargainers must consider the impressions they give not only in terms of toughness but also in terms of reasonableness. The optimum image is toughness moderated by reasonableness. This implies a modification of the practical implications suggested by level-of-aspiration theory. It is important for a coalition to be tough or firm enough to avoid exploitation by others and to demonstrate its resolve while remaining reasonable enough so that opponents feel it has some willingness to resolve the conflict.

Despite the foregoing modification of level-of-aspiration theory, the basic ideas underlying the theory remain sound. Toughness has been found to be effective (1) in the early stages of the bargaining, when parties' aspirations are not fully crystallized and are subject to greater manipulation; (2) when parties have little information on each other's priorities or utilities (the bluffing that is intrinsic to the theory becomes transparent if the opponent has complete information); (3) when parties are not under severe time constraints (sufficient time makes a tough stance less of a surprise and also makes it appear less aggressive); (4) when the user of tough tactics has greater power than the target of toughness (see, for example, Chertkoff and Esser, 1976; Liebert and others, 1968; Michener and others, 1975a; Pruitt and Drews, 1969; Rubin and Brown, 1975). The theory provides a sound starting point for analyzing intercoalition bargaining in organizations just as it provides a foundation for actors making tactical decisions.

From the standpoint of the organization, the major difficulty is that the theory applies only when just one of the coalitions follows its dictates. If both (or all) coalitions adopt tough tactics in bargaining, the likely result is an impasse. If this occurs across a multitude of intercoalition conflicts, the organization could become riddled with many seemingly unresolvable conflicts. Level-of-aspiration theory, therefore, points to a major dilemma for organizations: how to establish structural conditions that encourage coalitions to resolve conflicts effectively. One way to do this, of course, is by the forceful intervention of third parties. However, such efforts can be costly and lead to an expansion of conflicts beyond their prior scope by involving even more coalitions in each conflict. Another approach is to structure the relationship between two coalitions so that conflict will be resolved by the parties themselves before it becomes too damaging to the organization as a whole.

The latter approach implies that the organization or its representatives create conditions that minimize the toughness of the tactics adopted by conflicting coalitions. Based on our earlier discussion of bargaining relationships, one possibility is to move the bargaining relationship in the direction of an explicit integrative one. Any shift toward explicit or integrative bargaining should reduce the use of tough tactics in the bargaining. This may be a major reason why explicit integrative relationships produce the greatest likelihood of conflict resolution. In sum, we suggest the following hypotheses:

Hypothesis 40. An increase in the explicitness of the bargaining relationship will reduce the mutual toughness in bargaining between conflicting coalitions.

Hypothesis 41. An increase in the integrative or a decrease in the distributive elements of the bargaining relationship will reduce the mutual toughness of bargaining between conflicting coalitions.

The conditions under which toughness is more or less effective also have implications for minimizing impasses in organizational contexts (see, for example, Pruitt and Drews, 1969; Yukl, 1974a). First of all, time limits will inhibit toughness, because coalitions will have less room to maneuver and should foresee the deleterious effects of tough tactics. In an organizational context, outside parties or subgroups (such as superiors) can apply time pressure by establishing explicit time limits. Another approach is to pressure one or more of the conflicting coalitions to accomplish other tasks that just happen to be contingent on quick and effective resolution of the conflict.

Hypothesis 42. An increase in the temporal constraints, established directly or indirectly, will reduce the mutual toughness of bargaining between conflicting coalitions.

Aside from setting time constraints, the organization or its representatives may manipulate the availability and flow of information between conflicting coalitions. Simply requiring more information exchange could enable both coalitions to infer each other's intentions, aspirations, and so forth more accurately and confidently. Such information would enable both parties to identify deception and bluffs more clearly and would thereby inhibit the inclination of the coalitions to maintain tough tactics. The information issue is very complex, however. The organization must consider the type of information, how it is communicated, from whom it comes, and other aspects of it. In addition, a coalition or subgroup could undermine their areas of control within the organization if they released information that serves as one basis for regulation of an opposing coalition's activities. Nevertheless, on a general level, we expect:

Hypothesis 43. An increase in the information available to each coalition (about the opponent) will reduce the mutual toughness of bargaining between conflicting coalitions.

Finally, an organization might mitigate impasses by creating conditions of mutual dependence between key coalitions within it. Dependence is a major dimension of power, and it affects the costs of not reaching agreement. When a coalition has only minimal or narrow dependence on its opponent, it can adopt and maintain a tough stance in bargaining. In this context, the basic dilemma of bargaining (to yield as little as possible but still reach agreement) is less of a dilemma. The optimum stance for a coalition with little dependence on its opponent is to maintain toughness and see what the opponent does. If the opponent yields substantially, then conflict resolution may produce more benefit (or fewer costs) than an impasse; otherwise, an impasse might be perceived as the best option. High levels of mutual dependence, on the other hand, should make it difficult for coalitions to maintain toughness over time as the prospect of an impasse becomes more real. The bargaining dilemma is increased when there are higher levels of dependence because an impasse entails significant costs. Thus, one way to alter the costs of an impasse to the coalitions is to alter their dependence or interdependence.

The issue of dependence in bargaining is more complex and critical than our brief discussion here indicates. Dependence can provide the cornerstone for a comprehensive theory of bargaining tactics, linking different tactics to different elements of the bargaining context. In this section, we have simply elaborated a single dimension of tactical action, toughness, which underlies much of the bargaining literature. In Chapter Seven, we expand our treatment of bargaining tactics and offer a theory of those tactics based on power-dependence theory. Before we examine dependence in bargaining more fully, however, we will analyze the constituent-representative dimension of bargaining.

Constituent-Representative Dimension of Bargaining

This section might be construed as an unnecessary digression because it involves some shift in the unit of analysis. While our focus is intercoalition bargaining, constituent-representative relationships imply a concern with intracoalition relationships.

Constituents are the members of a coalition, and *representatives* are the persons formally or informally selected to represent the coalition in bargaining. This shift in our unit of analysis is appropriate because theory and research on collective bargaining indicate that constituent-representative relationships can provide a major obstacle to conflict resolution. Real, imagined, or even anticipated pressure from constituents can reduce the flexibility of representatives and, thereby, affect both the nature of the bargaining relationship and tactical action. The pressure of constituents often moves the bargaining relationship in the direction of distributive bargaining while enhancing the toughness of both parties. Given the implications of constituent-representative relations on the topics already covered in this chapter, our discussion would be incomplete without a brief treatment of the issues raised by the presence of constituents.

In intercoalition bargaining within organizations, the constituent-representative relationships may be very subtle and informal. Constituent pressure does not necessarily imply or require a formal relationship between constituents and representatives, like that found in union-management bargaining. In the absence of a formal relationship, members of the coalition may still look to others (those with the most critical positions within the organization) for leadership and expect these leaders to represent their opinions on organizational committees or the like. Similarly, members of key decision-making groups or committees may perceive themselves as having constituencies even though their ties to these constituencies are very informal. In sum, we expect much more variation in the nature of constituent-representative relations in intercoalition bargaining than in bargaining between entities such as unions and management. For some insight into the issues raised by constituent-representative relations, we will briefly present the major implications of the social psychological and collective bargaining literature on this topic.

Deutsch (1969) suggests that constituencies produce a narrowing of vision in negotiations. Specifically, actual, expected, or even very subtle forms of pressure from constituencies are likely to (1) reduce the search for alternative ways to approach or resolve issues, (2) reduce the ability of representatives to take each other's roles and interpret the situation from the opponent's standpoint, and (3) inhibit overall quality of communication. The reason is that constituent pressure (real or imagined) leads bargainers to approach their activities with more single-mindedness and less flexibility. This narrowing of vision typically leads to excessive toughness on the part of both parties. Deutsch is essentially suggesting that constituents make conflict resolution more difficult and less likely, because representatives will be more reluctant to make concessions or seriously attempt to reach compromise positions. All other things being equal, constituencies may facilitate an orientation that defines issues as distributive and views bargaining as a purely zero-sum power game.

The implication of Deutsch's notion is that conflict resolution within organizations can depend, in part, on the manner in which the structure of the organization limits the interactions of constituents and representatives. In this sense, the structure of an organization can serve to either facilitate or inhibit the narrowing of vision implicit in constituent-representative relations. We can get some ideas about the relevant dimensions of the organization by examining the social psychological conditions that increase or decrease this narrowing of vision.

The bargaining literature indicates that four major conditions bear on the narrowing of vision: (1) the involvement of constituents in planning and conducting actual negotiations, (2) the accountability of representatives to their constituents after the bargaining, (3) the formalization of the constituent-representative relationship, and (4) the loyalty or commitment of the representative to the coalition and its goals. Each of these variables should be interpreted in light of its effects on the autonomy of the representatives. One of the most basic ideas from the literature is that representatives with more autonomy are able to adopt a more flexible approach to negotiations, adapt to the emergent events or issues in the actual bargaining, and resolve the conflict more effectively (Rubin and Brown, 1975). Thus, the most basic proposition guiding our analysis is:

Hypothesis 44. The greater the autonomy of representatives, the less narrowing of vision and, hence, the less mutual toughness there will be in intercoalition bargaining.

With this hypothesis as a backdrop, we will examine each of the above conditions.

Constituent Involvement. The nature and magnitude of the input representatives receive from constituents can vary considerably within organizations, as can the mode of communicating input. Some coalitions have formal, regularized procedures for constituents to convey ideas, priorities, and the like to representatives. In other coalitions, representatives meet regularly with other coalition members on an informal basis to determine the sentiments of constituents. In both of these cases, the involvement and participation of constituents, whether formal or informal, can be characterized as relatively high. Alternatively, representatives may plan and develop tactics and goals relatively independently of their constituents. Constituents might formally or informally grant such discretion or autonomy to their representatives, or it may be forced upon them by inadequate lines of communication or by the positions of representatives and constituents in the authority structure of the organization.

The participation or involvement of constituents is important because it places constraint on the behavior of representatives and influences the direction of the coalition. Constituents can limit the range of options to be considered by their representatives and inhibit their discretion to respond to emergent, unexpected elements of the bargaining process. Constituents can also extract implicit or explicit commitments from the representatives to push certain ideas or proposals. Overall, the participation of constituents, regardless of their formal power, is likely to communicate expectations to the representatives, and representatives are likely to feel obligated to act within these expectations. This felt constraint should be greater under circumstances of greater participation and input by constituents. These notions are supported in a study by Druckman (1967) that compared a context where representatives met prior to the negotiations either with their own constituents or with the opposing representatives. Druckman's findings indicate that involvement of constituents in the planning produced tougher bargaining. Based on this research and the reasoning we presented above:

Hypothesis 45. The greater the involvement and participation of constituents in planning the negotiations, the less the autonomy of representation and the greater the narrowing of vision.

Accountability of Representatives. Prior theoretical treatments of constituent-representative relations have heavily emphasized the accountability of representatives. Accountability refers to the degree to which constituents can make representatives account for, justify, or defend the actions they took in negotiations. The specific nature or basis of the accountability can vary. In informal settings, mere contact with constituents subsequent to negotiations can allow constituents to ask the representative about the negotiations and request explanations for various aspects of the ultimate resolution. Research in experimental contexts indicates that even this minimal degree of accountability tends to harden representatives' bargaining and increase the likelihood of an impasse (see Gruder, 1971). The most extreme form of accountability occurs where the representative's position as representative is on the line (Bartunek, Benton, and Keys, 1975). To be more specific, a number of conditions will vary the pressure exerted by accountability: the level of contact with constituents, the level of constituents' knowledge about the negotiations, and the degree to which constituents can apply sanctions, such as removal or public chastisement, against the representative (Rubin and Brown, 1975). The hypotheses suggested by these ideas are:

Hypothesis 46. The greater the accountability of the representative, the less the autonomy of the representative and the greater the narrowing of vision in the bargaining.

Hypothesis 47. The greater the future contact with constituents, the greater the representative's narrowing of vision in the bargaining.

Hypothesis 48. The greater the constituents' knowledge about the negotiations, the greater the representative's narrowing of vision in the bargaining.

Hypothesis 49. The greater the ability of constituents to apply sanctions to the representative, the greater the narrowing of vision in the bargaining.

Formality of Constituent-Representative Relations. Formalization of constituent-representative relations is a two-edged sword, which must be considered in conjunction with constituent involvement and the accountability of representatives. On the one hand, formalization can protect representatives from excessive constraint and can legitimize substantial autonomy. On the other hand, formalization can severely limit the representative's autonomy. For instance, formal rules and procedures may specify that participation or input from constituents is merely advisory or may make it binding on the representative. Informal patterns may similarly call for more or less involvement and accountability. In sum, formalization alone should have little bearing on the degree of autonomy accorded a representative. It is the specific *content* of the formal or informal patterns, traditions, and procedures that is most critical.

There is, however, an important exception, grounded in the nature of intercoalition bargaining within organizations. In organizations, there are many examples of rather explicit constituent-representative relations with a combination of formal and informal procedures. The most obvious case is collective bargaining between management and labor; another example is the bargaining that occurs between different departments on committees. Such committees may be designed to bring together persons representing different viewpoints, and implicitly different constituencies, within the organization to discuss conflict issues. In fact, a system of standing and ad hoc committees is a key means an organization may use to mitigate and control conflict not only between different individuals vying for power in the organization but also between the different coalitions or interest groups they represent. Often, the tie between particular members on a committee and their constituencies is loose, unspecified, and unformalized. It is these circumstances that must be contrasted with more formal, publicly recognized constituencies.

In general, there appears to be a minimal threshold of formalization beyond which only differences in the content, rather than the degree, of formalization are important. Below this threshold, there is a substantial increase in the autonomy of the representative; in fact, the representative is a representative only in a token sense. The difference between the areas below and above the threshold is essentially a difference between minimum formalization (above the threshold) and virtually no formalization (below the threshold). Without a minimum degree of formalization, the constituent-representative relationship is not publicly recognized or legitimized, obligations on the part of either constituents or representatives are undefined, and any contact or communication between representatives and constituents is incidental to the constituent-representative relationship. Aside from the fact that that there is no formal content to the relationship, informal aspects are not sufficiently developed to specify the obligations of constituents and representatives. This kind of relationship is probably typical of newly emerging coalitions of a tacit, temporary nature, but it might also occur in some long-standing subgroups within an organization.

Consider the case of a woman who is appointed to an important committee whose other members are all men. If there is no organized coalition of women within the organization, her representation of the women merely implies that she is a member of a wide-ranging category of persons. She may see herself as a representative of women in general, rather than of a women's caucus, faction, or coalition. Other women have no claim on or control over her, but they may still see her as a representative in a very general sense. In the absence of minimum formalization, this type of representative has the greatest autonomy to maneuver and press for demands that she interprets to be in the interests of the group she represents. Beyond the minimum level of formalization, the constituent-representative relationship is qualitatively transformed into a publicly recognized and legitimized connection, in which constituents have the right to develop expectations for the representative and engage in some level of evaluation and monitoring of the representative's activity. At this point, the fusion of formal and informal procedures, norms, and activities into specific contents becomes more important than the degree of formality or informality.

A summary of our discussion of formalization in constituent-representative relations suggests the following basic propositions:

Hypothesis 50. Below a minimal threshold of formalization, the greater the formalization of constituent-representative relations the greater the "narrowing of vision."

Hypothesis 51. Above a minimal threshold of formalization, changes in the formalization of constituent-representative relations will have no effect on the autonomy of the representative or "narrowing of vision."

Loyalty of the Representative. Social psychological research on constituent-representative relations (Rubin and Brown, 1975) suggests the following major hypothesis:

Hypothesis 52. The greater the loyalty or commitment of the representative to the group, the greater the "narrowing of vision."

The most basic implication of this proposition is that an in-house representative will be more adamant in defense of the group goals and more resistant to compromise than an outsider. The reason is that an insider will be more loyal to the group than a representative from outside. Professional negotiators, having less of a commitment to the group, being less involved in and able to empathize with constituents, will ostensibly be more able and willing to yield concessions to the opposition in order to reach a mutually satisfactory agreement.

This proposition is empirically supported at a very general level, but it overlooks some important issues. First of all, loyalty and commitment are not necessarily interchangeable. We need to distinguish commitment to the group as a group from commitment to the goals of the group. Loyalty in the strictest sense refers only to the former—the willingness of the representative to subordinate his or her own opinions or goals to those of the group. The loyalty dimension of commitment should clearly increase the "narrowing of vision," while commitment to the group's goals, if not combined with loyalty, need not lead to this result. Loyalty implies unequivocal obedience to the demands of constituents (or to the representative's interpretation of what is in the constituents' interest); a commitment to the group's goals implies a more contingent and pragmatic approach to the bargaining. Commitment to a coalition's goals, in the absence of loyalty, should engender a somewhat softer bargaining stance.

However, there is a countervailing factor at work: Representatives who can demonstrate their loyalty and commitment to the group goals may also be given a freer hand in the negotiations. For example, an in-house negotiator in labor-management contexts may be given more autonomy by constituents than professional negotiators from the outside. The reason is that constituents expect the in-house negotiator's loyalty and commitment to constitute enough constraint; they may therefore be more receptive to giving that bargainer discretion in adapting to the exigencies of the bargaining process. This means that an important paradox is overlooked by hypothesis 52. On the one hand, greater loyalty and commitment should increase the toughness of the bargaining; on the other hand, greater loyalty and commitment may also enable representatives to reduce the involvement of constituents. In sum, loyalty and commitment have two (simultaneous) contrasting effects. By increasing autonomy, they facilitate conflict resolution; but they themselves tend to narrow the representative's vision, inhibiting conflict resolution.

Summarizing our discussion, four basic aspects of constituent-representative relations increase the mutual toughness of the bargaining: (1) the involvement of constituents in planning the bargaining, (2) the accountability of representatives to the constituents, (3) the formalization of constituent-representative relationships within the coalition, and (4) the loyalty and commitment of representatives to the coalition and its goals. All these conditions have a bearing on the autonomy and discretion of the representatives; and, as the autonomy of the representatives decreases, there is an increasing likelihood of mutual toughness and an impasse in the bargaining.

Each of these constraints on constituent-representative relations can be affected by the structure of the organization. For example, the formal lines of communication within the organization can facilitate or inhibit contact between the representatives of major coalitions and their constituents. Lower levels of contact will reduce the involvement of constituents in the planning phase before bargaining and reduce the ability of constituents to hold the representatives accountable. Loyalty of the representatives to the coalition can be altered by pressures for loyalty by other subgroups within the organization. One rather persistent fear of constituents is that representatives will be coopted by either the opponents or third parties. Finally, the nature and degree of formalization in the larger organization might affect the degree and content of formalization of the constituent-representative relations. Overall, by constraining the pressures of constituents on representatives, the structure of an organization can affect both the nature of the bargaining relationship and the tactical actions in intercoalition bargaining.

Summary

We began this chapter with the assumption that conflict and bargaining are inextricably intertwined in organizational contexts. Relations in organizations are inherently mixed motive in nature, which implies that bargaining, the concrete manifestation of conflict, is also intrinsic to intraorganizational relations. Coalitions are the mechanisms that crystallize and bring conflicting interests to the foreground, while intercoalition bargaining is the process through which organizational members act on and deal with their conflicting interests. This distinction between intracoalition and intercoalition bargaining is analogous to Marx's distinction between a *class in itself* and a *class for itself.*

We have developed a typology of bargaining relationships, analyzed the tactical dimension of bargaining, and examined constituent-representative relations within coalitions. Our typology of bargaining is derived from two previously unlinked dimensions of bargaining: integrative versus distributive bargaining and tacit versus explicit bargaining. The first dimension deals with the finiteness of the resources at stake in the bargaining, while the latter deals primarily with the communicative aspects of bargaining. From these two dimensions, we can distinguish formal from informal bargaining, cooperative from competitive bargaining. We classified organizational relationships in terms of four categories: tacit integrative, tacit distributive, explicit integrative, and explicit distributive. Different types of bargaining relationships are grounded in different aspects of the organization. They have divergent effects on both the tactics of bargaining and the likelihood of conflict resolution.

The essence of bargaining is tactical action. We have portrayed bargaining as an impression-management or information-manipulation game, in which deception and bluff are critical elements. This standpoint contrasts with the rather sterile view of bargaining propagated by game theory models, but it is consistent with most social psychological treatments. Using Siegel and Fouraker's (1960) level-of-aspiration theory, we identified the degree of toughness as the most basic tactical dimension of bargaining. Level-of-aspiration theory predicts that tactics that convey a high level of toughness are more effective, but this can create significant problems of conflict resolution for organizations. Consequently, we considered how the structure of an organization or the actions of other subgroups can reduce mutual toughness and the impasses it creates in intercoalition bargaining.

The final section of the chapter examined the impact of constituent-representative relations on intercoalition bargaining. Our discussion suggested that constituent participation, accountability of representatives, formal constituent-representative relations, and loyalty of representatives to the coalition increase mutual toughness and lead to impasses. These ideas have implications for the ways in which dimensions of the organizational structure can moderate intercoalition bargaining.

Our next task is to elaborate the cursory treatment of bargaining tactics we offered in this chapter. Given the centrality of tactical action to bargaining, we need a theoretical framework that leads to a more comprehensive analysis of bargaining tactics. This is the goal of Chapter Seven.

7

Theory of Bargaining Tactics

The formal or informal structure of an organization can be conceptualized in terms of dependence or interdependence relations. From our treatment of power as dependence presented in Chapter Two, we can argue that the distribution of power across coalitions is, in part, a function of these dependence relationships. The dependence relations are constrained by the organizational structure but they also constitute some of the underlying issues of intercoalition bargaining. Consequently, the dependence relationship should be a prime basis for tactical action in bargaining. It sets the stage for bargaining, generates the underlying issues in conflict, and is the ultimate foundation for tactical action. Given the importance of dependence to intercoalition bargaining, this chapter will develop a theory of tactical action that is grounded in the social exchange conceptualization of dependence.

The importance of tactics in bargaining needs little documentation, given our treatment of bargaining in Chapter Six.

However, the literature on tactics is surprisingly scattered and fragmented. This state of the literature is evident in the social psychological material on bargaining as well as in collective bargaining research. The problems in these two bodies of literature are somewhat different. In the social psychological literature, there is a vast body of research on the effects of particular tactics on particular behaviors in highly controlled experimental settings (Rubin and Brown, 1975). There is, however, little consensus about how to classify tactics (see, for example Michener and Suchner, 1972; Raven, 1974; Tedeschi and Bonoma, 1972), and the implicit or explicit concepts of power underlying the research on tactics are too simple. For instance, power tends to be defined and operationalized as the ability to fine or sanction another. While this is a critical aspect of power, it fails to treat several other aspects of power and leads to a rather constricted tactical analysis.

The study of collective bargaining can potentially provide useful information to supplement social psychological research on tactics. This literature, however, has tended to emphasize the collective as opposed to the bargaining aspect of the topic. Not only is a framework for analyzing power and tactics lacking, but there is actually very little research on tactics. Furthermore, available research and conceptualizations in this tradition suffer from the same basic defects as found in the social psychological literature. The studies adopt an essentially unidimensional concept of power, such as the cost of a strike or the cost of not reaching an agreement within a specified period. This leads to limited analyses of bargaining tactics. There are discussions on tactics but, once again, not unified by an overarching theory of power relationships.

The classic volume by Walton and McKersie (1965) might be construed as an exception. They provide the most comprehensive treatment of bargaining in the current literature. Yet, as valuable as their work may be for certain purposes, it reduces to a fragmented exegesis of particular tactics or specific manifestations of power in isolation from other tactics and the broader power context. It is truly astonishing how seldom power is mentioned in this seminal work on labor-management collective bargaining. Furthermore, for our purposes, the Walton and McKersie approach is inadequate because it focuses solely on labor-management bargaining, and this leads to institutionally specific analyses. The theory does not adequately identify the general features of tactical action that apply across institutional, situational, or intraorganizational spheres.

The inadequacies of the available literature become even more apparent if we consider what a theory of tactics should ideally accomplish. First, a conceptualization or theory of power must underlie and guide the analysis. Neither the social psychological nor the collective bargaining work contains an underlying approach to power except in a very rudimentary sense. Second, the conceptualization of power upon which a theory of tactics is based must be multidimensional rather than unidimensional. If anything is clear from the long-standing conceptual debates on power (discussed in Chapters Two and Three), it is that unidimensional concepts are very limited in scope. Power and tactics are inherently complex, multidimensional phenomena and require a comparable conceptualization. Third, the conceptualization of power should capture the dynamics of the use of power, by examining the various ways bargainers can gain, use, and lose power. Specifically, a theory of tactics should provide a classification of the tactics through which bargainers can change the power relationship and should identify empirical links among different dimensions of power and the tactics of using power.

We also suggest that a theory of tactics, and the concomitant conceptualization of power, should be based on examination of the interdependence of social units. This is not a new idea; it is implicit or explicit in the social psychological (Michener and Suchner, 1972; Raven and Kruglansk, 1970; Thibaut and Kelley, 1959) and collective bargaining (see Walton and McKersie, 1965) literature. However, the tactical implications of dependence have not been fully developed, especially as they apply to bargaining. To identify the implications of dependence or interdependence for tactical action, we must turn not to the bargaining literature but rather to more general sociological literature. The framework that comes closest to meeting the requirements we have listed is the power-dependence theory of Emerson (1962, 1972a, b) and Blau (1964). However, previous treatments and applications of the theory have not paid sufficient attention to the tactical aspects of bargaining.

The remainder of this chapter develops a power-dependence approach to the tactics of bargaining. We first present the framework for analyzing power, elaborating our discussion of dependence in Chapter Two. We then evaluate the tactical elements of the theory, that is, the ways in which bargaining can change the power relationship. Finally, we develop propositions linking elements of the power relationship to bargaining toughness (for example, the likelihood that bargainers will adopt tougher or softer concession tactics) and to decision-making processes underlying tactical choices.

Power-Dependence Theory

Power-dependence theory, originally articulated by Emerson (1962) and revised somewhat by Blau (1964) and Emerson (1972a, b), is a particularly suitable starting point for our analysis. First of all, the theory offers a multidimensional conceptualization of power that links power to dependence and differentiates the specific bases of dependence in a social relationship. Second, the theory offers a foundation for identifying the major tactical options in most social situations.

As noted in Chapter Two, power-dependence theory stipulates that power is a function of dependence, and dependence, in turn, is based on (1) the availability of alternative outcome sources, and (2) the degree of value attributed to the outcomes at stake. A strict interpretation of the theory holds that the power of a party is determined by the *other's* dependence on the party, not the party's dependence on the other. For example, assume that two coalitions, arbitrarily labeled *Alpha* and *Beta*, are bargaining over some scarce resource within an organization. They are negotiating over how much X Alpha should give Beta and how much Y Beta should give Alpha. Within an organization, the relevant outcomes, X and Y, might symbolize the information or knowledge necessary to maintain control over or influence certain policy decisions.

The theory indicates that there are four dimensions of power in the above situation, as shown in Figure 2: Alpha's

Figure 2. Model of a Power-Dependence Relationship Between Two Coalitions

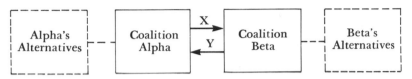

alternatives, Alpha's outcome value, Beta's alternatives, and Beta's outcome value (*value* refers to the importance of or need for the outcomes rather than their actual magnitude—see Chapter Two). The power of Alpha is determined by the dependence of Beta, that is, Beta's alternatives and the value Beta attributes to the outcomes at issue; conversely, the power of Beta is grounded in Alpha's dependence, that is, Alpha's alternatives and the value Alpha attributes to the outcomes in question. With reference to the diagram, the importance of X and Y to the parties and the alternatives available to the parties will ostensibly determine the relative advantage of the coalitions.

The theory implies a non-zero-sum conception of power; in other words, an increase in Alpha's power does not necessarily decrease Beta's power and vice versa. Each party's power is independently determined by the *other's* dependence, and the relative power of the parties is, therefore, analytically distinct from the total power (the mutual dependence or the sum of both parties' power) in the relationship. The same relative power could occur in the context of higher or lower levels of total power. For example, both coalitions in a bargaining relationship could independently contact and solidify relationships with other subunits within the organization and thereby decrease their mutual dependence without altering their relative power vis-à-vis one another. These non-zero-sum implications of the theory are important because, as is clear from our analysis in Chapter Six, bargaining situations are inherently non-zero-sum in nature: In a zero-sum or positive-sum context, bargaining is either impossible or unnecessary.

Overall, the theory offered by Emerson and Blau is an interesting and fairly complete framework for moving beyond more simplistic, piecemeal approaches to tactical action. However, as we consider the tactical implications of the theory, a number of conceptual ambiguities and gaps become apparent that must be addressed before we present our theory of bargaining tactics. The major problems lie in the conceptualizations of dependence, alternatives, and value. Specifically, there are two interrelated problems: (1) The theory does not clearly identify the relationship between or joint effects of the outcome alternatives and outcome value dimensions, and (2) the comparison process underlying the theory is left implicit, while it should be the cornerstone of the theory. Each of these problems is discussed, in turn, below.

The theory treats the outcome alternative and outcome value dimensions of a given party as analytically distinct phenomena. While this is a justifiable premise, there is an important caveat. Empirically these analytically distinct dimensions can become closely intertwined. This is suggested by both classical economics and operant (instrumental) learning psychology. In classical economics, the alternative dimension is tantamount to scarcity. In a somewhat analogous way, operant notions in psychology indicate that the value of a reinforcer is determined, in part, by the reinforcement history. Prior deprivation (that is, very high scarcity) will increase the value of a reinforcer, while prior satiation (that is, very low scarcity—abundance) will decrease the value of the reinforcer (Staats, 1975). The exact form of the deprivation-satiation function is a matter of some debate in psychology, but overall this notion suggests that extreme levels of scarcity (at the low or high end) will affect the value of a reinforcer. The point is that, in concrete empirical circumstances, alternatives and value can become highly interrelated.

The potential interrelationship of outcome alternatives and outcome value is not a devastating problem for the theory for two reasons. First, the analytic distinction remains important, especially for an analysis of tactics (which will become clear later). Second, the theory is not concerned with the relationship of alternatives and value but rather with the effects of these dimensions on other behavior in a relationship. Nevertheless, the foregoing caveat suggests that the joint effects of these dimensions warrant greater attention than has been given to this issue. In the absence of further specification, one could probably infer an additive relationship from the Emerson and Blau treatments of the theory. In contrast, we posit a multiplicative relationship based, in part, on the implication of operant notions. We also base it on the assumption that the combination of high alternatives and low value will make a bargainer particularly immune to influence from the opponent, while the combination of low alternatives and high value will make the bargainer especially vulnerable to influence. These are conditions under which the bargainer is quite independent of or highly dependent on the opponent. If we use alt_b to mean Beta's alternatives, V_b to mean the value Beta attributes to the outcomes, alt_a to mean Alpha's alternatives, and V_a to mean the value Alpha ascribes to the outcomes, we can predict each bargainer's power by these equations:

$$\text{Alpha's power} = \text{Beta's dependence} = \frac{1}{alt_b} \times V_b$$

$$\text{Beta's power} = \text{Alpha's dependence} = \frac{1}{alt_a} \times V_a$$

The equations represent the core of power-dependence theory: The power of Alpha is determined by the alternatives of Beta (or the reciprocal thereof) weighted by the importance of the outcomes to Beta, and the power of Beta is determined by Alpha's alternatives weighted by the importance of the outcomes to Alpha.

The most critical problem of the Emerson and Blau power-dependence theory is its failure to treat systematically the comparison process underlying the theory. The theory explicitly assumes that parties are comparing what they can do or receive *within* a relationship with what they can do or receive from *outside* the relationship. Yet the dimensions along which the immediate relationship is compared to the alternative are unspecified. An application of the dimensions of dependence to this issue confronts some serious conceptual difficulties.

The basic problem is that, as it stands, the theory confuses the dimensions of dependence with the process of comparing outcomes within and outside the relationship. In the Emerson and Blau treatment, the alternatives dimension is a global representation of what a party might receive from outside the relationship, while the value dimension fails to distinguish the immediate from the alternative relationship. The alternatives dimension implies outcome *quantity* and this, of course, can be applied to outcomes within and outside the relationship. That is, it is implicit in the theory that actors compare the quantity of outcomes they can receive within a relationship to those they can receive from outside the relationship. The value dimension implies outcome *weight*—it implies that actors compare the importance of the outcome from the relationship to the importance of outcomes they can receive from alternative relationships. In other words, the value or weight dimension can also be applied to outcomes within versus outside the relationship. The comparison process for value is especially critical because there are likely to be multiple outcome dimensions in most conflicts. With regard to these outcomes, bargainers will set priorities that should have an important bearing on the comparison of the alternative and current relationships.

The implication is that there are two dimensions within each dimension of dependence specified in the Emerson and Blau analysis: quantity and weight. Quantity refers to the level or number of outcomes expected from alternatives versus the immediate relationship; weight refers to the priority given to the outcomes. To examine more closely this revision of the theory, we will revise Figure 2 (discussed above) as shown in Figure 3.

The two coalitions are negotiating over how much bene-

Figure 3. Revised Model of a Two-Coalition Power-Dependence
Relationship

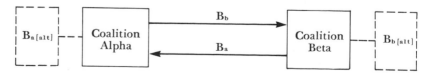

fit, designated B, they will provide each other. They are primarily concerned with the benefit from *within* the relationship: B_b refers to the benefit that coalition Alpha is providing coalition Beta; B_a refers to what coalition Beta is providing coalition Alpha. The anticipated benefit from alternatives for each coalition are shown on the other side of each in the diagram. Coalitions evaluate the benefit in terms of quantity and weight. Each term for benefit is a product of quantity (Q) multiplied by weight (W) for the particular outcomes. Consequently the anticipated (or prospective) benefit of each coalition's alternatives is determined by the following equations:

$$B_{a[alt]} = Q_{a[alt]} \times W_{a[alt]}$$

$$B_{b[alt]} = Q_{b[alt]} \times W_{b[alt]}$$

The benefit of Alpha's alternative (first equation) is determined by the quantity of outcomes available from Alpha's alternatives and the weight Alpha accords these outcomes. The benefit of Beta's alternative (second equation) is evaluated similarly.

The same dimensions, quantity and weight, are used to evaluate the benefit from within the immediate relationship:

$$B_a = Q_a \times W_a$$

$$B_b = Q_b \times W_b$$

With this background, we can now specify the nature of the comparison process underlying power-dependence theory. Specifically, the core equations of the theory that we offered above should be modified as follows:

$$\text{Alpha's power} = \text{Beta's dependence} =$$

$$(Q_b \times W_b) \times \frac{1}{(Q_{b[alt]} \times W_{b[alt]})} = \frac{B_b}{B_{b[alt]}}$$

$$\text{Beta's power} = \text{Alpha's dependence} =$$

$$(Q_a \times W_a) \times \frac{1}{(Q_{a[alt]} \times W_{a[alt]})} = \frac{B_a}{B_{a[alt]}}$$

In other words, Alpha's power depends on the degree to which Beta receives greater benefit from the relationship with Alpha than Beta can get from alternative groups. Similarly, Beta's power is positively related to the degree to which Alpha receives greater benefit from the relationship with Beta than Alpha can get from alternative groups. The implication of the equations is that the ratio of an actor's benefit within the relationship to benefit from alternatives is the basis for the opponent's power. Thus:

Hypothesis 53. All other things being equal, a decrease in an actor's benefit from within the relationship versus that actor's benefit from alternatives (B/B_{alt}) or an increase in the opponent's benefit from within versus the opponent's benefit from alternatives will increase the actor's power in the relationship.

This basic idea underlies a number of works on the social psychology of conflict and bargaining (see Cook and Emerson, 1978; Komorita, 1977; Michaels and Wiggins, 1976; Schellenberg, 1965; Thibaut and Faucheux, 1965; Thibaut and Kelley, 1959). However, the implications of the theory for a tactical analysis of bargaining have not been fully explicated. For example, as indicated in Chapter Six, level-of-aspiration theory (Siegel and Fouraker, 1960) identifies one of the critical aspects of bargaining relationships: concession behavior. Concession behavior is important because it transmits information to the other side about an actor's own aspirations; such information can be manipulated to the actor's advantage. None of the works cited above considers how dependence and power can affect aspirations or manipulative uses of concession behavior. Thus, even though power-dependence theory has been applied to conflict relationships, there are glaring gaps in its applications to anything that can even roughly be called bargaining.

Our goal, of course, is to develop the implications of power-dependence theory for bargaining. Our discussion is divided into two general segments. First, we present the bearing of the theory on a very basic tactical issue in bargaining—concession behavior. We expand on our discussion in Chapter Six by examining level-of-aspiration theory from the power-dependence standpoint and thereby identify how dependence should affect bargaining toughness. Second, we use the dimensions of dependence to develop a comprehensive scheme for analyzing the tactical action of bargaining and, relatedly, power struggle in organizational contexts.

Dependence and Concession Behavior in Bargaining

There are two interrelated implications of the power-dependence approach. The first is simply that concessions are likely to be a function, in part, of the dependence relationship. Level-of-aspiration theory posits the effects of a party's concession stance, while power-dependence theory can elucidate the sources or bases of the concession stances and predict the level of toughness in bargaining. The second implication is that the congruence of a concession stance with the power-dependence relationship will affect the success of the concession stance. Bargainers may, in practice, select concession tactics without considering the power-dependence relationship. Therefore we need to consider what happens if a bargainer adopts a concession tactic that does not take account of the power-dependence relationship.

Social psychological evidence (see Michener and others, 1975a; Rubin and Brown, 1975) enables us to begin with the following rather simple hypothesis:

Hypothesis 54. The greater a bargainer's power, the higher his or her aspiration level, and the tougher his or her concession stance.

Although this notion is far from new, power-dependence theory elaborates it by identifying the specific bases of dependence underlying a bargainer's power. From this basic idea, it follows that toughness should be negatively related to a bargainer's dependence on the opponent and positively related to the opponent's dependence on the bargainer. Specifically:

Hypothesis 55. An increase in a bargainer's dependence on the opponent will decrease that bargainer's toughness and increase the opponent's toughness.

Hypothesis 55 leads to four more specific statements indicating the effect of the four basic dimensions of dependence on each bargainer's toughness. Table 11 contains these predictions. Each one assumes that all other things are equal, for

**Table 11. Predicted Effects of Dimensions of Dependence
with Bargainer's Toughness**

Dimension of Dependence	Alpha's Toughness	Beta's Toughness
Alpha's benefit from alternatives ($B_{a[alt]}$)	+	—
Beta's benefit from alternatives ($B_{b[alt]}$)	—	+
Value Alpha attributes to outcomes (B_a)	—	+
Value Beta attributes to outcomes (B_b)	+	—

example, that other dimensions of dependence are not simultaneously changing. It should be remembered that each dimension of dependence in the table is a function of the product of outcome quantities and weights. The benefit equations we presented earlier should provide the basis for predicting the combined effects of the various dimensions of dependence. This is important when the dependence relationship is in flux and more than one dimension is undergoing change at once. For example, if the benefit of Alpha's alternatives improves but there is a concomitant and equal increase in the value Alpha ascribes to the bargaining outcomes, these contradictory pressures on Alpha's stance would balance each other and yield no change in toughness. Thus, the predictions in Table 11 should be interpreted in light of our revised core equations above. As the table demonstrates, any change in one dimension indicates a change in the difference between benefit from outside the relationship and benefit from within it and, hence, a change in the B/B_{alt} ratios. These hypotheses reduce to and can be generated from the following equations:

$$\text{Alpha's Net Power} = B_b/B_{b[alt]} - B_a/B_{a[alt]}$$

$$\text{Beta's Net Power} = B_a/B_{a[alt]} - B_b/B_{b[alt]}$$

The dependence relationship is the foundation on which bargainers develop aspiration levels and make tactical decisions about the appropriate bargaining stance. The dimensions of dependence reflect points of strength and weakness in each party's situation, and information on these points can be exploited to a greater or lesser degree by different bargaining postures. The dependence relationship constrains concession behavior, but it also defines the opportunity for manipulating self-presentation by concession behavior.

Bargainers, however, need not and will not always act in accord with the dependence relationship. The reason is that the dependence relationship is inherently ambiguous. Parties do not have complete or perfect information on the dimensions of dependence. Like most aspects of bargaining contexts, therefore, the power relationship is itself subject to manipulation and negotiation. In fact, the power-dependence relationship is typically a hidden or underlying agenda item, if not an explicit, recognized part of the agenda.

As a consequence, there may be a congruent or incongruent relationship between the dependence relationship and a bargainer's concession stance. Congruence can have an important impact on the effectiveness of the concession tactic. On the one hand, if the opponent's dependence on the bargainer is low, then a tough bargaining stance could drive the opponent out of the relationship entirely. A softer stance would be necessary to continue the relationship and keep alive the prospect of conflict resolution. On the other hand, adopting a softer stance than is congruent with the dependence relationship will yield an agreement somewhat less favorable to the bargainer's interests than a tougher stance would yield. The notion that dependence affects toughness, therefore, suggests a corollary hypothesis:

Hypothesis 56. The greater the congruence of a concession tactic with the dependence relationship, the greater the tactic's effectiveness.

Effectiveness in this context means the ability of a tactic to yield the best possible agreement from the bargainer's standpoint. Based on this criterion, tactics that produce substantial yielding by the adversary but no agreement are less effective than those that maximize the opponent's concessions and do produce an agreement.

There is, however, an important qualification to hypothesis 56: It may not apply unless there is a sufficient level of mutual dependence in the relationship. Consider a situation in which both bargainers are relatively independent of each other. While they may enter negotiations, both will probably adopt a tough bargaining stance, and the likelihood of agreement will be lower than in circumstances of greater mutual dependence. If both parties adopt the congruent stance (that is, toughness), the result will not fit our criterion of tactic effectiveness. The failure of negotiations under such circumstances can be attributed to the dilemma of individual versus collective rationality, a dilemma treated in the game theory literature (Rapoport, 1966). For both bargainers, the individually rational stance is to be very tough, but, if both bargainers adopt this stance, the result may be collectively irrational. As the level of mutual dependence in the relationship increases, the disparity between the individual and the collective rational stance begins to disappear. Under conditions of high mutual dependence, the congruent bargaining stances (less toughness) are likely to be individually rational and also yield a collectively rational solution. The overall point is that hypothesis 56 is likely to apply only beyond some minimal threshold of mutual dependence.

Classification of Tactics

The dimensions of dependence are not constant, fixed aspects of a relationship but are under continuous tacit and explicit negotiation. A scheme that treats this dynamic, manipulative aspect of power relationships is crucial to a conflict model of organizations. Power-dependence theory, of course, offers such a framework. It provides not only a theory of power but also a theory of power struggle, by integrating tactical action into the power scheme. The first step in developing these tactical aspects of the theory is to conceptualize and classify the tactical options of bargaining.

Tactics are behaviors that can change the power relationship. A bargaining context invariably offers parties a range of tactical options. One of the key dilemmas of bargainers is that they must wade through a plethora of options and make informed tactical decisions. The decision process is complicated by the fact that tactical action is a two-edged sword. On the one hand, it can overcome the resistance of an adversary and produce favorable bargaining results. On the other hand, it can antagonize the opponent and lead to damaging counteraction or, worse, a conflict spiral through which each party does substantial harm to the other. To deal with this dilemma effectively, therefore, parties carefully consider their tactical options and their opponents', and they are likely to base their tactical choices on the fit between the tactic and the underlying power relationship.

The literature on bargaining includes a number of attempts by social psychologists to develop a generic conceptualization of tactical options. These classification schemes create a rather muddled picture because their theoretical underpinnings tend to vary and are not always specified. Even the interpretations within a given theoretical tradition vary somewhat. Some of the schemes are rather explicitly grounded in some kind of dependence framework (Bacharach and Lawler, 1980; Blau, 1964; Emerson, 1962, 1972a, b; Lawler and Bacharach, 1976; Michener and Suchner, 1972; Thibaut and Kelley, 1959); others are based on a field theory (French and Raven, 1959; Raven, 1974; Raven and Kruglanski, 1970); and still others are ad hoc efforts to integrate the widest range of tactics into one scheme (compare Tedeschi and Bonoma, 1972). In many cases, the links between the tactics and changes in the power relationship are ambiguous, nonexistent, or irrelevant to the scheme (see French and Raven, 1959). We are naturally concerned with schemes based on a dependence framework where such links provide the backbone of the classification.

There have been four major attempts to translate the elements of power-dependence theory into a scheme for analyzing tactics (Bacharach and Lawler, 1980; Blau, 1964; Emerson, 1962; Lawler and Bacharach, 1976; Michener and Suchner, 1972). Each scheme mixes different units of analysis—some tactics seem to be tactics of individuals, others could be used by individuals or groups, and still others are uniquely the tactics of groups (such as coalitions). Our approach is to develop a more general scheme applicable across units of analysis. The particular unit of analysis is the organizational coalition, but we see the tactics as applicable to conflicts between individuals as well. There are other differences among prior power-dependence schemes particularly in the labels and specific content assigned to particular tactics. However, virtually all of these classification schemes recognize the following four basic tactics:

1. *Improving the quality of the bargainer's alternatives.* This tactic reduces the bargainer's dependence on the opponent and thereby limits a foundation for the opponent's influence. Some have labeled this *extending the power network* (Emerson, 1962; Michener and Suchner, 1972); others have labeled it *seeking alternatives* or *threatening to leave the relationship* (Bacharach and Lawler, 1980; Blau, 1964; Lawler and Bacharach, 1976). Despite different labels, the underlying tactic is essentially the same.
2. *Decreasing the quality of the opponent's alternatives.* This tactic increases the opponent's dependence on the bargainer and hence the bargainer's own power. Labels for this tactic include *coalition formation* (Emerson, 1962) and *outcome blockage* (Michener and Suchner, 1972). Once again, however, the basic tactic remains the same.
3. *Decreasing the value of what the opponent gives to the bargainer.* This tactic involves a reevaluation of the outcomes received in the relationship. Devaluation of what the opponent provides the bargainer reduces the bargainer's dependence and decreases the opponent's power. Labels for such tactics have included *withdrawal* and *conflict avoidance* (Bacharach and Lawler, 1980; Emerson, 1962).
4. *Increasing the extent to which the opponent values what the bargainer provides.* This involves manipulation of the opponent's perception of the bargainer and serves to increase the opponent's dependence on the bargainer, increasing the bargainer's power. This has been called *ingratiation, self-enhancement,* and *status giving* in different schemes (Bacharach and Lawler, 1980; Emerson, 1962; Lawler and Bacharach, 1976; Michener and Suchner, 1972).

The four basic tactics simply involve changes in the four dimensions of dependence identified in the Emerson and Blau theory. Tactics 1 and 3 are attempts by a bargainer to change his or her own dependence and thereby reduce the opponent's power. Tactics 2 and 4 are attempts by a bargainer to increase his or her own power by increasing the dependence of the opponent. Where two coalitions are vying for power within an organization, these four tactics are theoretically available to both parties. The specific ways in which these four general tactics will be manifested in a concrete situation will depend on the particular situation.

Our revision of the theory suggests a further subclassification of tactics based on the previously discussed quantity and weight dimensions. Each of the four tactics can be accomplished by a manipulation of either outcome quantities or outcome weights. Table 12 contains this elaboration of the four

Table 12. Application of Basic Tactics to Quantity and Weight Dimensions

Basic Tactic	Quantity Dimension	Weight Dimension
1. Improving quality of bargainer's alternatives	Increasing what alternative is willing to give bargainer	Shifting the weight toward what alternative is willing to give bargainer
2. Decreasing quality of opponent's alternatives	Decreasing what opponent's alternative is willing to give opponent	Shifting the weights of opponent away from what opponent's alternative is willing to give
3. Decreasing value of opponent to bargainer	Refusing inducements opponent offers bargainer	Attaching lower weight to what opponent gives bargainer
4. Increasing value of bargainer to opponent	Giving more inducements to opponent	Persuading opponent to give more weight to what bargainer gives

basic tactics. Keep in mind that the tactics are presented from the standpoint of *one* of the bargainers and that the opponent would have the same tactical options.

The table suggests that a coalition can improve its own alternatives by altering the quantity or weight attached to the alternatives. Another way might be simply to expand the number of alternatives the coalition has at its disposal. For example, assume that a coalition (Alpha) in an organization is attempting to influence a policy soon to be decided. It needs certain kinds of information to make an effective case, and it is negotiating with another coalition (Beta) possessing the information. One way for Alpha to increase its power in the bargaining is to seek out other units that could provide the same or substitute information. Presumably, the more Alpha increases its chances of getting needed information from alternatives, the more it will be able to extract from Beta in the current negotiations.

However, an alteration in the quantity dimension is not the only way for Alpha to improve its own alternatives. A second possibility is to revise the weight it gives to the kind of information the alternatives can supply. For example, suppose that the initial contacts with Beta indicate that Beta is quite resistant to providing information and would require a larger concession than Alpha is prepared to offer. One possibility is for Alpha to reevaluate the kind of information it needs and increase the weight given to information available from an alternative group.

In the case of tactic 2, decreasing the opponent's alternatives, Alpha might engage in the same kinds of actions, except the target of the action is now the quantity or weight of Beta's alternatives. For example, the quantity dimension would be reflected in direct contact or an alliance with groups comprising Beta's alternatives. This could reduce the willingness of these groups to provide outcomes to Beta. The weight dimension might be altered by feeding Beta knowledge (true or false) about the adequacy of the outcomes that Beta can get from its alternatives.

Tactic 3, decreasing the value of the opponent to the bargainer, can also take two forms. Alpha might simply refuse some of the information ostensibly provided by Beta. This would imply to Beta that Alpha can do without that benefit and that the exchange relationship should be redefined accordingly. One rationale for this tactic might be that the benefit comes with too many strings attached and obligates Alpha to provide something in return that Alpha prefers to keep. The second form, decreasing the weight dimension, involves no actual change in the resources provided by Beta but simply a cognitive reevaluation of them by Alpha. For example, instead of altering the weight given to information provided to Alpha by alternative groups, Alpha might simply redefine the information Beta has to offer as not that critical. Combining implications of the weight dimension for this tactic with those for tactic 1, the reevaluation process could result in either a change in the weight Alpha gives to information available from its own alternatives or a change in the weight Alpha gives to Beta's information. We should note that the weights given outcomes are not zero-sum in nature; in other words, an increase in the weight of outcomes from the alternative does not necessarily imply a decrease in the weight given to outcomes from Beta. Alpha may simply readjust one or both of these weights. The exact relationship between these options is an empirical one that does not bear on our analysis here.

The options under tactic 4 are the simplest to detail. The quantity dimension is merely how much to give the opponent, that is, how much Alpha should yield or how tough it should be in the negotiations. With more inducement (concessions), Alpha might extract more concessions from Beta; yet the exact rate of exchange may not yield concessions from Beta in direct proportion to Alpha's inducements. The weight dimension suggests another way to accomplish the goal of extracting more concessions without providing more inducements. Specifically, Alpha could convince Beta that what Alpha is currently providing in the relationship or offering in the bargaining is worth more than Beta previously thought. For example, Alpha could offer to exchange a little information for a substantial amount from Beta while arguing that the information it provides to Beta is of considerable value and that quantity is not, therefore, a valid criterion for evaluating and comparing the concessions. Another possibility is to argue that ancillary information Alpha is already providing Beta on a regular basis is of such value that an exchange of little for much in the current negotiations is justifiable on equity or other normative grounds.

In brief, each of the eight tactics involves a modification of one of the terms of our revised theory of power-dependence (see the revised core equations earlier in this chapter). While we have discussed the tactics in isolation from one another, bargainers are not likely to choose only one of the eight or evaluate one tactic apart from the others. Various combinations of tactics are likely to be used depending on the specific circumstances and, of course, the power-dependence relationship. We argue that parties in bargaining tend to evaluate and attempt to alter many of the dimensions at once. This is inherent in our approach, because we emphasize the comparison process more than Emerson and Blau do. For example, we would expect bargainers to compare simultaneously the various quantity dimensions within and outside the relationship for both themselves and their opponents and also to compare simultaneously the weights given by themselves and the opponents (inferentially) to the outcomes from within and outside the relationship. Now that we have classified and described the tactics, it is time to turn to the issue of tactic choice and effectiveness.

Choice of Tactics

Although bargainers in "natural" settings simultaneously evaluate and select tactics from a relatively wide range of options, theory and research have neglected this multiple-tactic decision process. Most of the research on tactics is social psychological, and the standard experimental settings are designed to investigate one tactic at a time (see reviews in Kipnis, 1974; Michener and Suchner, 1972; Raven and Kruglanski, 1970; Tedeschi and Bonoma, 1972). At this point, we know very little about how bargainers simultaneously evaluate different tactics, whether different criteria are used to make decisions about different tactics, and what tactics are likely to be combined in a given setting.

Kipnis (1974) has done some work on multiple-tactic decision making, with a specific focus on how superiors deal with dissident or troublesome workers. Drawing on a medical metaphor, he argues that there is a *treatment of choice* for different forms of worker resistance. The treatment is ostensibly adapted to the type of resistance and the circumstances surrounding it. Specifically, superiors diagnose the reason for a subordinate's resistance and adopt the tactics that are most likely to negate that reason. The basic idea, therefore, is that bargainers will estimate the probable success of each tactical option and base their tactical choices on these subjective probabilities of success.

We will base our treatment of tactical decisions on two hypotheses, the first of which comes from Kipnis (1974).

Hypothesis 57. Coalitions will select those tactics to which they attach the greatest probability of success.

This premise is applicable to contexts where the coalition combines more than one tactic or focuses on a single tactic. The manner in which the coalition ranks tactics in terms of their success probabilities will determine the choices. The second hypothesis is:

Hypothesis 58. Coalitions will use the dimensions of dependence to attach subjective probabilities of success to tactics.

In other words, coalitions will fit the tactics to the specific nature of the power relationship. This implies that the dimensions of dependence will serve as major criteria for multiple-tactic decisions.

Hypothesis 58 is most critical for our purposes, and it warrants some elaboration. It is, in turn, based on three other assumptions:

Hypothesis 59. Coalitions will use the quality of each other's alternatives and the value of the bargaining outcomes to identify points of strength and weakness in each other's situations.

A group with poor alternatives is quite vulnerable to tactics addressed at this weakness (all other things being equal). Similarly, a group that attaches high value to the bargaining outcomes is likely to be subject to greater manipulation by its opponent.

Hypothesis 60. Different tactics deal with different sources of strength or weakness in a coalition's or an opponent's situation.

The four basic tactics (and the variants subsumed within them) are directed at the four sources of a coalition's or an opponent's dependence. Each tactic, therefore, can enhance a coalition's strengths or reduce its weaknesses.

Hypothesis 61. Coalitions will attempt to maximize their points of strength and minimize their points of weakness within the power relationship.

Coalitions will try to maximize their own power (maximize the opponent's dependence on them) and minimize the opponent's power (minimize their own dependence on the opponent).

To summarize, these assumptions indicate that coalitions will attempt to improve their power position, that tactics deal with different dimensions of power, and, therefore, that bargainers will use different dimensions of power to evaluate and make decisions about different tactics.

Four general hypotheses are suggested by the above assumptions. In each hypothesis, the dependent variable is one coalition's tactics. The label *coalition* can refer to either party, which means that each of these four hypotheses can be translated into two more specific (or eight total) propositions—one for each bargainer in a two-party context. Given that the general hypotheses deal only with the more general tactic categories, it should be noted that the four basic hypotheses also suggest two more subdivisions, one for the outcome quantity dimensions and one for the outcome weight dimensions. Consequently, we will state the two more specific propositions under each general one:

Hypothesis 62. The poorer a coalition's alternatives, the more likely the coalition is to adopt tactics that improve the quality of its own alternatives.

Hypothesis 62a. The poorer a coalition's alternatives, the more effort the coalition will devote to contacting and carrying on simultaneous negotiations with alternative groups (outcome quantity).

Hypothesis 62b. The poorer a coalition's alternatives, the more effort and consideration the coalition will give to reevaluating what is already available from alternative groups (without further negotiation with those groups) (outcome weight).

Hypothesis 63. The more value a coalition ascribes to the outcomes at issue, the more likely the coalition is to adopt tactics that will devalue those outcomes.

Hypothesis 63a. The more value a coalition ascribes to the outcomes at issue, the more effort the coalition will devote to cutting off or refusing outcomes currently being received from the opponent (outcome quantity).

Hypothesis 63b. The more value a coalition ascribes to the outcomes at issue, the more effort and consideration the coalition will give to reevaluating those outcomes (outcome weight).

Hypothesis 64. The better the opponent's alternatives, the more likely the coalition is to adopt tactics that will decrease the quality of the opponent's alternatives.

Hypothesis 64a. The better the opponent's alternatives, the more effort the coalition will devote to contacting and carrying on negotiations with the opponent's alternative groups (outcome quantity).

Hypothesis 64b. The better the opponent's alternatives, the more effort the coalition will devote to manipulating the weight the opponent accords the outcomes available from alternatives (outcome weight).

Hypothesis 65. The lower the value the opponent ascribes to the outcomes at issue, the more likely the coalition is to adopt tactics that increase their value to the opponent.

Hypothesis 65a. The lower the value the opponent ascribes to

the outcomes at issue, the greater the concessions the
coalition will make to the opponent in the bargaining
(outcome quantity).

Hypothesis 65b. The lower the value the opponent ascribes to
the outcomes at issue, the more effort the coalition will
devote to manipulating the weight the opponent gives to
the outcomes within the relationship (outcome weight).

In sum, the hypotheses indicate that the likelihood of a
given tactic depends on specific level of the dimension of dependence that the tactic can alter. Next, we must consider the implications of these propositions for the combined, simultaneous
use of more than one tactic.

The hypotheses have fairly straightforward implications
for combined strategies. The likelihood of two or more tactics
being combined should depend on their respective levels of dependence. That is, among the available tactics, those that deal
with the most troublesome dimensions of dependence will constitute the most likely combination. If Alpha's power position is
weakest along the dimensions of its own alternatives and Beta's
value assignment to the outcome, then we would expect Alpha's
most likely tactic combination to involve simultaneous improve-
ments in the quality of Alpha's alternatives and attempts to
enhance the value Beta attributes to the outcomes at issue.
Thus, the following hypothesis is suggested:

Hypothesis 66. Coalitions are likely to attack those dimensions
that make them most dependent on their opponent and
those that make the opponent least dependent on them.

If there is only one troublesome dimension, then a coalition will
tend to focus its effort on one of the tactic categories.
More than one tactic will be simultaneously adopted to the
extent that more than one dimension is troublesome for a coalition.

It should be noted, finally, that all of these propositions
require an "all other things being equal" clause. While the subjective probabilities of success represent the basic rationale

underlying the hypotheses, any concrete bargaining setting will include other dimensions that could modify the application of these hypotheses. Some tactics may be more or less likely to succeed depending on particular aspects of the bargaining context. For example, consider the tactic of changing the opponent's alternatives. The feasibility of this tactic depends on the lines of communication between the bargainer and the opponent's alternatives, among other things. Structural or other obstacles in a concrete case could make it difficult to adopt this tactic even though it would theoretically address the most troublesome aspect of the dependence relationship.

The rules and traditions of an organization are also likely to constrain the tactical action of bargainers. This must be taken into account in any concrete application of the hypotheses. Tactics that alter a coalition's own dependence may be more legitimate within some organizations than tactics that alter the opponent's dependence. For example, decentralized organizations may establish formal or informal norms that call for different coalitions to respect each other's autonomy. Depending on the strength of such norms, an attack on the opponent's alternatives or value may be construed as an illegitimate intrusion on the affairs of another subgroup and may lead to outside intervention. In such a context, there could be a strong bias in favor of tactics that alter only the coalition's own dependence, that is, tactics that expand, affirm, or develop the autonomy sanctioned by the larger organizational context. The point is that our tactic scheme is, by its very nature, abstract and heuristic, and it should be treated as such in concrete applications and empirical tests.

This section has presented a theory of tactical choice. The cornerstone of the theory is the conceptualization of power and tactics in the power-dependence framework. In contrast to Emerson and Blau, our purpose has been to propose empirical links between the dimensions of dependence and tactical choices. We will now use and revise notions in the power-dependence approach to analyze the dynamics of tactical action over time.

Dynamics of Tactical Action

Tactical action in bargaining is actually a continuous process of action and counteraction, by which parties attempt to improve their power positions. The theory of tactical action, presented in the last section, indicates that there are certain tactical tendencies at any given time, but it does not examine the dynamic process. Examining this dynamic process is important, because tactical choices at any given point should be a function of not only the conditions of power-dependence but also the prior tactical action of the opponent. Clearly, bargainers will adjust their action not only to the conditions of dependence but also to their opponent's tactical efforts to deal with the power relationship.

There have been two relatively recent attempts to develop a conceptual apparatus for grasping the dynamic aspects of power struggle: Mulder's (1977) power-distance-reduction theory builds on a nonutilitarian foundation, while Emerson's (1962, 1972b) theory of balance attempts to adapt power-dependence theory for this purpose. Neither of these efforts is adequate for our purposes.

Mulder's theory stipulates that power and its use are governed primarily by a nonutilitarian motivation. Specifically, power is an end in itself, and this is enough to maintain tactical action over time. In other words, parties play a power game, not just because of the benefit derived from it but also because the game takes on a momentum of its own. Playing the game ostensibly becomes valued in and for itself. Yet the tendency to use power depends on the relative power of the conflicting parties. Considering only a context in which parties differ in power, Mulder's theory predicts that (1) the party with less power is more likely to use power (that is, attempt to reduce the difference between itself and the other) the smaller the difference in power between the two; and (2) the party with more power is more likely to use power (that is, increase the distance between itself and the other) the greater the existing difference in power. The most basic assumption is that the more power a party has (whether a lower- or higher-power party in the particular rela-

tionship at issue), the more power that party will try to get vis-
à-vis the other.

Mulder's theory raises several problems (see Lawler,
1979, for a more extensive treatment). First, while nonutilitarian motivations are admittedly important to consider in any
theory of power struggle, the exclusion of utilitarian motivations here appears unwarranted. The consequence of this can be
seen in the second of Mulder's propositions. One can make a
convincing case for the reverse of this proposition, based on the
following assumptions: (1) Higher-power parties will feel more
threatened as lower-power parties gain power, and (2) parties
will attempt to increase the distance between themselves and
those who are most threatening to their position in the organization. As it stands, Mulder's (1977) second proposition is
highly questionable at best.

A second and even more compelling problem is that Mulder's theory deals only minimally with the tactical aspects of
power struggle. There is no classification of power tactics, and
little attention is given to how parties act out this power struggle. In sum, Mulder's theory of power struggle contains conceptual and empirical difficulties that render it an inadequate foundation for examining the dynamic aspects of tactical action.

Emerson's (1962, 1972b) approach to the dynamics of
tactical action is reflected in his treatment of the power-balance
principle. Emerson argues that the tactics of power are essentially balancing tactics, and the ultimate result of action over
time is to create a situation of power balance. Power balance
means equal power and, therefore, Emerson offers a very con-
soling, utopian notion: Power relationships gravitate toward
power equality. More specifically, he suggests that the use of
power by the higher-power party is inevitable, but to use power
is to lose it, since equality is the ultimate consequence of power
use and counteruse. While this is a provocative notion, there are
so many situations in which the use of power does not result in
movement toward equality that the theory appears to have little
prospect of empirical confirmation.

We suggest an alternative starting point, specifically, that
bargainers resist their opponents' efforts to change the power-

dependence situation. Consider the following hypothesis as an addition to those on tactical choice:

Hypothesis 67. An attempt by a coalition to change the power-dependence relationship will engender counteraction by the opponent designed to maintain the same relative power between the coalitions.

This hypothesis suggests that power relationships are resistant to change, that counteraction will be directed at restoring the status quo. It should be viewed not as a descriptive principle but as an heuristic one with which to compare empirical instances. The assumption implies that the "status quo" is a minimal, satisficing goal of the "responder" and a major reference point for all parties to the conflict. Countertactics may in concrete instances involve retaliation, that is, attempts to further undermine the opponent's power position beyond that in the former relationship. However, from the standpoint of our theory, retaliation will engender further countertactical action by the opponent, and the ultimate consequence of a continuous series of actions and counteractions over time is a *tendency* toward the status quo.

This status quo assumption appears more realistic than the starting points of either Mulder or Emerson. However, it can be quite misleading. The proposition is not intended to suggest that power relationships do not change or that tactical action is ultimately futile. In the absence of tactical action or counteraction, a coalition is likely to be overwhelmed by adversaries. The point is that, despite short-term shifts in the power relationship—victories and defeats, successful and unsuccessful uses of power—there is a *tendency* over long periods of time for the relative power in a relationship to remain the same. This is merely a tendency, not a fixed, a priori outcome of a long-term conflict relationship. This tendency can be undermined by changes in the intraorganizational or environmental context and also by varying rates of tactic success across parties in the conflict.

It is critical to realize that this tendency toward the status quo applies only to the *relative* power of bargainers not to the *total* power in the relationship or to the sum of both parties' power. In sum, hypothesis 67, in conjunction with hypothesis 61, indicates that bargainers make every effort to create more relative power for themselves but, at the same time, are careful to avert the opponent's attempts to do likewise. The result of both parties adopting this posture is a tendency toward the status quo. Thus, in contrast to Emerson, we are positing that existing power inequalities will be as resistant to change as existing power equalities.

Counteraction not only accounts for the resistance to change in the relative power but can also either solidify or bifurcate the relationship by changing the level of mutual dependence. To elucidate this, we must distinguish two basic types of counteraction: blockage and matching. A *blockage* response obstructs or prevents a change in the power relationship. Take a situation where a coalition (Alpha) is attempting to improve its alternatives by engaging in simultaneous negotiations with its alternative groups. To block this action, the opponent (Beta) might apply pressure on Alpha's alternative groups. A *matching* tactic is essentially identical to the opponent's tactic. Matching is a strict variant of Gouldner's (1960) reciprocity principle and it implies that the actions of both bargainers fall within the same tactic category. The action need not be identical or even similar on a very specific level, as long as it can be subsumed under the same category. In the above example, the matching tactic would be for Beta to undertake some kind of action to increase its own alternatives in response to Alpha's attempt to improve its alternatives.

Table 13 summarizes the effects of these two countertactics on mutual dependence. For the sake of simplicity, the tactical choices are classified simply as decreasing the bargainer's own dependence on the opponent and increasing opponent's dependence on the bargainer. As the table indicates, there are two variants of matching and two variants of blockage tactics. From the perspective of coalition Alpha, blockage implies either decreasing its dependence in response to Beta's tactic that increased Alpha's dependence or increasing Beta's dependence in response to Beta's decrease in its own dependence. Similarly,

Table 13. Effects of Countertactics on Mutual Dependence

Tactical Choice of Coalition Beta	Tactical Choice of Coalition Alpha	
	Decrease Self's Dependence	Increase Opponent's Dependence
Decrease self's dependence	Matching: decrease in mutual dependence	Blockage: no change in mutual dependence
Increase opponent's dependence	Blockage: no change in mutual dependence	Matching: increase in mutual dependence

there are two variants of matching tactics distinguished by what tactic by Beta Alpha is responding to. This analysis assumes that the original tactic and countertactic are equally successful. To the extent that the tactics of the actor and opponent differ in success, there will be some departure from these predictions.

The most interesting point about countertactics is that the pattern of countertactical action bears on the future of the relationship. Blockage tactics prevent a change attempted or accomplished by an opponent; they do not alter the mutual dependence. Matching tactics, however, tend to either increase or decrease mutual dependence. If coalitions emphasize changes in their own dependence, the long-term effect of this countertactical pattern could be destruction of the relationship or at least a substantial decrease in contact, communication, and negotiation. If coalitions emphasize manipulations of the opponent's dependence, there should be a gradual increase in mutual dependence over time. In this case, the two coalitions would tend to move closer together, find it increasingly easy to resolve conflicts by negotiation, and so forth, because of their enhanced dependence on one another. In sum, the following hypothesis is warranted:

Hypothesis 68. The greater the use of matching rather than blockage countertactics over time in a conflict relationship, the greater the change in the mutual dependence of the parties.

The exact nature of the change, of course, is contingent on whether bargainers are matching tactics dealing with their own dependence or their opponent's dependence. Hence, the following elaborations of hypothesis 68 are important:

Hypothesis 69. The greater the tendency to match tactics that deal with the dimensions of the bargainers' own dependence, the greater the decrease in mutual dependence over time.

Hypothesis 70. The greater the tendency to match tactics that deal with the dimensions of the opponents' dependence, the greater the increase in mutual dependence over time.

In sum, the effects of power struggle on the mutual dependence of the parties is contingent on the patterns of countertactical action. The greater the frequency of a given countertactical category, the greater the likelihood of the corresponding effect on mutual dependence.

Summary

Intercoalition bargaining within organizations takes place in the context of dependence or interdependence relations. The nature and degree of dependence between distinct coalitions is likely to vary across different segments of the organization, across conflict issues, or even within a given segment. This variation in dependence can account for much of the variation in tactical action and conflict resolution in organizations. The dependence or interdependence relationship may be said to embody the stakes of the parties in the intercoalition bargaining. These stakes should provide the primary foundation for tactical decisions and, indirectly, for ultimate conflict resolution. The purpose of this chapter was to develop a theory of tactical action that explicitly grounded different bargaining tactics in different dimensions of the dependence relationship.

Based on a critical examination of the power-dependence ideas in Blau (1964) and Emerson (1962, 1972a, b), we indicated that the dependence of coalitions on each other is based on a comparison of the immediate relationship with relationships available from alternative groups. Specifically, coalitions

will compare the outcomes available from outside the immediate relationship to those available from within it. The coalitions use two dimensions in this comparison process: the quantity of outcomes from within and outside, and the weight or
importance of the outcomes. Our analysis identified eight basic
dimensions of dependence in two-party relationships and led to
an eightfold classification of tactical action. Each category of
tactics implies a change in the dependence relationship—either a
decrease in the bargainer's dependence or an increase in the opponent's dependence.

Our hypotheses linking the dimensions of dependence to
tactical action imply the following:

1. Coalitions in intercoalition bargaining will use the dimensions of dependence to identify the points of strength or
   weakness in their own and their opponent's dependence
   situation.
2. Coalitions will attempt to minimize their points of weakness
   and maximize their points of strength over time.
3. A coalition's tactical choices will reflect its evaluations of
   strength and weakness. The tactical action of a given coalition will be designed to change those aspects of the dependence relationship that are most troublesome to it.
4. Attempts by a coalition to change the dependence relationship to its opponent's disadvantage will be met by counteraction designed to prevent a change in the relative dependence of the coalitions on each other. The *relative*
   dependence will tend toward the status quo over long periods of time.
5. Countertactical patterns can take one of two forms: matching or blockage. The type of countertactical pattern adopted
   will affect the parties' mutual dependence in the relationship, which in turn will determine the long-term prospects
   for conflict resolution.

Overall, our theory provides a conceptual means to analyze power struggles among a multitude of coalitions within an
organization. A power struggle is activated by attempts to alter

the dependence relationship, and its long-term effects on the organization are determined by the nature of the countertactical patterns. Our discussion shows that the impact of a power struggle on an organization is not necessarily disintegrative. Some countertactical patterns actually solidify intraorganizational relationships by increasing the mutual dependence (interdependence) of disparate coalitions. Consequently, from the standpoint of the organization as a whole, power struggle is a two-edged sword.

This chapter has examined the power relationship underlying intercoalition bargaining. We argue that the power relationship is the prime foundation for tactical action and that a dependence approach to power leads to a general framework for linking power and tactical action. There is a noteworthy gap in our analysis, however. We argued in Chapter Two that sanctions also represent a key dimension of power. Indeed, most conceptualizations of power are built around the notion of sanctions. As a consequence, we need to incorporate this element of tactical action into our analysis. Chapter Eight will address this issue.

8

Coercion in Intraorganizational Bargaining

▀▄▀

Coercion is the capability to punish or threaten punishment of another. It may take the form of withdrawing or limiting rewards as well as administering costs (see French and Raven, 1959; Gamson, 1968, 1975). Coercion can be an alternative to or an integral part of bargaining. As an alternative to bargaining, coercion can be construed as an attempt by its user to gain compliance or concessions from an opponent without giving anything in return. For example, superiors may use coercion to eliminate poor performance, dissident action, or rule breaking by subordinates. The coercion or force is essentially a substitute for, or an attempt to avoid, bargaining with subordinates over the issues in conflict. In an actual bargaining context, however, coercion might be used at key points to engender a softer concession stance by the opponent. In bargaining, it can become a tactic for speeding up the process of conflict resolution. Regardless of whether it is used as an alternative to bargaining or as an adjunct to a bargaining encounter, several basic issues are confronted by the users and targets of coercion, and these general issues are the focus of this chapter.

The foundation of any formal organization is ultimately coercive. This coercive foundation may be shrouded in rules and informal norms that make "might right." However hidden, the coercive element is still there in one form or another. This is a crucial and often missed point in Weber's (1947) analysis of organizations as imperatively coordinated systems. Writers in the field of organizations typically emphasize the systemic or coordinated aspects of organizations while neglecting the imperative aspect.

Viewing organizations as imperatively coordinated, we must examine how their coercive elements facilitate control, reduce dissent, and play a role in intercoalition bargaining. Our focus is somewhat broader than Weber's. We are concerned with coercion not only as a solution to the control problem in organization (that is, as a means by which superiors can control subordinates) but also as a factor in bargaining between coalitions at similar levels in the organizational hierarchy.

Given the obvious importance of coercion to intraorganizational relationships, it may seem paradoxical that our classification of tactics (in Chapter Seven) does not contain any explicitly coercive tactics. None of the tactics, for example, involves a reduction in the outcomes of the opponent. Such a reduction in outcomes could be the ultimate consequence of a shift in the dependence relationship induced by tactics of decreasing the bargainer's dependence or increasing the opponent's dependence. However, coercion implies direct manipulation of the opponent's outcomes, not an indirect consequence of shifts in dependence, and it must be treated as a separate tactic.

An integration of coercion into the scheme is not difficult and raises issues that are generally neglected in the literature on power and tactics. To accomplish this integration, we must distinguish coercive *potential* from the *use* of coercion, and we must treat coercion in the context of the dependence relationship. The dependence relationship places important constraints on coercion, and these have not been adequately detailed in extant literature on power and tactics.

Coercion in the Context of Dependence

The relationship between coercion and dependence can best be illustrated if we return to the diagram of an exchange relationship we presented as Figure 3 in Chapter Seven. Recall

Figure 4. Model of a Power-Dependence Relationship

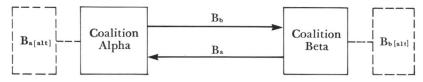

that Alpha is giving the benefit B_b to Beta, Beta is giving B_a to Alpha, and this exchange is taking place in the context of the alternatives available to both parties ($B_{a[alt]}$ and $B_{b[alt]}$. Given this conceptualization, coercion is the ability of either party to reduce the benefit given to the other by either withdrawing some of the current benefit or by adding new costs that reduce the other's overall benefit. Coercive *potential* refers to the maximum amount of punishment that can be administered to the opponent (the total amount of benefit that can be withdrawn and the total costs that can be added). The *use* of coercion is the actual modification of the benefit to the other. That is, for coalition Alpha, use of coercion is a reduction in B_b, and for coalition Beta, use of coercion is a reduction in B_a.

The first implication of this analysis is that the dependence relationship places practical limits on the coercive potential of both coalitions. A coalition could conceivably reduce its opponent's outcomes to a level below what the opponent can extract from its alternatives, but such action would undoubtedly drive the opponent out of the relationship. In this sense, Alpha's coercive potential is limited by Beta's alternatives ($B_{b[alt]}$), and Beta's coercive potential is limited by Alpha's alternatives ($B_{a[alt]}$). The coercive potential, at least on a practical level, becomes essentially equal to the other party's dependence. For instance, the largest punishment Alpha can administer to Beta, without destroying the relationship, is $B_b - B_{b[alt]}$.

This is also tantamount to Beta's dependence on Alpha. In sum, the coercive potential of a party is equal to the dependence of the opponent on the party.

Turning to the use of coercion, we can see why no coercive tactics were included in the previous chapter. Coercion actually decreases the dependence of the target on the user. In terms of Figure 4, if Alpha uses a coercive tactic, then there is a reduction in the benefit of Beta (B_b) from the relationship, and Beta therefore becomes less dependent on Alpha. In contrast, the tactics identified in the prior chapter all involve changes in the dependence relationship that ostensibly improve the power position of the bargainer by enhancing coercive potential. Yet use of this potential in a coercive manner actually reduces the future power position of the user. This means that coercion might be quite effective in an immediate case or instance of conflict, but it will tend to have negative long-run consequences for the user's power in the relationship.

Overall, it is clear that coercion should be viewed in the context of the dependence relationship. The dependence relationship places boundaries on the potential coercion available to a party, and the actual use of coercion involves a reduction in the dependence of the target on the user. It appears that coercion should be more effective as the dependence of the target on the user increases, and it should be most effective when the target is highly dependent on the user. However, even under conditions of relatively low dependence, coercion can be effective if the user takes care to apply a level of coercion that will not drive the target out of the relationship.

The power-dependence framework provides a backdrop for analyzing and conceptualizing the limits of coercion, but it does not fully treat the multitude of conditions underlying the success or failure of a coercive tactic. For this, we must turn to the rather large body of theoretical and empirical literature on coercion. The focus of this literature has been the key variant or aspect of coercion: threat. This literature has not been guided by a consistent framework, but we can still make considerable use of the disparate theoretical and empirical threads. The remainder of this chapter will examine the elements of coercion, contrast the theoretical viewpoints on the effects of coercion, and link the social psychological literature to organizations by discussing the communication of threats in organizational contexts.

Elements of Coercion

There are actually three elements underlying coercion. First, there is a coercive *potential* from which a user can select a level of damage or punishment. Second, there is typically a *threat* intervening between the potential and actual punishment. A threat is an expression of an intent to do harm (Deutsch and Krauss, 1962). It warns the target of prospective damage to come if the target does not comply with the wishes of the user. Threats may be veiled or quite explicit, and they need not involve interpersonal communication. The third element, of course, is enforcement of the threat: actual *punishment*. This presumably occurs only if the stipulations implied in the threat are not carried out by the target, that is, if there is noncompliance.

These three elements can and should be arranged in a sequential manner: accumulation of coercive potential leads to use of the potential in the form of a threat, which leads to enforcement of the threat if the target does not comply. From a tactical standpoint, the most critical aspects of this sequence are the *potential* and *threat* dimensions. There are several reasons for this. First, the coercive potential is the backbone of a threat. A sizable potential makes a threat credible and worthy of attention by the target. Second, the threat can enable the user of coercive potential to avoid the costs of punishment. Enforcement of the threat not only reduces the dependence of the other but also may deplete resources of the user. Third, punishment is actually symptomatic of the failure of coercion. It occurs only if application of the potential, in a threat, does not have the intended consequences. Thus, from the standpoint of the coercer, the optimum situation is to accumulate substantial coercive potential (for instance, through modifications in the power-dependence relationship) and successfully use threats to influence the target, while avoiding the need to administer punishment.

Consider, for example, a superior group or coalition within an organization that is attempting to facilitate and maintain the compliance of subordinates. The success of the control system should be reflected in the frequency with which the superiors actually apply sanctions to deviant workers or groups. Frequent sanctions imply that either the coercive potential of the superior coalition is insufficient to buttress its threats or even though the potential is sufficient, the administration of the threats, perhaps through organizational rules or the action of supervisors, is simply defective. Depending on the diagnosis of the problem, the coalition may seek to change its coercive potential or its system for communicating threats.

The accumulation or development of coercive potential is essentially covered in our theory of bargaining tactics in Chapter Seven. At this point, our concern is with the use of the coercive potential or threat tactics. Threats can be communicated by verbal (written or oral) or nonverbal means. A threat tells targets that they will be punished if a particular behavior is not forthcoming. There must be at least a loose contingency suggesting not that punishment is inevitable but that it depends on the action of the targets. In other words, a threat implies that the targets' behavior will determine when and whether they will receive punishment. The targets ostensibly control the occurrence of punishment, because they have the choice of compliance (no punishment) or noncompliance (punishment). The clarity of the contingency implied in the threat as well as the exact nature of the threat communication are empirical issues to which we will return later. Our next task is to examine theories of coercion.

Theories of Coercion

There is support for two contradictory viewpoints on the effectiveness of coercion or threats. First, work in the areas of deterrence and subjective-expected-utility theory suggests that threats can be very effective means of influence (see Morgan,

1977; Schelling, 1960, 1966; Tedeschi, Schlenker, and Bonoma, 1973). This standpoint suggests that effectiveness depends on the utility to the target of compliance versus noncompliance; with sufficient modifications in utility, threats will be effective. A second standpoint, based on a variety of social psychological research, suggests that threats and coercion are relatively ineffective means of influence (see Rubin and Brown, 1975, for a review). From this standpoint, threats lead to a conflict spiral in which the issue of losing face becomes more important to the parties than strictly utilitarian issues.

The deterrence notion has implications for both the potential and the threat dimensions of coercion. The essential idea with regard to coercive potential is that the greater the potential of conflicting parties, the less the likelihood of actual damage, that is, the greater the deterrence of aggression (Morgan, 1977; Schelling, 1960, 1966). Parties with high coercive potentials, therefore, will deter each other from using coercion. This rather simple notion captures the logic underlying the post-World War II foreign policy of the United States and the arms race with the Soviet Union. Within organizations, it suggests that coalitions that are highly dependent on one another will be less inclined to use coercion in their negotiations. High mutual dependence (high coercive potential for both parties) will ostensibly make punitive action too risky. Thus, an organization that induces relations of high mutual dependence among its members will minimize conflict of a punitive or coercive form.

This basic notion of deterrence neglects the problem of credibility. In order for a coercive potential to deter another's aggression, it must also be credible (Schelling, 1966). Credibility refers essentially to the target's perception of a party's willingness to use the capability. A high potential for damage cannot provide a foundation for deterrence unless it is perceived as likely to be used under specified conditions. Consequently, to predict the deterrence, we must consider not only the magnitude of the damage but also the probability that a party will inflict such damage.

From the standpoint of deterrence theory, threats are important primarily because they bear on the credibility of a coercive potential. A threat can accomplish this in a number of ways. First, it can make the opponent more aware of the coercive potential. Second, it can clarify the amount of the potential that an actor is willing to use, by specifying the nature of the prospective damage. Third, it can clarify the specific conditions under which an actor is prepared to use the potential. For example, suppose a coalition (Alpha) within an organization regularly provides certain types of information to another coalition (Beta). Within the limits of the dependence relationship, Alpha has the potential of withdrawing certain benefits (information) from Beta. Assume that these two coalitions are in conflict over a general policy issue and are in the process of negotiating the policy. One of Alpha's options is to administer a threat to Beta designed to extract more concessions from Beta about the emerging policy. The threat could do all or only some of a series of steps: It could simply remind Beta of the valued resources that Alpha could withdraw; it could specify more explicitly that Alpha is prepared to withdraw a certain amount or certain types of information from the total given to Beta; or it could further specify what Beta can or must do to prevent a reduction in these valued resources. Obviously, a threat can facilitate deterrence in various ways depending on the social context and specific problems confronted by the actors.

The deterrence notion calls attention to the utilitarian consequences of coercion. These utilitarian aspects essentially translate into subjective expected utility. Recall that subjective-expected-utility theory contends that an actor's choices depend on the magnitude of the outcomes weighted by the probability that they will materialize. Actors are assumed to choose lines of behavior that maximize their utility (magnitude multiplied by probability). Similarly, the deterrence notion suggests that deterrence is contingent on having a big stick and being willing to use it (or at least conveying this to the opponent). Based on subjective expected utility, deterrence should vary positively with the magnitude multiplied by the probability of punitive action. Applied to the deterrent effects of a threat tactic, subjective-expected-utility theory leads to the following basic hypothesis (Tedeschi, Schlenker, and Bonoma, 1973):

Hypothesis 71. The greater the magnitude of damage implied in
a threat multiplied by the probability of implementation
of the threat, the greater the effectiveness of the threat
tactic.

This basic hypothesis has formed the foundation for a
large number of experiments by Tedeschi and his colleagues (see
Tedeschi, Schlenker, and Bonoma, 1973, chap. 3, for a summary). This research supports the basic notion, with a few qualifications. First, the multiplicative effect of magnitude and probability does not always occur. In some studies, the effects are
additive. Second, and more important, the research as a whole
suggests that threat credibility (the probability of carrying out
the threat) is the key determinant of effectiveness. Third, the
credibility of a threat is contingent on a number of other conditions. It is positively related to the status or prestige of the user
and the user's frequency of following through on threats in the
past, and it is negatively related to the costs to the user of carrying out the threat. In other words, a threat is most effective if it
is buttressed by substantial coercive potential, the user has high
status, the user has a history of carrying out threats in the past,
and the costs to the user in carrying out the threat will be small
(Tedeschi, Schlenker, and Bonoma, 1973).

Deterrence and related subjective-expected-utility ideas,
therefore, paint a rather optimistic picture of threat effectiveness. A user must consider how conditions surrounding a threat
might affect the perceived magnitude and credibility of the tactic, but such tactics can be quite useful nonetheless. The conflict-spiral notion presents a far gloomier picture. This theoretical idea is ultimately based on the classic work of Deutsch and
Krauss (1962). They argue that coercive potentials have negative effects on a bargaining relationship that transcend and
undermine deterrence. In the face of substantial coercive potentials, some party will at sometime use the potential by means of
a threat, and this will lead to counteruse by the opponent. The
result is a conflict spiral through which all parties essentially
lose.

The conflict spiral has implications directly opposite to deterrence. While deterrence theory suggests that the level of aggression will decrease as the coercive potentials of parties in-crease, the conflict-spiral hypothesis is that greater coercive potential will engender greater aggression and counteraggres-sion. There are two rationales for the conflict-spiral notion. First, greater coercive potential provides a temptation that is too great to resist over time—at some point, someone will use the potential. Second, compliance under a threat entails a loss of face. It implies weakness, to the opponent and to significant third parties. Consequently, a threat will be met by a counter-threat, which is, in turn, met with a counterthreat, and so forth. The conflict increases until parties destroy each other, until one of them risks deescalation, or until a third party mediates the conflict or interferes with the spiral. This notion implies that an organization that gives its segments substantial coercive poten-tial that can be used against each other will inadvertently create a more conflict-ridden atmosphere. The conflict-spiral idea also implies that coercive potential will obstruct serious bargaining and distract parties from the real issues at hand. Thus, high coercive potential would also make it more difficult to regulate or resolve conflicts by bargaining.

Interestingly, this conflict-spiral hypothesis has also re-ceived substantial support in social psychological research. Deutsch and Krauss (1962) document the spiral in their classic work. While they have been criticized on theoretical and meth-odological grounds, the basic pattern they posit has been ob-served in enough subsequent research to lead Rubin and Brown (1975) to offer the following related hypothesis based on an ex-tensive review of social psychological evidence: The greater the total power in a relationship, the lower the bargaining effective-ness. In addition, the face-saving rationale is a plausible interpre-tation for the conflict spiral. A heightened concern for face has been shown to increase the toughness of bargaining and to lead a party even to "cut off its nose to save its face" (Brown, 1968, 1977). Based on our discussion of the conflict-spiral hypothesis, the following hypothesis is warranted:

Hypothesis 72. A threat tactic will be less effective to the extent that compliance leads to a loss of face.

We are left at this point with two contradictory notions, both with substantial empirical support. The deterrence notion places primary emphasis on the utilitarian consequences of compliance versus noncompliance to threats; the conflict-spiral notion places primary emphasis on the implications of compliance versus noncompliance for intangible issues such as loss of face. The question that needs to be asked is: Under what conditions will utilitarian or loss of face implications be of greatest importance? Clearly, deterrence sometimes works and the conflict spiral sometimes occurs. Our task is to gain some understanding of when one or the other is most likely to occur.

The major task is to determine when loss of face becomes an issue for conflicting parties. We will use attribution theory to deal with the conditions under which loss of face is an important problem (see Jones and Davis, 1965; Jones and others, 1971). Attribution theory is a social psychological attempt to determine when and how persons attribute dispositions or qualities to another. The theory begins with the assumption that party O will attribute qualities or dispositions to party P based on P's behavior. The qualities attributed to P might include success, failure, general or specific competences, weakness, goodness, or any other general characteristic or dimension along which persons might be arrayed. Attributions can generally be grouped into positive and negative categories, and the specific content of these categories is tied to the particular social context.

Our concern is with the tendency of persons to make negative attributions to actors who comply with an opponent's threat. The attributions relevant to our focus can be summarized as *weakness*. In conflict settings, weakness tends to be a socially devalued quality implying that the person or group lacks independence, is unwilling to stand up for itself, and is generally incompetent in dealing with certain social circumstances. Attribution theory is relevant to a target's compliance with a threat insofar as the target will anticipate the reactions of others (hypothetical or real) to its compliance. We are assuming that targets of a threat will evaluate themselves on the same criteria they would expect others to use, regardless of whether others will in fact know of or respond to the target's compliance.

From the standpoint of attribution theory, the inferences made about P as a person based on P's behavior are not made in isolation or on absolute grounds. The behavior of P is evaluated in light of the social context within which P is operating. One of the central ideas of attribution theory is that persons will evaluate the behavior in context and attempt to identify the causes of the behavior. The attributions of causality can be of two general types: internal and external. Attributions of internal causality imply that the behavior is caused by characteristics of the actor; attributions of external causality mean that the behavior is caused by the social context. These attributions index the degree to which actors are seen as responsible for their own behavior. Internal causality implies that actors are fully responsible for their behavior and, therefore, that the behavior clearly says something about the actors. Attributions of external causality, on the other hand, relieve actors of responsibility, that is, the behavior says more about the social context than about the actors. The theory thus suggests that persons will view internally caused behavior as reflecting more on the actors than externally caused behavior and be more likely to use such behavior to make inferences about the actors (see Jones and Davis, 1965).

Applied to the inferences to be drawn from compliance with a threat, attribution theory suggests that compliance will reflect badly on persons or group only if it is viewed (by the target and others) as internally caused. Where the constraints of the social context make compliance appear the reasonable or rational thing to do or something almost anybody would do, compliance will be readily attributed to the social setting rather than to the target. Since attributions about actors are more likely when the actors' behavior is perceived as internally caused, we expect the loss of face issue to be salient primarily under these same conditions. The loss of face issue can be con-

strued as the issue of how responsible actors are for their behavior. Face may be lost when actors perceive themselves and
expect others to perceive them as highly responsible for their
behavior. This means that targets of a threat can comply without a loss of face to the extent that they are not viewed (by
themselves or others) as personally responsible for the compliance. Thus, our attribution analysis and application implies the
following hypothesis:

Hypothesis 73. A threat tactic will be more effective the more
the target's compliance is likely to be attributed to external rather than internal causes.

Applied to organizations, this proposition suggests that
the allocation of responsibility to diverse persons or coalitions
can affect their receptivity to threats. The salience of the loss of
face issue will be greater when coalitions have considerable discretion and responsibility in the areas of conflict. Any aspect of
the organizational structure that constrains a coalition's ability
to respond in kind to threats or that limits the options of threat
targets will make compliance more palatable by giving the targets a rationale or justification for compliance. Thus, constraints on the discretion, responsibility, and tactical options of
threat targets will increase the effectiveness of threat tactics.

At this point, we need to discuss more precisely what
aspects of the organizational structure will constrain a target's
responsibility for compliance and, thereby, increase the effectiveness of threats. First, we will examine superior-subordinate
relationships with a focus on authority differences. Next, we
will discuss the bearing of our attribution hypothesis on conflict
and bargaining between coalitions of relatively equal power.

A number of structural conditions can make threats by
superiors against subordinates more or less effective. First of all,
we must consider the differences in coercive potential. It is interesting that the social psychological research that supports
deterrence theory is typically conducted in settings where one
party has much more coercive potential or power than the
other. In fact, in the work of Tedeschi, Schlenker, and Bono-

ma (1973), the subordinate has virtually no power in the setting. Under circumstances of a wide disparity in power, the target can clearly attribute compliance to the situation. In contrast, research supporting the conflict spiral tends to observe it primarily in conditions of equal power between parties (see Deutsch and Krauss, 1962; Deutsch and others, 1967; Rubin and Brown, 1975). However, the conflict spiral has also been observed in contexts where there is a power difference but the subordinate has at least some level of coercive potential with which to respond in kind to the superior (Michener and Cohen, 1973; Rubin and Brown, 1975). From this literature, we infer that compliance entails a loss of face only when the target's coercive potential allows the target a viable counterthreat option. The overall implication is that large differences in coercive potential will facilitate compliance, but as the differences get smaller the tendency toward compliance will decrease substantially. The relationship between power differences between parties and compliance by subordinates may actually be curvilinear, with a sharp drop in compliance in the transition from high to moderate power differences.

A second aspect of the organization consists of the norms and rules that govern the use of threats and coercion by superiors. Specifically, we are referring to the authority relationship of superior and subordinate. Social psychological evidence suggests that the status and prestige of the user of coercion has a positive effect on threat compliance (Tedeschi, Schlenker, and Bonoma, 1973; Tedeschi and Bonoma, 1972). Similarly, when an authority in an organizational context has the legitimized right or obligation to use coercion or the target has an obligation to comply with the wishes of the authority, compliance is possible without a loss of face. In this case, the responsibility of the target is likely to be formally limited by the organizational rules. Yet the authority is not likely to have unlimited rights to use coercion, and there must be some congruence between the rights of the user and the obligations of the target before the target feels relieved of responsibility for compliance. If the authority oversteps the formal boundaries of the position, then the target would presumably feel greater pressure not to comply and would have to find another justification for compliance (such as the power of the user).

To summarize, our discussion of power and authority suggests the following specific hypotheses:

Hypothesis 74. Large differences in coercive potential will reduce the salience of the loss of face issue.

Hypothesis 75. The greater the authority of the user, the less salient the loss of face issue.

Hypothesis 76. The greater the congruence of the user's organizational rights (authority) to coerce and the target's organizational obligations to obey, the less salient the loss of face issue.

These propositions focus on superiors' threats to subordinates, and they suggest some of the mechanisms through which organizations alleviate the loss of face problem and enhance the ability of superiors to command compliance. The implication is that superiors in key organizational positions can successfully use threats against subordinates when there is a large difference in coercive potential between themselves and the targets, when their position of authority legitimizes the use of coercion, and, in particular, when their rights to coerce and the formally specified obligations of the subordinates are congruent with regard to the concrete issue in question.

The hypotheses are applicable primarily to superior-subordinate relationships. Our integration of the theories of coercion also applies to conflicts between coalitions of relatively equal power. As noted earlier, the deterrence and conflict-spiral hypotheses have different implications for the effect of organizational structure on conflict. The deterrence notion suggests that a decentralized organization that gives substantial coercive potential to disparate segments or coalitions (in other words, one that induces high mutual dependence) will minimize intercoalition conflict. The rationale for this is that coalitions in a decentralized organization will develop substantial autonomy despite their mutual dependence on other coalitions. The manner in which they use this autonomy is critical to the day-to-day operation of the organization. They could use it to interfere with each other's activities, but their mutual dependence will inhibit interference and the concomitant use of coercion. The risks of mutual interference are simply too great. The conflict-spiral notion suggests that, given substantial coercive potential (mutual dependence), the parts of a decentralized organization will tend to interfere with each other's activities in an attempt to improve and secure their own positions in the organization. Consequently, the conflict-spiral hypothesis suggests that a decentralized organization will be more conflict-ridden (all other things being equal) than a more centralized organization. Our analysis of the loss of face issue tends to support the conflict-spiral notion. (It should also be noted that these implications for decentralization are consistent with and extend our analysis in Chapter Four.)

The loss of face issue should be quite salient if two relatively powerful coalitions are in conflict with each other, because both parties have a viable way to resist coercion, and compliance will therefore be attributed to weakness. To the extent that decentralization provides areas of substantial autonomy to coalitions and increases the mutual dependence of major organizational coalitions, the following hypothesis should apply:

Hypothesis 77. The greater the decentralization of the organization, the greater the use of coercion in intercoalition relations, the greater the frequency of conflict spirals, and the lower the amount and effectiveness of two-party bargaining as a method of conflict resolution.

To summarize, coercive tactics are rather dangerous means of limiting resistance and facilitating the compliance of adversaries. Threats can induce significant changes in the utility of compliance and noncompliance by manipulating the perceived magnitude and probability of certain outcomes; however, the loss of face problem can obstruct any inclination of targets to act in terms of these strictly utilitarian criteria. The loss of face problem is least important in superior-subordinate relationships, because organizations typically attach resources and per-

quisites to superior positions that minimize the loss of face for
complying subordinates. However, the issue of loss of face is
likely to be particularly salient in conflicts between coalitions
of relatively equal power. In that context, neither coalition can
comply with threats without a loss of face. At the same time,
both coalitions will be tempted to use their coercive potential.
The result is a conflict spiral that does damage to the coalitions
and the larger organization. The precise manner in which organizations structure and oversee the relationships of distinct coalitions can have a critical bearing on the patterns of conflict
between coalitions. Decentralized organizations may need more
developed conflict-resolution mechanisms to blunt these tendencies toward conflict between distinct coalitions.

Communication of Threats

The nature of the communication of threats is important
because it can have a significant bearing on the credibility of the
threat as well as the likelihood that the loss of face issue will
reduce the target's willingness to comply. In this section we will
examine the content of the communication (what is communicated) and the methods of communicating threats in organizations.

Regardless of how it is communicated, a threat message
contains three basic elements: (1) the user's behavior, that is,
the nature of the prospective damage, (2) the target's behavior,
that is, what the target can do to avoid punishment, and (3) a
contingency linking the user's behavior to the target's behavior.
The content of any threat message or communication, however
subtle or vague it may be, includes these three basic elements.
The specific nature of the communication takes the form of an
if-then statement: If Beta does (or does not do) X, then Alpha
will do (or not do) Y. X is the target's behavior, Y is the user's
response, and the if-then format establishes a contingent relationship between X and Y.

We are not implying that users actually articulate the if-
then statement in verbal form. The exact mode of communicating contingencies is quite variable, and threats are typically

communicated by a combination of verbal and nonverbal action. Threats are actually matters of impression management. The task of the user is to give an impression, perhaps in very subtle ways, that certain behavior by the target will be punished in certain ways by the user. The if-then format simply captures the critical elements of what happens to be communicated to the target. In other words, the if-then format is as much a part of the target's definition of the situation as it is an explicit part of the user's actual communication.

The content of the threat communication, defined in terms of our three elements, can have an important bearing on the effectiveness of the threat. The most critical aspect of a threat message appears to be its clarity. Clear messages with clear contingencies leave less room for misunderstanding and probably appear more credible to targets. This aspect can be examined in relation to each of the three elements. A threat should be more effective to the extent that it conveys to the target in a clear fashion how the consequences of the threat can be avoided. In other words, the more clearly a threat distinguishes compliance from noncompliance in the user's terms, the more information it provides the target on how to avoid the punishment. Thus:

Hypothesis 78. The more precisely and clearly a threat defines compliance for the target, the more effective the threat tactic.

There is a more complex relationship between clarity of the punishment and threat effectiveness. Clarity appears to be in the user's interest only if the user has substantial coercive potential and is willing to use that potential to its full extent. Where the potential is low or ambiguous, clarity may undermine the effectiveness of the threat. Ambiguity regarding the punishment, in this case, can lead the target to overestimate the coercive potential and ultimate level of punishment. Thus, the following hypothesis is suggested:

Hypothesis 79. Under conditions of high coercive potential, the greater the clarity of the punishment, the greater the effectiveness of the threat; under conditions of ambiguous or low coercive potential, the lower the clarity of punishment, the more effective the threat.

With low coercive potential, clarity serves only to emphasize the weakness of the threat, while it emphasizes the power behind the threat under conditions of high coercive potential.

The contingency between the target's behavior and the user's punishment is relevant primarily to the issue of threat credibility. To exemplify this issue, consider two general types of contingencies: deterministic and probabilistic (Tedeschi, 1970). Deterministic messages imply a very strong contingency —that it is certain punishment will follow noncompliance. Probabilistic messages imply a looser contingency. A deterministic threat might convey, "If Beta does X, then Alpha will definitely do Y," while a probabilistic one might imply, "If Beta does X, then Alpha might do Y." Given the importance of threat credibility to effectiveness, we posit the following:

Hypothesis 80. The stronger the contingency (between the target's behavior and the punishment) in the threat, the more effective the threat tactic.

Stronger contingencies imply a firmer commitment by the user to induce or maintain the compliance of the target (Schelling, 1960). The strength of commitment conveyed in a specific context should affect the credibility of the threat independent of the user's prior history of following through on threats. A prior history of not following through on similar strong commitments would, however, undermine the effect of commitment. In general, conveying an especially strong commitment may be a means of overcoming credibility problems in a concrete situation.

As a whole, hypotheses 78-80 indicate that users of threats will gain compliance more effectively if they administer clear threats and convey a strong contingency between target behavior and user punishment. However, there are other considerations that could make less clarity and a looser contingency tactically more advantageous to users. The reason is that a threat binds the users as well as the targets. A clear threat commits the user to follow through in specific ways and in response to specific behaviors of the target, thereby actually reducing the discretion of the user. Similarly, a strong contingency makes it more imperative that the user punish noncompliance (enforce the threat). More ambiguous threats leave the user more room to maneuver in the event of the target's noncompliance. With a looser contingency, a user can decide not to punish noncompliance and yet not suffer as great a loss in future credibility as if a strong contingency had been ignored. Unclear communication of what constitutes compliance and noncompliance gives the user the option of deciding afterwards what behavior to punish; the user can then consider more completely the specific conditions surrounding compliance or noncompliance.

The likelihood of the user making ambiguous threats will depend on two interrelated conditions: the cost of enforcement and the extent to which the threat is a bluff. When there are substantial costs in enforcing a threat, the user is likely to be wary of making explicit, clear commitments about the nature of noncompliance, the level of punishment, or even whether punishment will occur. To maximize flexibility in responding to the target, the user would tend to leave a loophole or some leeway to invoke post hoc definitions to fit the context of the target's behavior. In a related way, the party who uses a threat as a bluff, with no intention of following through on it, is likely to use an ambiguous threat with a loose contingency in order to minimize the effects of the bluff on credibility of future threats if the bluff is called. In sum, we would expect the following:

Hypothesis 81. The greater the costs of enforcement to the user of a threat, the greater the ambiguity of the threat.

Hypothesis 82. If a party uses a threat as a bluff, the threat will tend to be ambiguous.

Summarizing this section, we have examined the content of threat communications. Our discussion suggests that different types of content will tend to affect the success of the threat tactic and the extent to which the user is bound by the threat.

A sizable and credible threat can limit the freedom or autonomy of the user as well as the target. Having examined the general conditions of effectiveness, we now turn to the manner in which threats are likely to be communicated within organizations. The method of communication is important, because different methods are related to the conditions of success detailed in this chapter.

Methods of Communicating Threats

The social psychological work upon which the previous sections are based stresses one general method of communicating threats: behavioral. The theory and research focus on situations in which one person or group is administering threats to another person or group, and the primary method is some combination of verbal and nonverbal communication to the opponent. While this is obviously a major means of threatening others, organizations have the capacity to threaten in less obvious and direct ways. More specifically, organizations contain social structures that communicate threats in impersonal, subtle ways. For example, the organizational position of a supervisor may include coercive potential and an explicit or implicit set of conditions under which the supervisor is expected to enforce threats (punish subordinates). The structural position administers the threats, and it is primarily enforcement that is left up to the supervisor. Although the supervisor may be able to affirm the threat embodied in the organizational structure, the threat is essentially independent of the supervisor's behavior. In sum, there are actually two forms of communicating threats in formal organizations: behavioral and structural.

An organization is able to command considerable compliance from its members in part because of the structural mode of threat administration. We argued at the beginning of this chapter that organizations are ultimately based on coercion. The primary means by which this coercive foundation manifests itself throughout the organization is in the structure of relationships among social positions. Embedded in this structure are the active components of coercion: threats. In fact, structure might be viewed as simply a set of legitimized threats that, in often subtle ways, establish contingencies between the behavior of the members and the response of the organization or some subgroup within it. This is not to suggest that rewards or incentives are unimportant. Rewards and incentives provide a key foundation for dependence and the coercive potential of the organization vis-à-vis its members or of one coalition vis-à-vis another; further, the withdrawal or reduction of rewards is a prime mechanism of coercion. Rewards are inseparable from and actually a part of the coercive foundation of organizations.

With regard to the two basic methods of administering threats, therefore, we begin with the following hypothesis:

Hypothesis 83. Structural methods of administering threats are more effective than behavioral methods.

The rationale for this proposition is that structurally induced threats avoid the loss of face problem (all other things being equal) more than behavioral threats. There are three interrelated reasons for this. First of all, structurally induced threats are inherently impersonal. They do not constitute a personal attack on a given individual or group but rather are ostensibly applicable across members or classes of members. The impersonal character of these threats should mitigate any loss of face from compliance, since all or at least many organizational members are similarly constrained.

Second, it is difficult if not impossible for the target of a structural threat to identify the person or group responsible for the threat. The source is inherently ambiguous, and responsibility is dispersed across various individuals or subgroups within the organization. In the absence of a clear source, the target may consider attacking a symbolic representative of the organization, such as an immediate supervisor. Given the diffusion of responsibility, however, the immediate supervisor can legitimately shift responsibility elsewhere. The threat may be blamed on that amorphous entity the administration, but it is still not clear what parts of the administration bear primary responsibility. The conflict spiral seems to require that the target be able to identify the source of the threat—otherwise, it is not clear who deserves retaliation. Thus, diffusion of responsibility for the threat makes it easier for the target of a threat to comply without a loss of face.

Third, structurally induced threats imply a separation of threat administration and threat enforcement, that is, a separation of the use of threats from the act of following up threats with actual punishment in the event of noncompliance. As implied above, threats are administered by the structure, for example, by rules specifying rights and obligations of members, and are not attached to any person or group. On the other hand, the enforcement of threats is inherently a behavioral phenomenon, requiring the intervention of specific parties. For example, the immediate supervisor may enforce the contingencies of punishment implicit or explicit in the organizational structure, but the supervisor typically will not establish the contingencies. In fact, the supervisor may not even agree with the contingencies established by the organizational structure. This is important to the loss of face issue, because it enables immediate supervisors to shift responsibility for the threats, as well as for enforcement, to higher levels in the organization. The targets of threat and enforcement will tend to attribute less blame to the enforcers, and the enforcers can argue that they are only doing their job. The targets will likely perceive themselves as having little choice but to comply and will perceive the enforcers as having little choice but to levy punishment in the event of noncompliance. To summarize, intentionally or unintentionally, organizations that separate threat administration from threat enforcement are likely to enhance the influence of the enforcers.

The foregoing provides a rather extensive rationale for a very general proposition: Structurally induced threats are more effective than behaviorally induced threats. Embedded within the rationale are a number of other propositions that suggest when structurally induced threats are more or less successful:

Hypothesis 84. The more impersonal the threat, the greater the compliance of the target.

Hypothesis 85. The more diffuse the responsibility for the threat, the greater the compliance of the target.

Hypothesis 86. The greater the separation of threat administration and threat enforcement, the greater the compliance of the target.

Each of these propositions is intended to apply to structurally induced threats. However, it should be noted that behaviorally induced threats may also vary in impersonality, and users may be more or less able to shift responsibility from themselves. Consequently, these same ideas can serve as guides to individuals or groups attempting to influence other individuals or groups.

The nature of structurally induced threats varies with the nature of the organizational structure. Formalization and centralization appear to have particularly important implications for the threat system of an organization. Formalization implies greater codification of rules, more specified and delimited treatment of rights and obligations, and stricter enforcement of the formal rules. If we conceptualize the structure as, in part, a system of implicit and explicit threats, then formalization should affect the clarity, credibility, and impersonality of the threats embedded in the structure. That is:

Hypothesis 87. The greater the formalization of an organization, the greater the clarity of the contingencies in the threat communication.

Hypothesis 88. The greater the formalization of an organization, the greater the credibility (the likelihood of enforcement) of threats.

Hypothesis 89. The greater the formalization of an organization, the greater the impersonality of the threats.

Given that clarity, credibility, and impersonality increase the effectiveness of a threat, the following hypothesis can be derived from the previous ones:

Hypothesis 90. The greater the formalization of an organization, the greater the effectiveness of structurally induced threats.

The rationale for the last hypothesis is implied in hypotheses 87-89. Greater formalization will engender clearer and more definite statements about what constitutes compliance and noncompliance in the organization. Formalization will also increase the perceived probability of enforcement, in part, because it more severely constrains the options of users. In other words, formalization will facilitate standardized treatment of deviance and impose demands on the enforcers that maximize the credibility of the threats. Not only does enforcement have official sanction but also the nature of enforcement will be more precise, exact, and binding with greater formalization. Finally, formalization will increase the impersonality of threat administration (and enforcement, for that matter) in the same way it enhances impersonality throughout the organization.

In contrast to formalization, centralization bears on different aspects of structurally induced threats. A decentralized structure implies greater difficulty in locating the parties responsible for the administration of threats. We suggest the following implications:

Hypothesis 91. The greater the decentralization, the greater the diffusion of responsibility for threat administration.

Hypothesis 92. The greater the decentralization, the greater the separation of threat administration and threat enforcement.

While other structural conditions, such as size and the number of hierarchical levels, may further specify these hypotheses, the overall conclusion is:

Hypothesis 93. The greater the decentralization, the greater the effectiveness of structurally induced threats.

Decentralization tends to create conditions that make it difficult for targets to identify the source of a threat clearly and know where to direct their retaliation; in addition, it implies a clearer separation of threat administration and enforcement than in centralized organizations. The model in Figure 5 summarizes our hypotheses about the effectiveness of structurally induced threats.

Figure 5. Impact of Formalization and Centralization on Structurally Induced Threat

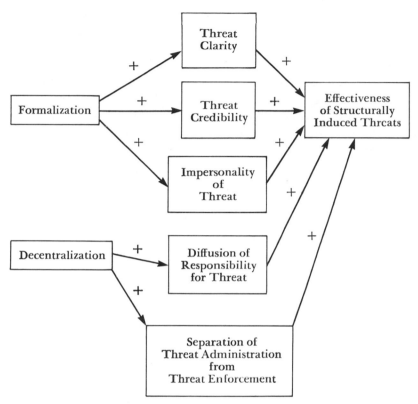

On the surface, the implications of hypothesis 93 appear paradoxical. Our earlier discussion indicated that larger power differences between the user and the target of a threat mitigate the loss of face problem and enhance threat effectiveness. Would this not also suggest that threats are generally more effective in centralized than decentralized organizations? As noted earlier, decentralized organizations tend to incorporate conditions such as more equal distributions of power that appear to underlie the conflict spiral.

This dilemma can be resolved if we return to our distinction between structurally induced and behaviorally induced threats. Behaviorally induced threats tend to be made either when structurally induced ones are ineffective or when structurally induced ones are left undeveloped and relegated to the discretion of the most powerful coalitions or individuals in the organization. A highly centralized organization is likely to leave threat administration to the discretion of powerful groups and, hence, behavioral threats are likely to be the dominant mode of threat communication. In the case of behavioral threats, highly centralized organizations should yield greater threat effectiveness for the reasons detailed earlier in this chapter. Ultimately, the success of such threats is based on the concentration of coercive potential in the most powerful groups.

Decentralization should render behaviorally induced threats less effective for three basic reasons. First, a more equal distribution of coercive potential increases the danger of a conflict spiral. Second, assuming that decentralization accords greater autonomy to component parts of the organization, the use of coercion is more likely to be construed as an illegitimate intrusion of one coalition on the other, making compliance even less palatable. Third, decentralization implies a diffusion of responsibility for the administration of threats. In fact, decentralization may actually countermand the use of coercion in the day-to-day activities of the organization. While these aspects of decentralization decrease the effectiveness of behaviorally induced threats, they are precisely the conditions that make structurally induced threats more effective. Thus, centralization increases the effectiveness of behaviorally induced threats, and decentralization enhances the effectiveness of structurally induced threats.

Summary

This chapter analyzed the use of coercion in organizational contexts. Consistent with a social psychological approach, we have emphasized the action or tactical dimension of coercion. That is, our concern has been not so much with coercive capability or potential but rather with the manner in which coalitions or other actors use coercive tactics. Such tactics differ from those analyzed in Chapter Seven in that coercion engenders a *decrease* in the dependence of the target on the user of coercion. These divergent consequences for the dependence relationship make coercive tactics a separate class of tactics.

The most crucial element of coercion is the threat. A threat is an expression of intent to do harm to another. Threats are means for activating or making salient a coercive potential and for avoiding the costs of enforcement, that is, of carrying out punishment. Since actual punishment reduces the dependence of the target on the user, it is generally in the interest of the user to avoid that step. If effective, threats are cheap means of influence, because they make actual punishment unnecessary. On the other hand, an ineffective threat places the user in a dilemma. Enforcement of the threat may undermine the user's future influence by reducing the target's dependence; yet, failure to enforce the threat may reduce the credibility of the user's future threats. Given our tactical focus, the basic purpose of this chapter was to examine conditions under which threats are effective means of influence.

Two social psychological notions afford contradictory images of coercive tactics. Deterrence theory stipulates that the coercive potential of two parties is inversely related to their actual use of coercion. Based on subjective-expected-utility theory (see Chapter Five), aggression will most likely be deterred if both parties have high coercive potential and perceive each other as likely to use the potential under given conditions. Threats make the coercive potentials salient and communicate the conditions under which the actors will use coercion. An alternative notion, which we term the conflict-spiral hypothesis, indicates that high coercive potential will create a temptation so great that eventually one of the parties will use or threaten to use the coercion. The use (or threatened use) of coercion, in turn, will unleash an upward spiral of retaliatory coercive action. The basic reason for the spiral is that coercion arouses an issue of loss of face: Compliance or submission to coercion entails a loss of face for the target. Parties will ostensibly refuse to comply to save face, even when this is costly to them. Applied to organizations, deterrence theory suggests that, within decentralized organizations, intercoalition bargaining will contain little use of coercive tactics; the conflict-spiral notion indicates that the conditions surrounding decentralization are precisely those that will arouse the loss of face issue and engender more frequent and severe conflict spirals. An interpretation of the loss of face issue in terms of attribution theory supports the implications of the conflict-spiral notion.

The mode of communication is also important to the effectiveness of threats. We distinguished two modes of communicating threats: behavioral and structural. Behavioral threats are induced by verbal or nonverbal communication in the context of social interaction. They are inherently attached to particular individuals or coalitions. Structurally induced threats are built into the actual structure of the organization. Formal rules, for example, can be construed as systems of structurally induced threats. We contend that structurally induced threats are less likely to arouse the loss of face issue and thus are more effective than behavioral ones (all other things being equal). The rationale for this hypothesis is that structurally induced threats are more impersonal, make responsibility for the threats more ambiguous, and tend to imply some separation of threat enforcement from threat administration within the organization. All these conditions make the loss of face issue less salient to those who must decide whether or not to comply with the threat.

Focusing on structural threats, the last section of the chapter examined the impact of decentralization and formalization. We argue that decentralization is positively related to the effectiveness of structurally induced threats, because decentralization induces greater structural separation between threat administration and threat enforcement while diffusing responsibility for the threats throughout the organization. Formalization is also positively related to the effectiveness of structurally induced threats. It increases the clarity, credibility, and impersonality of the threats, and all of these conditions enhance threat effectiveness.

9

Influence Networks and Decision Making

^^^

Influence Network as an Emergent Property of Organizations

One of the main criticisms that can be directed at our discussion is that, while our political perspective stresses intra- and inter-group political processes, we have failed to emphasize the emergent organizational properties implied by intraorganizational political analyses. It may be argued that we have held to an implied network metaphor of the organization; while we have suggested directions for studying the groups in the network and relationships within the network, we have yet to accentuate the network as an emergent property of the total organization.

Most of the comparative sociological research on organizations in the past decade produces an image that is distinctly at odds with the images emanating from our discussions. The recent empirical work has been dominated by a number of comparative studies: research by Pugh, Hickson, and their colleagues on British industrial organizations (for example, Pugh and

203

others, 1968, 1969), Hage and Aiken's (1970) research on nine-
teen welfare organizations, Blau and Schoenherr's (1971) research on state employment organizations, and Aiken and
Bacharach's (1978) research on local government organizations.
These studies have tended to focus primarily on the structural
characteristics of organizations, such as size, technology, and
complexity, rather than on the more dynamic political processes we have stressed here. The failure to deal with these
processes has been one of the main drawbacks of contemporary
comparative organizational research.

Empirically, this failure has been manifested in the oversimplified treatment of decision making. For example, Blau and
Schoenherr (1971) are purportedly concerned with decision-
making processes in organizations; however, in their investigation of these processes, they confine themselves to obtaining
reports from key informants about who has the authority to
make decisions. Other comparative researchers such as Hage and
Aiken (1970) and Pugh and his colleagues (1968) also limit
their concern to determining who has the authority to make decisions. Methodologically, these previous studies have aggregated individual reports of authority to develop a composite
score of organizational centralization or decentralization. Specifically, Blau and Schoenherr (1971) asked department heads
in the organizations in their sample to rate the authority they
had to make specific decisions on a scale of one to four; then,
they aggregated these individual ratings and derived an average
score for the entire organization. This score was used as an indi-
cation of organizational centralization or decentralization. Blau
and Schoenherr discovered that certain organizational characteristics, such as size and complexity, affect the level of organizational centralization or decentralization. However, viewing decision making as a structural component refers to the official
decision-making power that flows from the various positions in
the organizational system. Indeed, as we have argued, due to its
formal, structural properties, the study of authority to make
decisions in organizations may be based solely on positional criteria, such as those revealed in organizational charts, eliminating
the need to examine interaction processes. By contrast, influ-

ence is the more elusive aspect of organizational power. Influence relationships do not always coincide with the authority structure; one may be independent of the other. Therefore, the formal, structural characteristics of the organizational system do not always provide clues to the sources of influence. To identify the sources of influence, the links among key coalitions or interest groups become critical. Thus, the theoretical value of concentrating on the influence network as opposed to the authority structure is that it offers a more complete, political picture of the organizational system. Given this emphasis on influence relationships, a network metaphor may provide the most useful methodological technique for examining these relationships. The influence network that exists among coalitions is the emergent organizational property of primary interest to the political analysis of organizations.

A social network is a patterned set of relationships among actors or groups in a social space. The ties upon which the relationships are based and from which the social network emerges may be of several different kinds. While we have chosen to concentrate on influence as the primary tie, there may be other important ties, for example, friendship. A coalition may in fact be further defined as a dense clustering of reciprocal relationships within any network. The point is that each researcher, informed by specific theoretical interests, selects a specific type of tie for investigation. We have adopted a political model, which leads us to concentrate on influence as the primary tie among coalitions in the organizational network.

Emergent Properties of the Influence Network

Seven emergent properties of the influence network may be identified:

1. *Connectedness* refers to the degree to which any coalition of a network can or cannot influence another member either directly or indirectly. Thus, an organizational system in which each of the coalitions is connected directly or indirectly may be described as low in fragmentation; con-

versely, an organizational system in which direct or indirect connections are often lacking may be described as high in fragmentation.

2. *Density* refers to the proportion of direct contacts to possible direct contacts.

3. *Number* is simply the number of coalitions within the influence network.

4. *Centrality* refers to the degree to which one coalition is the center of a network.

5. *Overlap* examines whether coalition membership is overlapping or mutually exclusive. Specifically, the distinction embodied in this dimension is whether key interest groups belong to more than one coalition in the network.

6. *Structural congruence* examines the degree to which influence network groups coincide with the formal organizational subunits in membership. Implied here is the question of whether the influence network coincides with the authority structure.

7. *Dominance* concerns the question of whether the same coalition prevails over different decision areas. This last dimension raises important methodological and theoretical considerations, specifically, the need to discover whether each dimension discussed above varies by decision area.

Having described the seven dimensions of the influence network, the following hypotheses attempt to illustrate the relationship among organizational structure, work processes, environment, and these dimensions. Our list of hypotheses is intended to be illustrative rather than exhaustive.

Hypothesis 94. The more structurally complex the organization, the greater the overall connectedness, the greater the network density, the greater the number of coalitions, the lower the centrality of any single coalition, the greater the overlap among coalitions, the lower the coincidence between the influence network and the authority structure, and the less likely it is that any single coalition will prevail over all issue areas.

This proposition is based on the assumption that, as organizations become increasingly complex (that is, greater in size, in vertical and horizontal differentiation, and so forth), the number of formal positions increases, thus enhancing the potential number of bonds between members. In effect, the network configuration produced by such organizational complexity may be characterized as pluralistic. Conversely, following the same logic, relative lack of structural complexity in an organization would probably give rise to a more monolithic influence network.

Hypothesis 95. The more autonomous the work activity of an organization, the greater the overall connectedness of the network, the greater the density of the network, the greater the number of coalitions, the lower the centrality of any single coalition, the greater the overlap among coalitions, the lower the coincidence between the influence network and the authority structure, and the less likely it is that any single coalition will prevail over all issue areas.

This hypothesis parallels that for structural complexity; however, the basic rationale is different. Here, the primary source of network complexity is uncertainty in the roles of organizational personnel. Thus, it may be argued that the more autonomous the work activity, the less routine the work activity, the less adherence there is to rules and regulations, and the more ambiguity organizational members experience in the conduct of their work roles. Such ambiguity is reflected in the relative lack of constraints in work activity, and it leads to more diversified influence networks.

Hypothesis 96. The more heterogeneous and complex the environment of an organization, the lower the level of overall connectedness, the lower the density of the network, the greater the number of coalitions, the lower the centrality of any single coalition, the greater the number of mutually exclusive coalitions, the less the coincidence between the influence network and authority structure, and the less likely it is that any single coalition will prevail over all issue areas.

The assumption underlying this hypothesis is that environmental heterogeneity and complexity give rise to competing sets of demands on the organization. As a result, we would expect a greater variety of coalitions to be formed to confront these demands appropriately, making for a diversified influence network.

Networks and Goal Consensus

The political model of organizations that forms the basis of our analysis assumes that each interest group attempts to maximize its own goals and priorities by having its views represented in policy decisions. The influence network is the mechanism used to assure this representation. It follows that the characteristics of the influence network will affect an interest group's attempt to achieve its goals.

Despite the importance of interest groups in a political analysis of organizations, it is only recently that subunit goals have been examined empirically (Balke, Hammond, Meyer, 1973; Huber, 1974; Kochan, Huber, and Cummings, 1975). A political analysis of organizations focuses on an interest group's efforts to realize its goals.

While there has been a dearth of empirical literature on the subject, goal consensus has been cast as an important predictor of conflict within an organization (March and Simon, 1958; Schmidt and Kochan, 1972). Further, the effectiveness of an organization depends on the ability of the system to coordinate the various goals held by actors within it (Pennings and Goodman, 1977). The influence network is the mechanism by which such coordination is achieved. Thus, an examination of the effects of influence network characteristics on goal consensus represents an effort to delineate the process by which goals are set and used in organizations. In essence, organizational effectiveness must be recognized as essentially a political process (Campbell, 1976, 1977; Cummings, 1977). The following hypotheses are meant to illustrate the relations between network characteristics and goal consensus.

Hypothesis 97. The greater the overall connectedness of the network, the greater the level of goal consensus.

Hypothesis 98. The greater the density of the network, the greater the level of goal consensus.

Hypothesis 99. The greater the number of coalitions, the lower the degree of goal consensus.

Hypothesis 100. The greater the centrality of any single coalition, the greater the degree of goal consensus.

Hypothesis 101. The greater the degree of overlap among coalitions, the greater the degree of goal consensus.

Hypothesis 102. The greater the coincidence between the influence network and the authority structure, the greater the degree of goal consensus.

Hypothesis 103. The greater the likelihood that a single coalition will prevail across issues, the greater the degree of goal consensus.

The underlying assumption of these hypotheses is that pluralistic demands within an organization may be met by the formation of a pluralistic influence network. The variety of responsive positions of groups may result in numerous participants in the influence network differing by issue over which coalition will dominate. Obviously, different coalitions may dominate different issues.

Summary

A network imagery portrays the morphology of organizational politics at the aggregate level. This cursory presentation illustrates the manner in which our perspective can be integrated with a holistic approach to organizations. A holistic political approach requires combining network and coalition imagery. An analysis of networks that fails to treat composite coalitions and interest groups is likely to result in a perspective as apolitical as traditional structural approaches.

Conclusion

Most debates in organizational analysis can be reduced to discussions of the appropriate unit of analysis. Do we analyze the organization as a whole, look at individual members of the organization and the role that the individual occupies, or consider the organization as a composite of groups?

An analysis of the organization as a whole assumes that the organization is a rational system of interdependent units functionally held together by a common goal. Attention is focused on organizational structure (size, vertical and horizontal differentiation, role specialization, span of control, and so forth) and work processes (communication, interaction, centralization, and the like). Empirically, the appearance of a harmonious whole is enhanced through the use of aggregate data as the basis of analysis. Such a perspective assumes a uniform effect of structure and process across the organization, combining scores to create one measure of each variable for the total organization (Bacharach, 1978).

210

There are several problems inherent in this perspective. One of the limitations of previous structural research is its failure to depict organizations as dynamic entities subject to conflict and change. Structure has been reified in such a manner that it, rather than action, has become the focal point of analysis. Even when attention is paid to processes, they are conceptualized as if they were organizational structures. For example, various social control processes are simply referred to as organizational formalization; similarly, various power processes are subsumed under the broad category of centralization.

A second perspective in the analysis of organizations emphasizes the individual, casting the organization as a composite of individual actors and individual actions. This perspective maintains that, in the final sense, to understand the organization, we need to understand the individuals acting within it. At its extreme, this perspective reduces itself to a phenomenological analysis of how actors construct their reality within the organization. In contrast to the twin assumptions of homogeneity and objectivity that guide the rational managerial perspective, the individualistic perspective assumes that organizations are heterogeneous and subjective. The crucial problem for researchers using this approach is to explain how individual actors coordinate their actions with others to accomplish shared objectives. The answer is that coordinated action results when actors share a conceptualization of the organizational reality. Coordination, then, is a product of the rationality used to conceptualize the organization.

In attempting to move from individual to aggregate analysis, some recent researchers have concentrated on identifying the ways in which individuals in an organization are coupled (Weick, 1976). However, an emphasis on coupling suffers from the same limitations as other modes of individual analysis of organization. Taken at face value, it is prone to reductionism. Moreover, while this perspective is based on a phenomenological bias that implies a focus on the individual, theorists tend to use the individual model as a metaphor for the functioning of the organization. When this happens, the proponents of this approach are as guilty of anthropomorphizing the organization as their sociological colleagues are of reifying the organization. Finally, the individualistic perspective tends to overemphasize the chaotic nature of action in organizations. While the rational managerial proponents err in failing to consider the internal dynamics of organization, the adherents of the individualistic approach fail to consider the political and structural contexts that impinge on an individual's cognitions and actions. This tendency to depoliticize cognition, when combined with the other limitations, leads investigators away from discovering the rules of politics that we view as integral to organizational life.

A final alternative is an organizational model that is based on the group as the unit of analysis; it envisions the work group as the primary focus for the study of organizations. This perspective affords an empirical middle ground between concentrations on aggregate and on individual data. It examines collectivities of individuals within an organization. To date, the potential of the group model has not been fully realized. Its use has been dominated by organizational psychologists whose primary concern has been with group autonomy, that is, with the group itself rather than the group's relationship with other work groups in the organization. Furthermore, the group has been viewed as a relatively formal entity whose activities within the organization are passive and of little interest to researchers. Realization of the full potential of the group perspective requires that the dynamics of group interrelationships become a focal point for future research.

The basic unit of traditional political analysis is the subgroup—for example, class interests, class relations, and class conflict; the basic unit of an apolitical perspective is the total system. As Gouldner (1967) observes, a major bone of contention between system theorists and more politically oriented sociologists is that the former accept the unit of a total system as an axiom while the latter view this unity as problematic. Nowhere in organizational research is the assumption of unity more overplayed and the assumption of the presence of subgroups more underplayed than in comparative intraorganizational analysis. With the exception of research specifically designed to identify the sources of conflict in organizations (see Kochan, Huber, and Cummings, 1975; Pondy, 1967;

Schmidt and Kochan, 1972; Walton, 1969), current comparative intraorganizational research has only peripherally treated
subgroups and has tended to ignore subgroup differences, thereby preventing any systematic examination of the political tensions inherent in organizations. A systematic organizational
analysis that ignores subgroups is by definition apolitical, for it
assumes a harmonious whole and overlooks the inevitable tensions among subgroups.

In attempting to accentuate a political perspective for
intraorganizational analysis, this volume has stressed interest
groups and coalitions as the basic units of analysis. Specifically,
we have discussed how interest groups and coalitions form and
operate to influence organizational outcomes.

The following assumptions about organizations underlie
our theoretical perspective:

1. Organizations are best conceptualized as political bargaining
   systems.
2. Specific decision-making spheres are the primary arenas for
   bargaining and conflict in organizations.
3. Within the decision spheres, most organizational politics involve the efforts of actors to mobilize interest groups and
   coalitions for the sake of influencing the decisions of those
   in authority.
4. On the basis of collective objectives, interest groups merge
   into coalitions and select tactics to achieve their common
   objectives.
5. The formation of coalitions and coalition alliances will depend on the nature of the organizational structure and on
   the distribution and control of organizational resources.

On the most general level our book is an analysis of two
interrelated phenomena which form the foundation of an
understanding of organizational politics: coalitions and bargaining. Coalitions are the organizational groupings around which
politics are carried out within organizations. As construed in
this volume, coalitions are not "natural" groupings automatically created by the formal structure of an organization. Coalitions are the socially constructed groupings that emerge from

"natural" groupings such as interest groups and work groups. As such, coalitions are likely to cut across and modify the day-to-day manifestations of an organization's formal structure. The basic reason for this is that coalitions are not a part of the formal structure but emergent products of the informal influence processes that are central to organizational politics.

Although the formal structure does not automatically create coalitions, it does have an impact on coalition processes. As indicated in Chapter Four, the hierarchy of authority creates tendencies toward coalition by subordinates against those individuals or groups with greater authority. These tendencies vary, however, with the nature of the authority structure. Using social psychology theory on coalitions, we argue that the nature and frequency of coalition processes will differ in centralized versus decentralized organizations. In brief, theories of coalitions suggest that decentralized organizations are more susceptible to rampant coalition processes. Coalition action should be more frequent, deal with more basic structural issues, and be a more integral part of the day-to-day politics within decentralized structures. The fact that such aspects of the formal structure affect coalition processes, however, does not mean that coalitions are an integral part of the authority structure. Coalitions are important because they can undermine, modify, or buttress the power relations formally established by the hierarchy of authority.

Given that coalitions are not natural groupings, Chapter Five analyzes the mobilization of coalitions from interest groups within the organization. Interest groups are natural groupings that join persons in similar professional or occupational categories together in relations of common interests; while coalitions join two or more interest groups, that is, persons and groups, from different sectors of the organization. Chapter Five indicates that the mobilization process is governed by subjective expected utilities. These utilities exercise a major influence when actors evaluate the resources under control of a given interest group against those available to the prospective coalition. Such basic considerations lead us to distinguish interest group from coalition politics and to argue that the convergence of functional goals and ideology determine whether interest group politics or coalition politics predominates. In addition, the frequency of coalition politics is affected by various aspects of the organization. A routine technology and uncertain environment should facilitate coalition politics, while professionalized groupings should inhibit coalition politics and foster interest group politics. Overall, the mobilization process underlying coalition action is grounded in the nature of the connections between interest groups that are established by the formal and informal structure of the organization.

We adopted a bargaining approach to the interaction of coalitions. While coalitions crystallize and bring conflicting interests of organizational subgroups to the foreground, the political action generated is tantamount to bargaining. This bargaining may be very subtle or hidden in organizational contexts; it may not even be recognized as such by the conflicting coalition. Nevertheless, we argue that bargaining remains the most appropriate metaphor for analyzing relations among coalitions within organizations.

The concrete implications of a bargaining approach are developed in Chapter Six through Chapter Eight. The sixth chapter identifies three basic parameters of bargaining: the nature of the bargaining relationship, tactical action, and the constituents' representative relations, that is, relations within each coalition. The relationship between each of these parameters and bargaining processes is detailed and we suggest how the organizational structure can indirectly affect conflict and its resolution by altering these parameters. On a general level, this chapter shows that social psychological work on bargaining can be helpful in analyzing intraorganizational conflicts. The seventh chapter extends these ideas by developing a general theory of bargaining tactics based on power-dependence notions. The theory articulates the links between power, tactical action, and conflict resolution, as well as providing a framework for analyzing power struggles in organizations. The main point of this chapter is that the dependence or interdependence relationships of coalitions are crucial to an understanding of bargaining processes and the dynamics of power struggle over time. Our theory in conjunction with social psychological work on deterrence further indicates that coercion is a problem-filled aspect of intraorganizational conflict. Chapter Eight identifies different dimensions of coercion, argues that threats are the most critical dimension, and demonstrates how centralization and formalization affect the mode of communicating threats and the ultimate success of coercive tactics. Overall, this chapter argues that, in an organizational context, the method of coercion is as important as its actual content.

This book has a number of implications for research on organizational politics. The chapters contain a large number of propositions that await testing, but beyond these specific propositions there are a number of implicit or explicit recommendations for research. With regard to macro work, the book suggests that more attention be given to the network of coalitions within organizations. On a practical day-to-day level, it is this network of coalitions that essentially defines the structure of an organization. A macrosociological understanding of organizational politics, therefore, implies that investigators identify the major coalitions, the interest groups composing these coalitions, and analyze the bargaining relationships between these subgroups. It should be emphasized that we are not simply positing a new reification, the coalition network. The fluidity of the coalition structure is one of the key empirical issues raised by our analysis. We have suggested some conditions that will determine its stability or fluidity and are hopeful that researchers will examine these and related ideas suggested by the coalition metaphor.

On a micro level, the book also provides a framework for analyzing the emergence and nature of conflict between particular segments within an organization. This specifically suggests that one must analyze the composition of the coalitions, that is, the nature of the interest groups joined together by the coalition, how the mobilization process developed, and the exact nature of the bargaining between the segments of concern. Throughout such an analysis, however, our perspective implies that investigators view the conflict as one between particular segments within a larger organizational structure. We have continually emphasized that the larger organizational structure establishes at least broad boundaries within which specific conflicts develop, are resolved, and often re-emerge.

Perhaps we should also emphasize that this volume does not call for a new methodology or even a shift in the methodological approaches that dominate the field of organizations. For example, just as investigators use questionnaires and structured interviews to gather information on organizational structure, such techniques can be used to acquire information on the coalition network or the relationship between specific coalitions and interest groups within the organization. Just as the dominant theoretical approaches in the field often imply longitudinal analyses but allow for "snapshots" at single instants, so does our theoretical approach have a similar flexibility. Overall, it should be clear that there is no single method of investigation that is appropriate to all the issues raised in the book; nor is the book the product of some methodological orthodoxy to which we are irrevocably committed. We have attempted to produce a theoretical work that is consistent with the leading comparative quantitative approaches, yet not the exclusive domain of such. Indeed, we would hope that while this volume provides new directions for quantitative research, our hypotheses and discussion will be elaborated and reflected by the type of insights that can only come from qualitative case studies.

In closing this volume we would like to suggest that our work has implications not only for organizational analysis but also for the field of collective bargaining. One of the limitations of the approach we have followed in this book is that in our effort to define generic concepts of power and bargaining in intraorganizational conflict, we have missed opportunities to link our observations and hypotheses to bargaining in particular organizational contexts. However, having offered a model of intraorganizational conflict that we claim is more realistic than those generated by other perspectives, we are now obligated to demonstrate how our model might be usefully and realistically applied to specific contexts. If our claim of realism has any strength, then one area for such application will be in research on collective bargaining between labor and management. There are several reasons for choosing to focus on collective bargaining, besides the obvious one that such bargaining fits the definition of conflict among coalitions over the exchange and distribution of resources in an organizational context. Students of collective bargaining are inclined to grant a measure of legitimacy to conflicting interests, therefore, their research has less tendency to define conflict as pathological and to define research questions in that light. This, in turn, has meant that collective bargaining research has generated a wide body of literature on the objective interests separating the parties and on variables associated with relative success in bargaining. As Kochan ("Collective Bargaining and Organizational Research," forthcoming) has noted, "Those interested in conceptualizing organizations as political systems composed of shifting coalitions and interest groups can benefit immensely from the rich descriptive research that already exists on collective bargaining."

Probably no other subject in the social sciences has generated such a rich descriptive literature with so little in the way of theory to integrate it. Much of the research on collective bargaining has been dominated by debates over the relative importance of economic, political, and structural determinants of wage goals, bargaining outcomes, and strikes. (See, for example, Ross, 1948; Dunlop, 1950; Levinson, 1966; Ashenfelter and Johnson, 1969). Most of this work concludes that some importance should be ascribed to each of these factors, but fails to specify in any systematic way how they relate to each other. That failure relates to another: a failure to demonstrate how environmental influences and bargaining outcomes are mediated by the bargaining process itself. Those who have concentrated on explaining and predicting bargaining outcomes have tended to attribute only marginal significance to the bargaining process, writing off the importance of tactical maneuvers with the assertion that experienced bargainers will be able to see through each other's tactics and thus cancel out their effects. Even Walton and McKersie, whose work (1965) brought some analytic coherence to what had previously been a largely impressionistic body of knowledge about the bargaining process, treat the characteristics of the bargaining environment as exogenous variables not subject to objective manipulation in the course of bargaining. The result of such research has been a characterization of bargaining as merely a process of impression management, with more or less influence over specific bargaining outcomes, but with little or no impact on the organizational and environmental dimensions that are essential to the relationship between the parties.

The concept of dependence-based power developed in this book can bring more coherence to the study of collective bargaining. It does not provide an alternative to the various economic, political, and institutional perspectives and levels of analyses that have dominated research in the area; but rather, it provides a framework for integrating the insights these different approaches have generated and for demonstrating how different aspects of the bargaining system relate to each other. It can do so for several reasons.

First, by starting with an abstract framework of distinct dependence dimensions, this model guards against the premature assumption that any two dimensions are necessarily related in a particular way. It is entirely possible, for example, that a slack labor market might mean there are few alternative sources of jobs for workers and many alternative workers for the employer. It is also possible, however, that high training costs or a sharp increase in the demand for the employer's product would make it important that the employer minimize turnover and avoid interruptions in the production process; or it is possible that the union's internal decision making would be dominated by workers who have little prospect of being laid off and for whom a high rate of general unemployment would be meaningless. Thus, a slack labor market might have an effect on one party's dependence in the relationship and not on the other's. By treating each party's dependence dimensions as conceptually distinct and then treating their possible interrelationships as uncertain, we can organize already available insights and formulate research questions more systematically.

Second, by defining bargaining power in terms of value,

alternatives, quantity, and weight dimensions, our model permits a definition of bargaining tactics that is broader than that
provided by those who focus exclusively on the activity at or
near the bargaining table. Some dependence dimensions may be
manipulated directly at the bargaining table, while others may
not be, yet all of them affect the bargaining process. We would
expect that the objective (that is, quantity) element of each
party's alternatives would be less subject to direct manipulation
during formal bargaining sessions than the quantity and weight
of a party's value dimension or the weight associated with its
alternatives, but trying to change the quantity of alternatives
available to oneself or the other party in order to improve one's
bargaining position would still constitute a bargaining tactic. A
union's efforts to secure government funding of national health
insurance or an employer's implementation of a less labor inten-
sive technology is just as much a bargaining tactic as the packag-
ing of proposals or the exchange of information during formal
bargaining. Our definition of bargaining tactics, therefore, provides a framework for considering subjects (like union and employer political action and lobbying) that have previously been
treated as tangential or irrelevant to the bargaining process.

Third, such a conception not only extends the definition
of bargaining beyond the bargaining table, but highlights the importance of what does (or can) go on at the bargaining table as
well. Just as readily as one that secures an objective change in
the quantity of its alternatives, a party that is able to convince
its opponent that it is prepared to resort to its own alternatives
(that is, a party that is able to change its opponent's perception
of the weight it attaches to those alternatives) can affect the
opponent's perception of its own power to press demands and
resist concessions. In fact, it is the linkage between the quantity
of alternatives available to each party and the weight each party
associates with its alternatives that makes the environment relevant to the bargaining process. The quantity-weight distinction
essentially mirrors the economic-political dichotomy that runs
through much of the collective bargaining literature, political in
this case referring to the internal political processes and influences within a union and a management organization. We would

argue that the debate over the relative importance of economic and political influences has been so inconclusive, in part because those conducting it have failed to demonstrate how either set of influences is brought to bear on the formal bargaining process. The model developed in this book affords an opportunity to integrate analysis of such aggregate influences with analysis of tactics used at the bargaining table itself, and thus, to bring some clarity (if not resolution) to that debate.

Fourth, one of the important differences between the perspective offered in this book and that offered by most studies of power and outcomes in collective bargaining is that ours directs attention to the parties' efforts to *change* their own and each other's dependence by improving or restricting access to resources outside the relationship, whereas other studies have tended to treat such access as *constraints* on the bargainers and therefore fixed and exogenous. (For an exception, see Levinson, 1966.) Our point is not that one or both parties will necessarily be able to control their own and each other's dependence, but that each of them will *try* to do so—and that in the course of their successful and unsuccessful attempts to improve outcomes through manipulation of dependence variables, they will reach a settlement that will reflect a new distribution of power. Whether a union (or employer) is a creature or a master of its environment is an empirical question that is too often obscured by the exogenous classification of environmental variables. Our model, therefore, ought to be particularly useful in analyzing how collective bargaining serves as a mechanism of change in the labor-management relationship.

Fifth, and more generally, power-dependence theory provides those engaged in research on collective bargaining an opportunity to draw upon a wide body of behavioral research and theory to formulate their hypotheses and interpret their findings. Strauss and Feuille (1978) have noted that one of the reasons collective bargaining research has such weak theoretical underpinnings is that it has been so institution specific, that it has been unable to specify the general properties of the process and structures under consideration. One of the consequences of having treated collective bargaining as a unique phenomenon is that such researchers have been unable to demonstrate how it *is* unique. One of the premises of industrial relations has always been that the process of collective bargaining is somehow as important as the particular outcomes it generates, yet for the most part it has not been defined or studied in those terms. The economic and legal paradigms that have guided research in collective bargaining have specified the structure of relationships, but not how those relationships emerge and change. The analytic device of assuming everything else being equal has obscured the *dynamic* nature of collective bargaining as a process. The basic contribution that behavioral science and power-dependence theory can make to the study of collective bargaining is a better appreciation of its nature as a process.

This book does nothing but provide a starting point for such an approach. We have no doubt that many of the propositions offered will seem obvious and unenlightening to those steeped in the institutional literature on collective bargaining or to those engaged in the process itself. We assume that some of our propositions (although we hope fewer) will sound like nonsense to them. But we are convinced that in the process of confirming, modifying, or rejecting our various propositions, students of collective bargaining can improve their understanding of the process. We are also convinced that our understanding of other forms of social exchange and of the concept of social exchange itself will benefit from such an approach to collective bargaining. We noted earlier that it is important not to assume that the various dependence dimensions are necessarily interdependent; they must be treated as conceptually distinct if we are to understand how they interact. That conceptual approach does not foreclose the possibility that some dimensions may be structurally related so that a change in one automatically constitutes or induces a change in another. Collective bargaining is an ideal area to test for such a possibility. We have said very little about how the kinds of resources being exchanged in bargaining might affect the process of bargaining; we have implied but not explored the possibility that having access to alternatives that one can obtain while remaining in the relationship may be fundamentally different than having alternatives that one can get only by leaving; we have said nothing at all about how bargaining over multiple outcomes might be different than bargaining over a single issue. Such questions inevitably arise in the context of collective bargaining, and they illustrate ways in which the model we have developed might be extended by its application to that area. We trust and hope that those already engaged in the study or use of collective bargaining will find many others.

References

Adler, F. "Operational Definitions in Sociology." *American Journal of Sociology,* 1947, *52,* 438-444.

Aiken, M., and Bacharach, S. B. "The Urban System, Politics, and Bureaucratic Structure: A Comparative Analysis of 44 Local Governments in Belgium." In L. Karpik (Ed.), *Organization and Environment.* London: Sage, 1978.

Aldrich, H. E. *Organizations and Environments.* Englewood Cliffs, N.J.: Prentice-Hall, 1979.

Aldrich, H. E., and Herker, D. "Boundary Spanning Roles and Organization Structure." *Academy of Management Review,* 1977, *2,* 217-230.

Aldrich, H. E., and Pfeffer, J. "Environments of Organizations." In A. Inkeles (Ed.), *Annual Review of Sociology.* Vol. 2. Palo Alto: Annual Reviews, 1976.

Allison, G. T. *Essence of Decision: Explaining the Cuban Missile Crisis.* Boston: Little, Brown, 1971.

Argyris, C. *The Applicability of Organizational Sociology.* Cambridge: Cambridge University Press, 1972.

Ashenfelter, O., and Johnson, G. E. "Bargaining Power, Trade Unions, and Industrial Strike Activity." *American Economic Review,* 1969, *59* (1), 35-49.

Axelrod, R. "Conflicts of Interest: An Axiomatic Approach." *Journal of Conflict Resolution,* 1967, *11,* 87-99.

Axelrod, R. *Conflict of Interest.* Chicago: Markham, 1970.

Bacharach, S. B. "Morphologie et Processus: Une Critique de la Recherche Organisationnelle Contemporaine" ["Morphology and Process: A Critique of Contemporary Organizational Research"]. *Sociologie Du Travail* [*Sociology of Work*], 1978, *20* (2), 153-173.

Bacharach, S. B., and Aiken, M. "Structural and Process Constraints on Influence in Organizations: A Level Specific Analysis." *Administrative Science Quarterly,* 1976, *21* (4), 623-642.

Bacharach, S. B., and Aiken, M. "Communication in Administrative Bureaucracies." *Academy of Management Journal,* 1977, *18,* 365-377.

Bacharach, S. B., and Aiken, M. "The Impact of Alienation, Meaninglessness, and Meritocracy on Supervisor and Subordinate Satisfaction." *Social Forces,* 1979, *57* (3), 853-870.

Bacharach, S. B., and Aiken, M. "Boundary Spanning in Public Bureaucracies." Unpublished manuscript. Ithaca, N.Y.: Cornell University, 1980.

Bacharach, S. B., and Lawler, E. J. "The Perception of Power." *Social Forces,* 1976, *55,* 123-134.

Bacharach, S. B., and Lawler, E. J. "Power Tactics in Bargaining." Ithaca, N.Y.: New York State School of Industrial and Labor Relations, Cornell University, 1980.

Baldridge, J. V. *Power and Conflict in the University.* New York: Wiley, 1971.

Balke, W. M., Hammond, K. R., and Meyer, G. D. "An Alternative Approach to Labor-Management Negotiations." *Administrative Science Quarterly,* 1973, *18,* 311-327.

Barnard, C. *The Functions of the Executive.* Cambridge, Mass.: Harvard University Press, 1938.

Barnes, J. A. "Networks and Political Process." In C. Mitchell (Ed.), *Social Networks in Urban Situations: Analyses of Personnel Relationships in Central African Towns.* Manchester, England: Manchester University Press, 1969.

Barry, B. "Review Article: Exit, Voice, and Loyalty." *British Journal of Political Science,* 1974, *4,* 79-107.

Bartos, O. J. "Determinants and Consequences of Toughness." In P. Swingle (Ed.), *The Structure of Conflict.* New York: Academic Press, 1970.

Bartos, O. J. "Foundations for a Rational-Empirical Model of Negotiation." In J. Berger, M. Zelditch, Jr., and B. Anderson (Eds.), *Sociological Theories in Progress.* Vol. 2. Boston: Houghton Mifflin, 1972.

Bartos, O. J. "A Simple Model of Negotiation: A Sociological Point of View." *Journal of Conflict Resolution,* 1977, *21,* 565-580.

Bartunek, J. M., Benton, A. A., and Keys, C. B. "Third Party Intervention and the Bargaining Behavior of Group Representatives." *Journal of Conflict Resolution,* 1975, *19,* 532-557.

Beer, M. "On Gaining Power and Influence for OD." *Journal of Applied Behavioral Science,* 1976, *12* (1), 44-51.

Bennis, W. "Practice vs. Theory." *International Management,* 1975, *30* (10), 41-42.

Benson, J. K. "Organizations: A Dialectical View." *Administrative Science Quarterly,* 1977, *22,* 1-21.

Bierstedt, R. "An Analysis of Social Power." *American Sociological Review,* 1950, *15,* 730-738.

Blau, P. M. *Exchange and Power in Social Life.* New York: Wiley, 1964.

Blau, P. M., and Schoenherr, R. A. *The Structure of Organizations.* New York: Basic Books, 1971.

Boulding, K. E. "Future Directions in Conflict and Peace Studies." *Journal of Conflict Resolution,* 1978, *22,* 342-354.

Bowlby, R., and Schriver, W. "Bluffing and Split the Difference Theory." *Industrial and Labor Relations Review,* 1978, *31,* 161-171.

Braverman, H. *Labor and Monopoly Capital.* New York: Monthly Review Press, 1974.

Brewer, J. "Flow of Communications, Expert Qualifications, and Organizational Authority Structures." *American Sociological Review,* 1971, *36,* 475-484.

Brown, B. R. "The Effects of Need to Maintain Face on Interpersonal Bargaining." *Journal of Experimental Psychology,* 1968, *4,* 107-122.

Brown, B. R. "Face-Saving and Face Restoration." In D. Druckman (Ed.), *Negotiations.* Beverly Hills, Calif.: Sage, 1977.

Burke, W. "Organizational Development in Transition." *Journal of Applied Behavioral Science,* 1976, *12* (1), 22-43.

Burt, R. S. "Positions in Networks." *Social Forces,* 1976, *55,* 93-122.

Burt, R. S. "Structure." *Connections,* 1978, *1* (2), 29-31.

Campbell, J. "Contributions Research Can Make in Understanding Organizational Effectiveness." In L. Spray (Ed.), *Organizational Effectiveness: Theory-Research-Utilization.* Kent, Ohio: Kent State University Press, 1976.

Campbell, J. P. "On the Nature of Organizational Effectiveness." In P. S. Goodman and J. M. Pennings (Eds.), *New Perspectives on Organizational Effectiveness.* San Francisco: Jossey-Bass, 1977.

Caplow, T. "A Theory of Coalitions in the Triad." *American Sociological Review,* 1956, *21,* 489-493.

Caplow, T. *Two Against One.* Englewood Cliffs, N.J.: Prentice-Hall, 1968.

Chertkoff, J. M. "Sociopsychological Theories and Research on Coalition Formation." In S. Groennings, E. W. Kelley, and M. Leiserson (Eds.), *The Study of Coalition Behavior.* New York: Holt, Rinehart and Winston, 1970.

Chertkoff, J. M., and Conley, M. "Opening Offer and Frequency of Concession as Bargaining Strategies." *Journal of Personality and Social Psychology,* 1967, *7,* 181-185.

Chertkoff, J. M., and Esser, J. K. "A Review of Experiments in Explicit Bargaining." *Journal of Experimental Social Psychology,* 1976, *12,* 464-486.

Cohen, M. D., March, J. G., and Olsen, J. P. "A Garbage Can Model of Organizational Choice." *Administrative Science Quarterly,* 1972, *17,* 1-25.

Collins, R. *Conflict Sociology: Toward an Explanatory Science.* New York: Academic Press, 1975.

Cook, K. S., and Emerson, R. M. "Power, Equity, Commitment in Exchange Networks." *American Sociological Review,* 1978, *43,* 721-739.

Crozier, M. *The Bureaucratic Phenomenon.* Chicago: University of Chicago Press, 1964.

Cummings, L. L. "Emergence of the Instrumental Organization." In P. S. Goodman and J. M. Pennings (Eds.), *New Perspectives on Organizational Effectiveness.* San Francisco: Jossey-Bass, 1977.

Cyert, R. M., and March, J. G. *A Behavioral Theory of the Firm.* Englewood Cliffs, N.J.: Prentice-Hall, 1963.

Dahl, R. A. "The Concept of Power." *Behavioral Science,* 1957, *2,* 201-218.

Dahrendorf, R. *Class and Class Conflict in Industrial Society.* Stanford, Calif.: Stanford University Press, 1959.

DeSwann, A. "An Empirical Model of Coalition Formation as an N-Person Game of Policy Distance Minimization." In S. Groennings, E. W. Kelley, M. Leiserson (Eds.), *The Study of Coalition Behavior.* New York: Holt, Rinehart and Winston, 1970.

DeSwann, A. *Coalition Theories and Cabinet Formation.* San Francisco: Jossey-Bass, 1973.

Deutsch, M. "Conflicts: Productive and Destructive." *Journal of Social Issues,* 1969, *25,* 7-41.

Deutsch, M. *The Resolution of Conflict.* New Haven, Conn.: Yale University Press, 1973.

Deutsch, M., and Krauss, R. M. "Studies of Interpersonal Bargaining." *Journal of Conflict Resolution,* 1962, *6,* 52-76.

Deutsch, M., and others. "Strategies of Inducing Cooperation: An Experimental Study." *Journal of Conflict Resolution,* 1967, *11,* 345-360.

Dill, W. "Environment as an Influence on Managerial Autonomy." *Administrative Science Quarterly,* 1958, *2,* 409-443.

Dill, W. "The Impact of Environment on Organizational Development." In S. Mailick and E. H. Van Ness (Eds.), *Concepts and Issues in Administrative Behavior.* Englewood Cliffs, N.J.: Prentice-Hall, 1962.

Druckman, D. "Dogmatism, Prenegotiation Experience, and Simulated Group Representation as Determinants of Dyadic Behavior in a Bargaining Situation." *Journal of Personality and Social Psychology*, 1967, *6*, 279-290.

Druckman, D. (Ed.). *Negotiations*. Beverly Hills, Calif.: Sage, 1977.

Duncan, R. "Characteristics of Organizational Environments and Perceived Environmental Uncertainty." *Administrative Science Quarterly*, 1972, *17*, 313-327.

Dunlop, J. T. *Wage Determination Under Trade Unions*. New York: A. M. Kelley, 1950.

Emerson, R. M. "Power-Dependence Relations." *American Sociological Review*, 1962, *27*, 31-40.

Emerson, R. M. "Exchange Theory, Part I: A Psychological Basis for Social Exchange." In J. Berger, M. Zelditch, and B. Anderson (Eds.), *Sociological Theories in Progress*. Vol. 2. Boston: Houghton Mifflin, 1972a.

Emerson, R. M. "Exchange Theory, Part II: Exchange Relations, Exchange Networks, and Groups as Exchange Systems." In J. Berger, M. Zelditch, and B. Anderson (Eds.), *Sociological Theories in Progress*. Vol. 2. Boston: Houghton Mifflin, 1972b.

Esser, J. K., and Komorita, S. S. "Reciprocity and Concession-Making in Bargaining." *Journal of Personality and Social Psychology*, 1975, *31*, 864-872.

Etzioni, A. *A Comparative Analysis of Complex Organizations*. New York: Free Press, 1961.

French, J. R., Jr., and Raven, B. H. "The Bases of Social Power." In D. Cartwright (Ed.), *Studies in Social Power*. Ann Arbor: University of Michigan Press, 1959.

Friedlander, F., and Brown, L. "Organization Development." *Annual Review of Psychology*, 1974, *24*, 313-341.

Gamson, W. A. "A Theory of Coalition Formation." *American Sociological Review*, 1961a, *26*, 373-382.

Gamson, W. A. "An Experimental Test of a Theory of Coalition Formation." *American Sociological Review*, 1961b, *26*, 565-573.

Gamson, W. A. "Experimental Studies of Coalition Formation."

In L. Berkowitz (Ed.), *Advances in Experimental Social Psychology*. Vol. 1. New York: Academic Press, 1964.

Gamson, W. A. *Power and Discontent*. Homewood, Ill.: Dorsey Press, 1968.

Gamson, W. A. "Power and Probability." In J. D. Tedeschi (Ed.), *Perspective on Social Power*. Chicago: Aldine, 1974.

Gamson, W. A. *The Strategy of Social Protest*. Homewood, Ill.: Dorsey Press, 1975.

Gergen, K. J. *The Psychology of Behavior Exchange*. Reading, Mass.: Addison-Wesley, 1969.

Gibbs, J. *Sociological Theory Construction*. Hinsdale, Ill.: Dryden Press, 1972.

Gouldner, A. "The Norm of Reciprocity: A Preliminary Statement." *American Sociological Review*, 1960, *25*, 161-179.

Gouldner, A. "Reciprocity and Autonomy in Functional Theory." In N. Demerath and R. Peterson, *System, Change, and Conflict*. New York: Free Press, 1967.

Gruder, C. L. "Relationships with Opponent and Partner in Mixed-Motive Bargaining." *Journal of Conflict Resolution*, 1971, *15*, 403-416.

Hage, J. *Techniques and Problems of Theory Construction in Sociology*. New York: Wiley, 1972.

Hage, J., and Aiken, M. "Relationship of Centralization to Other Structural Properties." *Administrative Science Quarterly*, 1969, *14*, 366-376.

Hage, J., and Aiken, M. *Social Change in Complex Organizations*. New York: Random House, 1970.

Hamermesh, D. "Who Wins in Wage Bargaining." *Industrial and Labor Relations Review*, 1976, *26*, 1146-1149.

Hamner, W. C. "Effects of Bargaining Strategy and Pressure to Reach Agreement in a Stalemated Negotiation." *Journal of Personality and Social Psychology*, 1974, *30*, 458-467.

Hamner, W. C., and Yukl, G. A. "The Effectiveness of Different Offer Strategies in Bargaining." In D. Druckman (Ed.), *Negotiations*. Beverly Hills, Calif.: Sage, 1977.

Harsanyi, J. C. *Rational Behavior and Bargaining Equilibrium in Games and Social Situations*. New York: Cambridge University Press, 1977.

Hinings, C. R., and others. "Structural Conditions of Inter-organizational Power." *Administrative Science Quarterly,* 1974, *19* (1), 22-43.

Hirschman, A. O. *Exit, Voice, and Loyalty.* Cambridge, Mass.: Harvard University Press, 1972.

Hirschman, A. O. "Exit, Voice, and Loyalty: Further Reflections and a Survey of Recent Contributions." *Social Science Information,* 1973, *13* (1), 7-26.

Homans, A. C. *Social Behavior: Its Elementary Forms.* New York: Harcourt Brace Jovanovich, 1974.

Huber, G. P. "Multi-Attribute Utility Models: A Review of Field and Fieldlike Research." *Management Science,* 1974, *20,* 1393-1402.

Jones, E. E., and Davis, K. E. "From Acts to Dispositions: The Attribution Process in Person Perception." In L. Berkowitz (Ed.), *Advances in Experimental Social Psychology.* Vol. 2. New York: Academic Press, 1965.

Jones, E. E., and others. *Attribution: Perceiving the Causes of Behavior.* Morristown, N.J.: General Learning Press, 1971.

Kaplan, A. "Power in Perspective." In R. L. Kahn and E. Boulding (Eds.), *Power and Conflict in Organization.* London: Tavistock, 1964.

Karpik, L. "Le Capitalisme Technologique" ["Technological Capitalism."]. *Sociologie du Travail [Sociology of Work],* 1972, *13,* 2-34.

Karpik, L. (Ed.). *Organization and Environment: Theory, Issues, and Reality.* London: Sage, 1978.

Katz, D., and Kahn, R. L. *The Social Psychology of Organizations.* New York: Wiley, 1966.

Kipnis, D. "The Powerholder." In J. T. Tedeschi (Ed.), *Perspectives on Social Power.* Chicago: Aldine, 1974.

Kochan, T. A. "Collective Bargaining and Organizational Behavior Research." Unpublished manuscript, Cornell University, 1978.

Kochan, T. A., Huber, G. P., and Cummings, L. L. "Determinants of Intraorganizational Conflict in Collective Bargaining in the Public Sector." *Administrative Science Quarterly,* 1975, *20,* 10-23.

Komorita, S. S. "A Weighted Probability Model of Coalition Formation." *Psychological Review,* 1974, *81,* 242-256.

Komorita, S. S. "Negotiating from Strength and the Concept of Bargaining Strength." *Journal for the Theory of Social Behavior,* 1977, *7,* 65-79.

Komorita, S. S., and Barnes, M. "Effects of Pressures to Reach Agreement in Bargaining." *Journal of Personality and Social Psychology,* 1969, *13,* 245-252.

Komorita, S. S., and Brenner, A. R. "Bargaining and Concession Making Under Bilateral Monopoly." *Journal of Personality and Social Psychology,* 1968, *9,* 15-20.

Komorita, S. S., and Chertkoff, J. "A Bargaining Theory of Coalition Formation." *Psychological Review,* 1973, *80,* 149-162.

Krauss, R. M., and Deutsch, M. "Communication in Interpersonal Bargaining." *Journal of Personality and Social Psychology,* 1966, *4,* 572-577.

Laumann, E. O., and Pappi, F. U. "New Directions in the Study of Community Elites." *American Sociological Review,* 1973, *38,* 212-230.

Laumann, E. O., and Pappi, F. U. *Networks of Collective Action: Perspectives on Community Influence Systems.* New York: Academic Press, 1976.

Lawler, E. J. "An Experimental Study of Factors Affecting the Mobilization of Revolutionary Coalitions." *Sociometry,* 1975a, *38,* 163-179.

Lawler, E. J. "Impact of Status Differences on Coalition Agreements: An Experimental Study." *Journal of Conflict Resolution,* 1975b, *19,* 271-277.

Lawler, E. J. Book Review of M. K. Mulder (Ed.), *The Daily Power Game. Administrative Science Quarterly,* 1979, *24,* 145-147.

Lawler, E. J., and Bacharach, S. B. "Outcome Alternatives and Value as Criteria for Multistrategy Evaluations." *Journal of Personality and Social Psychology,* 1976, *34,* 885-894.

Lawler, E. J., and Bacharach, S. B. "Power-Dependence in Individual Bargaining: The Unexpected Utility of Influence." *Industrial and Labor Relations Review,* 1979, *32,* 196-204.

Lawler, E. J., and Thompson, M. E. "Impact of Leader Responsibility for Inequity on Subordinate Revolts." *Social Psychology Quarterly,* 1978, *41,* 264-268.

Lawler, E. J., and Thompson, M. E. "Subordinate Response to a Leader's Cooptation Strategy as a Function of the Type of Coalition Power." *Representative Research in Social Psychology,* 1979, *9,* 69-80.

Lawler, E. J., and Youngs, G. A., Jr. "Coalition Formation: An Integrative Model." *Sociometry,* 1975, *38* (1), 1-17.

Lawler, E. J., Youngs, G. A., Jr., and Lesh, M. D. "Cooptation and Coalition Mobilization." *Journal of Applied Social Psychology,* 1978, *8* (3), 199-214.

Lawrence, P., and Lorsch, J. *Organizations and Environment.* Cambridge, Mass.: Harvard University Press, 1967.

Leiserson, M. "Power and Ideology in Coalition Behavior: An Experimental Study." In S. Groennings, E. W. Kelley, and M. Leiserson (Eds.), *The Study of Coalition Behavior.* New York: Holt, Rinehart and Winston, 1970.

Levinson, H. M. *Determining Forces in Collective Wage Bargaining.* New York: Wiley, 1966.

Liebert, R. M., and others. "The Effects of Information and Magnitude of Initial Offer on Interpersonal Negotiation." *Journal of Experimental Social Psychology,* 1968, *4,* 431-441.

Lipset, S. M., Trow, M., and Coleman, J. *Union Democracy.* New York: Doubleday, 1956.

March, J. G., and Olsen, J. *Ambiguity and Choice in Organizations.* Bergen, Norway: Universitetsfortaget, 1976.

March, J. G., and Simon, H. A. *Organizations.* New York: Wiley, 1958.

Marwell, G., and Schmitt, D. *Cooperation.* New York: Academic Press, 1975.

Mechanic, D. "Sources of Power of Lower Participants in Complex Organizations." *Administrative Science Quarterly,* 1962, *7,* 349-364.

Merton, R. K. *Social Theory and Social Structure.* New York: Free Press, 1949.

Meyer, M. W. "Size and Structure of Organizations: A Casual Analysis." *American Sociological Review,* 1972, *37,* 434-440.

Meyer, M. W., and others. *Environments and Organizations.* San Francisco: Jossey-Bass, 1978.

Michaels, J. W., and Wiggins, J. A. "Effects of Mutual Dependence and Dependency Asymmetry on Social Exchange." *Sociometry,* 1976, *39,* 368-376.

Michels, R. *Political Parties: A Sociological Study of Oligarchical Tendencies in Modern Democracy.* New York: Dover, 1959.

Michener, H. A., and Cohen, E. D. "Effects of Punishment Magnitude in the Bilateral Threat Situation: Evidence for the Deterrence Hypothesis." *Journal of Personality and Social Psychology,* 1973, *26,* 427-438.

Michener, H. A., Lawler, E. J., and Bacharach, S. B. "Perception of Power in Conflict Situations." *Journal of Personality and Social Psychology,* 1973, *28,* 115-162.

Michener, H. A., and Suchner, R. "The Tactical Use of Social Power." In J. T. Tedeschi (Ed.), *Social Influence Processes.* Chicago: Aldine-Atherton, 1972.

Michener, H. A., and others. "Factors Affecting Concession Rate and Threat Usage in Bilateral Conflict." *Sociometry,* 1975a, *38,* 62-80.

Michener, H. A., and others. "Minimum Resource and Pivotal Power Theories: A Competitive Test in Four-Person Coalitional Situations." *Journal of Conflict Resolution,* 1975b, *19,* 89-107.

Mills, C. W. *The Sociological Imagination.* Oxford: Oxford University Press, 1959.

Morgan, M. P. *Deterrence: A Conceptual Analysis.* Beverly Hills, Calif.: Sage, 1977.

Morley, I., and Stephanson, G. *The Social Psychology of Bargaining.* London: Allen and Unwin, 1977.

Mosca, G. *The Ruling Class.* New York: McGraw-Hill, 1939.

Mulder, M. *The Daily Power Game.* Leiden, Netherlands: Martinus Nijhoff, 1977.

Murnighan, J. K. "Models of Coalition Behavior: Game Theoretic, Social Psychological, and Political Perspectives." *Psychological Bulletin,* 1978, *85,* 1130-1153.

Nash, J. "Two-Person Cooperative Games." *Econometrica,* 1953, *21,* 128-140.

Nord, W. "The Failure of Current Applied Behavioral Science: A Marxian Perspective." *Journal of Applied Behavioral Science,* 1975, *10* (4), 557-578.

Pareto, V. *The Mind and Society.* New York: Harcourt, Brace and World, 1935.

Parsons, T. *The Structure of Social Action.* New York: Free Press, 1937.

Parsons, T. "Introduction." In M. Weber, *The Theory of Social and Economic Organization.* New York: Oxford University Press, 1947.

Parsons, T. *The Social System.* New York: Free Press, 1951.

Parsons, T. "Suggestions for a Sociological Approach to the Theory of Organizations." *Administrative Science Quarterly,* 1956a, *1,* 63-85.

Parsons, T. "Suggestions for a Sociological Approach to the Theory of Organizations." *Administrative Science Quarterly,* 1956b, *1,* 225-236.

Peabody, R. L. "Perceptions of Organizational Authority." *Administrative Science Quarterly,* 1962, *6,* 463-482.

Peabody, R. L. *Organizational Theory: Superior-Subordinate Relationships in Three Public Service Organizations.* New York: Atherton, 1964.

Pennings, J. M., and Goodman, P. S. "On the Nature of Organizational Effectiveness." In P. S. Goodman and J. M. Pennings (Eds.), *New Perspectives on Organizational Effectiveness.* San Francisco: Jossey-Bass, 1977.

Perrow, C. "A Framework for Comparative Organizational Analysis." *American Sociological Review,* 1967, *32* (2), 194-208.

Pettigrew, A. "Information Control as a Power Resource." *Sociology,* 1972, *6,* 187-204.

Pettigrew, A. *The Politics of Organizational Decision-Making.* London: Tavistock, 1973.

Pfeffer, J. "The Micropolitics of Organizations." In M. W. Meyer (Ed.), *Environments and Organizations.* San Francisco: Jossey-Bass, 1978.

Pondy, L. R. "Organizational Conflict: Concepts and Models." *Administrative Science Quarterly,* 1967, *12,* 499-505.

Pruitt, D. G., and Drews, J. L. "The Effect of Time Pressure,

Time Elapsed, and the Opponent's Concession Rate on Behavior in Negotiation." *Journal of Experimental Social Psychology,* 1969, *5,* 43-60.

Pruitt, D. G., and Lewis, S. A. "The Psychology of Integrative Bargaining." In D. Druckman (Ed.), *Negotiations.* Beverly Hills, Calif.: Sage, 1977.

Pugh, D. S., and others. "Dimensions of Organizational Structure." *Administrative Science Quarterly,* 1968, *13* (2), 65-105.

Pugh, D. S., and others. "The Context of Organizational Structures." *Administrative Science Quarterly,* 1969, *14* (1), 115-126.

Rapoport, A. *Two-Person Game Theory.* Ann Arbor: University of Michigan Press, 1966.

Rapoport, A. "Conflict Resolution in Light of Game Theory and Beyond." In P. Swingle (Ed.), *The Structure of Conflict.* New York: Academic Press, 1970.

Raven, B. H. "A Comparative Analysis of Power and Power Preference." In J. T. Tedeschi (Ed.), *Perspectives on Social Power.* Chicago: Aldine, 1974.

Raven, B. H., and Kruglanski, A. W. "Conflict and Power." In P. Swingle (Ed.), *The Structure of Conflict.* New York: Academic Press, 1970.

Reynolds, L. D. *A Primer in Theory Construction.* New York: Bobbs-Merrill, 1971.

Riker, W. H. *The Theory of Political Coalitions.* New Haven, Conn.: Yale University Press, 1962.

Roethlisberger, F. J., and Dickson, W. J. *Management and the Worker.* Cambridge, Mass.: Harvard University Press, 1939.

Ross, A. M. *Trade Union Wage Policy.* Berkeley, Calif.: University of California Press, 1948.

Rubin, J. A., and Brown, B. R. *The Social Psychology of Bargaining and Negotiation.* New York: Academic Press, 1975.

Schellenberg, J. A. "Dependence and Cooperation." *Sociometry,* 1965, *28,* 158-172.

Schelling, T. C. *The Strategy of Conflict.* New York: Oxford University Press, 1960.

Schelling, T. C. *Arms and Influence.* New Haven, Conn.: Yale University Press, 1966.

Schmidt, S., and Kochan, T. "The Concept of Conflict." *Administrative Science Quarterly,* 1972, *17,* 359-370.

Schopler, J., and Layton, D. B. "Attributions of Interpersonal Power." In J. T. Tedeschi (Ed.), *Perspectives on Social Power.* Chicago: Aldine-Atherton, 1974.

Selznick, P. *TVA and the Grass Roots: A Study of the Sociology of Formal Organization.* New York: Harper & Row, 1949.

Selznick, P. *Leadership in Administration.* New York: Harper & Row, 1957.

Shaver, K. G. *An Introduction to Attribution Processes.* Cambridge, Mass.: Winthrop Publishers, 1975.

Siegel, S., and Fouraker, L. E. *Bargaining and Group Decision-Making.* New York: McGraw-Hill, 1960.

Siegel, S., Siegal, A. E., and Andrews, J. M. *Choice, Strategy, and Utility.* New York: McGraw-Hill, 1964.

Simmel, G. *The Sociology of Georg Simmel.* (K. Wolff, Trans.) New York: Free Press, 1950.

Simon, H. A. "Notes on the Observation and Measurement of Political Power." *Journal of Politics,* 1953, *15,* 500-512, 514, 516.

Spray, S. L. *Organizational Effectiveness: Theory—Research—Utilization.* Kent, Ohio: Kent State University Press, 1976.

Staats, A. W. *Social Behaviorism.* Homewood, Ill.: Dorsey Press, 1975.

Stahl, I. *Bargaining Theory.* Stockholm: Economic Research Institute, 1972.

Stinchecombe, A. L. *Constructing Social Theories.* New York: Harcourt Brace Jovanovich, 1968.

Strauss, G., and Feuille, P. "Industrial Relations Research: A Critical Analysis." *Industrial Relations,* 1978, *17* (3), 259-277.

Stryker, S. "Coalition Behavior." In C. G. McClintock (Ed.), *Experimental Social Psychology.* New York: Holt, Rinehart and Winston, 1972.

Tannenbaum, A. S. *Control in Organizations.* New York: McGraw-Hill, 1968.

Tannenbaum, A. S., and others. *Hierarchy in Organizations.* San Francisco: Jossey-Bass, 1974.

Tannenbaum, R. "How to Choose the Leadership Patterns." *Harvard Business Review,* 1958, *26* (2), 95-101.

Tannenbaum, R., and Massarik, F. "Participation by Subordinates in the Managerial Decision-Making Process." *Canadian Journal of Economic and Political Science,* 1950, *16,* 408-418.

Tedeschi, J. T. "Threats and Promises." In P. Swingle (Ed.), *The Structure of Conflict.* New York: Academic Press, 1970.

Tedeschi, J. T., and Bonoma, T. V. "Power and Influence: An Introduction." In J. T. Tedeschi (Ed.), *Social Influence Processes.* Chicago: Aldine-Atherton, 1972.

Tedeschi, J. T., Schlenker, B. R., and Bonoma, T. V. *Conflict, Power, and Games.* Chicago: Aldine-Atherton, 1973.

Thibaut, J. W., and Faucheux, C. "The Development of Contractual Norms in a Bargaining Situation Under Two Types of Stress." *Journal of Experimental and Social Psychology,* 1965, *1,* 89-102.

Thibaut, J. W., and Kelley, H. H. *The Social Psychology of Groups.* New York: Wiley, 1959.

Thompson, J. D. *Organizations in Action.* New York: McGraw-Hill, 1967.

Vinacke, W. E. "Variables in Experimental Games: Toward a Field Theory." *Psychological Bulletin,* 1969, *71,* 293-317.

Von Neumann, J., and Morgenstern, O. *Theory of Games and Economic Behavior.* Princeton, N.J.: Princeton University Press, 1947.

Walton, R. E. *Interpersonal Peace Making: Confrontations and Third Party Consultation.* Reading, Mass.: Addison-Wesley, 1969.

Walton, R. E., and McKersie, R. B. *A Behavioral Theory of Labor Negotiations.* New York: McGraw-Hill, 1965.

Weber, M. *The Theory of Social and Economic Organization.* (A. M. Henderson and T. Parsons, Eds. and Trans.) New York: Oxford University Press, 1947.

Webster, M., and Smith, L. F. "Justice and Revolutionary Coalitions: A Test of Two Theories." *American Journal of Sociology,* 1978, *84,* 267-292.

Weick, K. *The Social Psychology of Organizing.* Reading, Mass.: Addison-Wesley, 1969.

Weick, K. "Educational Organizations as Loosely Coupled Systems." *Administrative Science Quarterly,* 1976, *21,* 1-19.

White, H., Boorman, S., and Breiger, R. "Social Structure from Multiple Networks. I. Blockmodels of Roles and Positions." *American Journal of Sociology,* 1976, *81,* 730-780.

Whyte, W. H. *The Organization Man.* New York: Simon & Schuster, 1956.

Wrong, D. H. "The Oversocialized Conception of Man in Modern Society." *American Sociological Review,* 1961, *26,* 184-193.

Wrong, D. H. "Some Problems in Defining Social Power." *American Journal of Sociology,* 1968, *73* (6), 673-681.

Young, O. R. (Ed.). *Bargaining: Formal Theories of Negotiation.* Chicago: University of Illinois Press, 1975.

Yukl, G. A. "Effects of the Opponent's Initial Offer, Concession Magnitude, and Concession Frequency on Bargaining Behavior." *Journal of Personality and Social Psychology,* 1974a, *30,* 322-335.

Yukl, G. A. "The Effects of Situational Variables and Opponent Concessions on a Bargainer's Perception, Aspirations, and Concessions." *Journal of Personality and Social Psychology,* 1974b, *29,* 227-236.

Zald, M. N. *Organizational Change: The Political Economy of the YMCA.* Chicago: University of Chicago Press, 1970.

Zetterberg, J. L. *On Theory and Verification in Sociology.* Totowa, N.J.: Bedminster Press, 1965.

Index